The Horror Spoofs of Abbott and Costello

The Horror Spoofs of Abbott and Costello

A Critical Assessment of the Comedy Team's Monster Films

by
JEFFREY S. MILLER

McFarland & Company, Inc., Publishers
Jefferson, North Carolina, and London

The present work is a reprint of the library bound edition of The Horror Spoofs of Abbott and Costello: A Critical Assessment of the Comedy Team's Monster Films, *first published in 2000 by McFarland.*

LIBRARY OF CONGRESS CATALOGUING-IN-PUBLICATION DATA

Miller, Jeffrey S., 1970–
 The horror spoofs of Abbott and Costello: a critical assessment of the comedy team's monster films / by Jeffrey S. Miller.
  p.   cm.
 Includes bibliographical references and index.

 ISBN 0-7864-1922-9 (softcover : 50# alkaline paper)

 1. Abbott, Bud. 2. Costello, Lou. 3. Monsters in motion pictures.   I. Title.
 PN2287.A217.M55   2004
 791.43'028'092273 — dc21   99-52498

British Library cataloguing data are available

©2000 Jeffrey S. Miller. All rights reserved

No part of this book may be reproduced or transmitted in any form or by any means, electronic or mechanical, including photocopying or recording, or by any information storage and retrieval system, without permission in writing from the publisher.

Cover art: Poster from the 1941 film *Hold That Ghost* (Photofest)

Manufactured in the United States of America

McFarland & Company, Inc., Publishers
 Box 611, Jefferson, North Carolina 28640
 www.mcfarlandpub.com

To my parents and grandparents for their
continued love and support.

and

To the Movie Club: Randy Gaumer, Bill Snyder,
Jim Hoffman, John Hoffman, Travis Flexer, Jeff
Lindenmuth, Jeff Boehm and our mascot Pepper
for allowing themselves to be forced into watching
countless Abbott and Costello films with me.

Acknowledgments

This book, my first, was a labor of love and I must take this opportunity to thank not only those who aided me and gave advice along the way but also those who gave continued support: Nevin and Karen Miller, Kenneth and Dorothy Uhler, Jason Miller, Randon Gaumer, William Snyder, John Plunkett, Sandy Gunter, Ed Naha, Chris Lewis, Tiffany Borders, Kathleen Whiting, Kris Barrett, Brian Chisholm, Jeff Evans, Eric Karp, Aaron J. Crausman, Fred Holliday, Elizabeth Penn Custer, Charles Massey (of Sutton, Barth, and Venari), Ron Borst, Stuart Gailbraith IV and Chris Costello.

Acknowledgement and thank-yous must also be made to the following institutions and their kind, courteous, and helpful staffs who provided services throughout the writing of this book: the Academy of Motion Picture Arts and Sciences Library, the American University Library and the American University Library's Media Services department, Eddie Brandt's Saturday Matinee, Rocket Video, Cinema Collectibles, Hollywood Movie Posters, and Video Monitoring Services.

A special thank-you to those who took some of their valuable time and talked to me over the phone or in person, giving me their special insight, recollections, and information: Sara Karloff, Bela Lugosi, Jr., Craig Stevens, and Paddy Costello Humphreys.

Contents

Acknowledgments	vii
Introduction	1

Part One. A Brief History of Bud Abbott, Lou Costello, and Universal's Monsters — 5

Part Two. The "Meet the Monsters" Formula — 29

Abbott and Costello Meet Frankenstein	29
Abbott and Costello Meet the Invisible Man	65
Abbott and Costello Meet Dr. Jekyll and Mr. Hyde	88
Abbott and Costello Meet the Mummy	114

Part Three. The Other Horror-Comedies — 137

Hold That Ghost	137
The Time of Their Lives	165
Abbott and Costello Meet the Killer, Boris Karloff	188

Appendix: Horror, Science Fiction, and Fantasy Scenes in Other Abbott and Costello Films	217
Notes	219
Bibliography	231
Index	235

Introduction

The comedy and horror genres have always been close cousins to each other. Films from each are meant to provoke a physical reaction in the viewer — comedy films make people laugh while horror films make people shiver and scream. Both reactions are uncontrollable reflexes. In fact, the laugh and the scream are similar in that both are emitted from the mouth and both are audible reactions to the action on the screen. If either reaction is produced, then the film is doing its job in entertaining the viewer.

A savvy director will punctuate his horror films with moments of comedy relief in order to lighten the tension of the film, as in the works of James Whale and Alfred Hitchcock. So it is only a natural course that horror-comedies should emerge. Horror-comedies are more than horror films with a few scenes of comic relief; they are works where each genre is equally represented. Arguments are bound to occur about whether a certain "horror-comedy" film is actually just a comedy or just a horror picture. A horror-comedy done right will satisfy the fan of each genre.

The horror-comedy can be broken into three types: black comedy, parody, and spoof. Black comedies are not always horror films; in fact, the greatest black comedy is probably *Dr. Strangelove, or How I Learned to Stop Worrying and Love the Bomb* (1964). Black comedies feature morbid scenes so outrageous they have to be funny. They also deal humorously with subject matter that is usually treated with more respect, and for this reason may sometimes be considered in poor taste by those who fail to see the humor. Examples include *Arsenic and Old Lace* (1944), *The Trouble with Harry* (1955), *The Old Dark House* (1932), and *Eating Raoul* (1982). Some writers even consider director James Whale's *Bride of Frankenstein*

(1935) to be a black comedy, and Alfred Hitchcock always referred to *Psycho* (1960) as one. Today, the black comedy can best be seen in the modern splatter films. Movies like *The Evil Dead* (1983), *Re-Animator* (1985), *Return of the Living Dead* (1985) and even the recent *Scream* (1996) feature gruesome, gory scenes of carnage and death played for laughs. This kind of dark comedy is very prevalent in today's horror works and is considered to be the hip approach to the genre. I call this type of film a "splaffter film" because it makes comedy out of the splatter film gore effects.

I differentiate between horror spoofs and horror parodies. A parody is a ridiculous imitation of another work or style that strives for a comic effect. A horror parody mocks all the conventions of the horror genre. There is nothing scary or frightening about this type of film; it is played strictly for laughs all around. Movies like *Young Frankenstein* (1974), *Love at First Bite* (1979), and recent films like *Re-Possessed* (1990) and *Silence of the Hams* (1993) are good examples.

The horror spoof treats the genre with respect. A spoof is a light, humorous imitation that makes good-natured fun of its target. It is deceptive in that it can be mistaken for the real thing until closer examination reveals the intended humor. Horror spoofs are films meant as comedies but containing horror sequences played straight.

The first horror spoofs were the "old dark house comedies" so prevalent in the period when silents were giving way to talkies. These spooky mysteries took the old dark house genre—films in which murders were committed by masked killers in old mansions—and added comedy elements (usually in the form of a timid hero or a scared servant). Examples include *The Cat and the Canary* (1927) and *The Bat Whispers* (1930). Later, comedy teams embraced the horror spoof because they found the combination of laughs and scares to be a surefire moneymaker. Also, ghosts and supernatural occurrences give a good clown something to work off of (Lou Costello is, of course, the master of the scared schtick). Almost every comedy team—including Laurel and Hardy, the Three Stooges, Our Gang, Wheeler and Woolsey, and the Ritz Brothers—made at least one horror spoof during their film careers, more often than not using the old dark house comedy as their format. (Abbott and Costello's would be *Hold That Ghost*.)

Bud and Lou were among the first to expand on that form and widen the scope of their spoofs (and their films *are* spoofs because the monster menaces are always played straight). Their spoofs satirize the entire Universal Monster series. In fact, most consider *Abbott and Costello Meet*

Frankenstein to be the greatest horror spoof of all time. Eventually, other comedy teams would follow the lead, and films like *The Bowery Boys Meet the Monsters* (1954) would result.

Today, there are few horror spoofs. Most filmmakers opt for silly parody or use gore to make a black "splaffter" comedy. Films like *Vampire in Brooklyn* (1995) and *Innocent Blood* (1992) try to keep up the tradition, but it seems that with the loss of the comedy team there is a loss of the classic horror spoof. No one is attempting to knock *Abbott and Costello Meet Frankenstein* from the top spot. And without a return to the well-timed wordplay and physical comedy of the great comic teams, it is unlikely that anyone could ever do so.

Part One

A Brief History of Bud Abbott, Lou Costello, and the Universal Monsters

Before one looks at the Abbott and Costello horror-comedies in detail, it is helpful to know something about the development of Abbott and Costello in their careers, and to examine the Universal Monster films as the starting point of the horror genre.

William Alexander "Bud" Abbott was born October 2, 1895, to Harry and Rae Abbott in Asbury Park, New Jersey. Both parents worked for Barnum and Bailey Circus — Harry as an advance man and Rae as a bareback rider — so Bud had a very early exposure to show business.

Shortly after Bud's birth, the family moved to Coney Island, where they lived for 18 years. Bud quickly dropped out of grade school to hang out on the Boardwalk. His first job, while still a child, was charging ten cents to lead patrons out of the Crystal Maze when they got lost.[1] Already, his con man persona was developing.

Harry soon quit the circus and began working for the organizers of the Columbia Wheel Burlesque Circuit. In 1911, Bud took a job at the box office in their Brooklyn theater. In the years that followed, he was promoted to assistant treasurer of the Casino Theater. There, he interacted with many great comedians who worked for a time at the theater, including W.C. Fields and Fanny Brice. From them he learned about timing and getting laughs.

While a teenager, Bud was shanghaied and forced to work on a Norwegian steamer for one year. After returning home, he spent the next ten to twelve years working in various burlesque theaters. Eventually, he worked not only behind the scenes but on stage. Comedian Billy Gilbert takes credit for giving Bud his first stage exposure when he asked Bud to replace his straight man for a few performances.

In 1918, Bud met Betty Smith, a chorus girl and stripper. A week after meeting, they married and moved to Cleveland. In 1923, Bud borrowed $1,500 from an uncle and started his own show.[2] For the next three years, Bud staged various shows for the National Theater. He often appeared in those shows as a straight man. He was coached by his cousin Al Golden, a well-respected straight man in his own right. Bud was so good in this role that word quickly spread, and soon everyone wanted to work with him. But he mostly worked with his wife, and together they traveled the circuits.

Louis Francis Cristillo was born on March 6, 1906, in Paterson, New Jersey, to Sebastian and Helene Cristillo. Always the class clown, Lou enjoyed entertaining his classmates in school. According to stories, one of Lou's teachers became angry with him and made him write on the blackboard 150 times, "I'm a bad boy." This became his trademark.[3]

Lou grew up loving the movies. In fact, his dream was to be a movie star like his idol Charlie Chaplin. He also loved sports. For a time, Lou played semiprofessional basketball and was, at one time, Paterson's foul shot champion. He was also an amateur boxer under the name Lou King, but his boxing career quickly ended when his disapproving father attended one of his bouts.

After graduating, Lou tried all the vaudeville agents but had no luck. So, in 1927, he moved to Hollywood. His family was against it, but his brother Pat stuck up for him and he was allowed to go. In silent pictures, Lou worked as a stuntman and an extra. But while doubling for Dolores Del Rio, he was badly hurt. He quit being a stuntman and decided to go to New York for voice lessons. Talkies were becoming popular, and Lou thought he could make his fortune there.

Unfortunately, Lou's money ran out somewhere around St. Joseph, Missouri. A local burlesque house was advertising for a Dutch comic, so Lou applied even though he did not know a word of the language. He had not even appeared in front of a live audience before! But somehow he got the job and showed a natural talent for comedy. It was at this time he changed his last name to Costello.

Lou moved back home, where he played the local burlesque houses for two years. In 1932, he appeared in stock burlesque in Los Angeles and tried for a second shot in the movies. Again, he did not make it.[4] He headed back east, working all the big cities along the way.

Meanwhile, Universal Studios was finally making an impact on the world of film. They were always considered one of the cheaper studios, not matching the extravagance of MGM but not quite in the depths of poverty row like Monogram. In 1930, their release *All Quiet on the Western Front* won the Oscar for Best Picture. Universal was getting noticed.

Until 1936, Universal was run by German immigrant Carl Laemmle, who liked to fill top level positions with members of his family. In fact, the running joke around the studio was a rhyme that went something like: "Uncle Carl Laemmle has a very big faemmle." Carl's son, Carl Laemmle, Jr., was the vice president in charge of production, and it was he who took a chance on some horror properties in 1931.

Carl, Sr., was against producing *Dracula*, thinking it would be in poor taste. But his son persisted and the film was made, resulting in a box office hit. Directed by Tod Browning and starring Bela Lugosi (in the role he played on stage), the film is today considered stiff and stagey, but at the time moviegoers had seen nothing like it. Unlike the old dark house thrillers, *Dracula* treated the supernatural as a very real presence instead of explaining it away. The tale of the vampire and his quest for fresh blood in London appealed to everyone, including women who, fascinated by the incredible performance of Lugosi, buried him in fan mail. As a result, Lugosi became Universal's first horror star. (Tragically, his star would fade when horror went out of vogue.)

The success of *Dracula* prompted Universal to release *Frankenstein* a few months later. Mary Shelley's story of a scientist bringing to life a man made up of dead body parts had previously been filmed twice, once by Thomas Edison in 1910 and once as *Life Without Soul* in 1915. Stories about the Universal production have practically become legends. Robert Florey was to direct the film, and he started putting together a script adapted from the stage play. But James Whale, newly arrived from England and coming off the success of *Journey's End* (1930), was the studio's new wonder. Offered his choice of any project currently in the works, he took *Frankenstein* away from a devastated Florey.

Studio executives wanted Lugosi to play the role of the Monster in their newest horror film. Stories say Lugosi refused the role when he found out the Monster had no dialogue. It was later revealed that Lugosi made a disastrous screen test with makeup patterned after Paul Wegener's *The Golem* (1920). Either way, for the rest of his life Lugosi would regret not playing the role. Whale cast bit player Boris Karloff as the Monster after spotting him in the studio commissary. Under the brilliant makeup by Jack Pierce, Karloff brought sympathy to the role and won the hearts of millions. With able performances by Colin Clive, Dwight Frye, and Mae Clarke, the film was even more successful than *Dracula*, and it made Karloff the studio's second horror star.

Karloff turned out to be a better actor than Lugosi, partly because the Hungarian-born Lugosi had never taken the time to properly learn the English language. The studio heads found Karloff to be much more of a gentleman, and he started receiving all the better horror roles they had to offer. For the rest of his life, Lugosi would stand in the shadow of Boris Karloff. Even when horror was out of vogue, Karloff would be getting work in other genres or on the stage while Lugosi would get nothing but poverty row pictures. Lugosi ended his life appearing in some of the worst films of all time, directed by current cult favorite Edward D. Wood, Jr. Yet Lugosi must still be admired, for he gave his all to any and every project, no matter how low on the ladder.

Over the next two years, Universal increased its horror output. In fact, horror was so popular the studio would insert one or two horror scenes into "straight" films and advertise them as pure horror movies, as they did with *The Man Who Reclaimed His Head* (1934) and *The House of Fear* (1939).

Universal's biggest horror releases of 1932 were *Murders in the Rue Morgue*, *The Old Dark House*, and *The Mummy*. *Murders* was Florey's directorial consolation prize but was nowhere near as good as *Frankenstein*. Lugosi appeared in the role of Dr. Mirakle, a mad scientist attempting to mate women with a killer ape. The other two pictures were Karloff vehicles and two of the greatest horror films ever made.

The Old Dark House was a black comedy named after the horror mysteries of the silent and early talkie periods. James Whale directed a once-in-a-lifetime ensemble of actors: Karloff, Raymond Massey, Melvyn Douglas, Gloria Stuart, Ernest Thesiger, Eva Moore, and Charles Laughton (in his first American film). The story deals with travelers forced to spend a night in an old house during a terrible storm. The house belongs to the Femms, a family of oddballs including a one-hundred-year-old patriarch, an effeminate son wanted by the law, a religious fanatic daughter, a pyromaniac son, and the mute butler Morgan (played by Karloff). Finally released on video, the film is a masterpiece and still chilling even today.

The Mummy featured Karloff as Im-Ho-Tep, an ancient Egyptian buried alive because he tried to bring his beloved princess back to life.

Found by archeologists in the present day, the Mummy is brought back to life by the Scroll of Thoth. Taking the name Ardeth Bey, he leads the archeologists to the burial grounds of his former lover. Upon realizing the soul of his beloved has been reincarnated in the lovely heroine (Zita Johann), he takes steps to make her live forever as a mummy like himself. Directed by former cameraman Karl Freund, Karloff is ably supported by *Dracula* stars Edward Van Sloan and David Manners. Although not as fast-moving as other Universal horror pictures (including its 1940 sequel, *The Mummy's Hand*), the film is a classic and repeated viewings make the picture's greatness apparent.

Nineteen thirty-three saw the release of another James Whale classic, *The Invisible Man*, one of the characters Abbott and Costello would eventually meet. Hollywood legend has it Universal wanted Karloff for the role but he turned it down when he found out he would not actually be seen until the film's final moments (similar to Lugosi's sentiments when asked to be the Frankenstein Monster). Claude Rains was cast as Jack Griffin, the scientist who turns himself invisible. But the serum affects his mind and makes him go mad. Intending to conquer the world, the Invisible Man kills again and again until brought down by the police who see his footprints during a snowstorm. The film is a great piece of work and John Fulton's effects are still incredible today. (Incidentally, the film made Claude Rains a star.)

In 1934, Universal teamed their two greatest horror stars, Boris Karloff and Bela Lugosi, in their first film together — *The Black Cat*. Directed by Edgar G. Ulmer, this cult classic features Lugosi as a former prisoner of war looking for his wife and daughter. Karloff is the Satan-worshipping traitor who caused Lugosi's imprisonment. Karloff married Lugosi's wife and, after she died, married his daughter. Although advertised as being based on the work of Edgar Allan Poe, the script had nothing to do with any of the author's famous stories. The film (which culminates in a scene that has Lugosi skin Karloff alive) was successful, however, and led to the two re-teaming the next year in *The Raven*.

In *The Raven*, Lugosi plays a famous surgeon obsessed with Poe. When his love for a patient is denied, he goes mad. Karloff portrays an escaped killer who wants Lugosi to change the way he looks. But Lugosi disfigures Karloff, blackmails him into helping to torture and kill the girl, her father, and her fiancé. Decadent and dark, these two films helped lead to the banning of horror movies in Britain.

In 1935, Universal added another monster to its stable with

the release of *Werewolf of London*. Henry Hull played the title role but he refused to let makeup wizard Jack Pierce cover him with too much makeup. The film did not do as well as Universal's other monster flicks and the werewolf would not become a major player until 1941 when Lon Chaney, Jr., essayed the role of *The Wolf Man*. Wary of trying something new, the studio now decided to do their first sequel.

Colin Clive, Boris Karloff, and director James Whale returned for *Bride of Frankenstein* (1935). Whale crafted the sequel as a black comedy which many prefer to its predecessor. The storyline has Dr. Frankenstein coerced by the evil Dr. Pretorius (Ernest Thesiger in his best role) into creating a mate for the Monster, who survived the burning windmill at the climax of *Frankenstein*. In fact, the film is all about the Monster as he terrorizes the countryside. Along the way, he learns his first words, taught to him by a friendly blind hermit. Elsa Lanchester appears as the Bride in the film's climactic moments. She rejects the Monster and he bitterly blows up the lab with he, she, and Dr. Pretorius in it.

Bride was successful so the studio produced another sequel, this time to *Dracula*. Bela Lugosi was originally supposed to appear in *Dracula's Daughter* (1936) but was dropped in favor of a wooden dummy. Gloria Holden starred in the title role with Edward Van Sloan returning as Van Helsing. It was a fine picture but turned out to be the studio's last horror film for close to three years.

Although producing scores of successful films, the studio's losses were still exceeding their profits. The losses were attributed to "the devastating effects of the Depression, an industry-wide strike that forced the studio to cease production for several months, and charges of gross nepotism."[5] The studio was verging on bankruptcy.

In 1935, Laemmle secured emergency funding by making a deal with J. Cheever Cowdin's Standard Capital Corporation and tycoon Charles R. Rogers. Part of the deal stated that the two would be given an option to buy the studio within three months if part of the loan was not repaid.[6] As a result, Laemmle lost the studio in 1936. Robert M. Cochrane became the new president and Rogers took Carl, Jr.'s, role as vice president in charge of production.

After *Dracula's Daughter*, the "New Universal" dropped all horror projects in favor of "low-budget action subjects, innocuous musicals, and comedies."[7]

While the first cycle of classic Universal horror films ran its course, events occurred that led up to the formation of the comedy team of Abbott and Costello.

The two were both working the burlesque circuits and probably met for the first time while working at the Republic Theater in New York in the early months of 1933. In 1934, Lou met and married chorus girl Anne Battler. Anne's career as a dancer was later halted when she suffered a broken neck in a car accident.

In 1935, Bud and Lou were both booked at the Eltinge Theater where they started to occasionally perform together. This led to their first official show as a comedy team in 1936. They were signed by the Minskys and spent April of that year touring in the show *Life Begins At Minsky's*. Unlike other burlesque comics, Bud and Lou used only clean material in their act. They were always proud of the fact that they used clean humor throughout their careers.

The duo honed their act over the next two years then became more legit by moving up to vaudeville in 1937. Burlesque was dying out and by doing vaudeville in the big cities, Abbott and Costello were able to earn more money.

In February 1938, they were signed to play the Loew's State Theater in New York. While there, they were seen by Ted Collins, the manager of popular radio star Kate Smith. He immediately wanted them to appear on her show. On February 3, 1938, they made their first radio appearance doing their routines. Listeners complained they had trouble distinguishing between the two voices so Lou adopted a higher pitched voice. Other than that, they were well received.

They eventually signed a contract and appeared on the show for 99 weeks until the summer of 1940. Part of their contract stated that they had to perform "Who's on First?" (their most famous routine) once a month, since it was unbelievably popular the first time they did it over the air. Years later, they received their own radio program and they continued the tradition of regularly performing the beloved bit.

In 1938, the duo appeared in stage shows at the prestigious Roxy Theater. The following year they were on Broadway in *Streets of Paris*. They received great reviews. By this time, their characters were down pat. Bud was the pushy, older-and-wiser, street-smart con man — the brains of the outfit. Lou was a naive, childlike patsy always getting in trouble. In reality, Lou was the driving force of the group. Although they won success after success, he still wanted more. He wanted to be a movie star.

Bud did not want to go to Hollywood but Lou finally convinced him it was the next logical thing for them to do. In 1940, they made the move and appeared in their first picture for Universal studios, *One Night in the Tropics*, a romantic musical co-starring Allan Jones and Bob Cummings.

The picture did not do well but the critics unanimously praised the work of Abbott and Costello. That was enough for Universal and they signed Abbott and Costello (A&C) to a contract.

Paddy Costello paints a vivid picture of what life was like when her father worked for Universal:

> Universal at the time wasn't like it is now. Not that huge, you didn't have the theme park or anything like that. It was much smaller — not in area — but it was great on a weekend or school holidays. Dad would always take us down there and we loved it. We were very good friends, very dear friends, with the man and his family, Frankie Van, who ran the gym there. We'd get bored or whatever and Dad would send us down to Frankie and we'd go to the gym and put the boxing mitts on and hit the punching bag — do all sorts of things. And Frankie had a daughter, too, who was our age so we were just like sisters. And they'd stick us in a projection room and have some poor guy show us every Johnny Mack Brown western that was ever made. We would pretty much just run around and do whatever we wanted to do. You had to know the rules. You knew when you could enter a set and when you couldn't enter or if you were not allowed to, you couldn't. So, like I said, he did take us there quite a bit. Oh, and on location, too, which was really a lot of fun. That was great fun. You'd go down, like into Calabasas, that's way out in the west valley, and it was all open land at that time. It's probably all houses now. But they did *Mexican Hayride* [1948] out there and some other films. And that was a lot of fun because you'd have caterers and people would want to do things in between to keep busy (in between when they were setting things up). They'd have softball games, all kinds of things going on. The people on the sets were always very good to us. They were very tolerant and we always had a lot of fun with them. The makeup man, if he wasn't busy, would put us in the chair and put scars on us, make us up. Everybody was great. The guy who was in charge of wardrobe — it was really neat. It was a great time. We had a lot of fun.[8]

By 1939, Universal was again close to going broke. Legend has it that a small theater in a large city was also close to going under. As a last ditch chance for survival, the shrewd owner booked a triple feature of *Dracula*, *Frankenstein*, and *The Son of Kong*. People came in droves to see the films and lines ran around the block. The theater was saved. Whether or nor the story is true, it is a fact Universal reissued both films that year and were surprised by how successful they were. Horror was back in vogue. To capitalize on it, the studio brought back Boris Karloff and Bela Lugosi for a second Frankenstein sequel, *Son of Frankenstein*.

It would be Karloff's last time playing the Monster. He felt the Monster had become a prop, that the character was nothing but a killing machine. Future films would prove him correct. Still, *Son* is a great film thanks to Lugosi's performance as Ygor, the demented shepherd who befriends the Monster. Lugosi's role was expanded by director Rowland V. Lee to the point where the down-on-his-luck actor stole the show. (Lugosi was financially hurt by the decline in horror popularity.) Rounding out the cast were Basil Rathbone as Frankenstein's scientist son and Lionel Atwill as the one-armed police inspector (one of his best performances). The film was a huge hit and Universal made plans to revive their other monster characters.

The same year Abbott and Costello made their first film, Universal released *The Mummy's Hand* and *The Invisible Man Returns*. The former was not the return of Im-Ho-Tep, but actually a new Mummy, Kharis, who spent the movie wrapped up in his bandages (unlike Karloff's Im-Ho-Tep/Ardeth Bey in the original). A rousing adventure, the film featured serial star Tom Tyler as the Mummy and George Zucco as the villainous Egyptian high priest who revives Kharis and sends him out to do his bidding. Dick Foran and Wallace Ford were the comic heroes who defeated the Mummy and killed Zucco. The film was successful enough to launch three more sequels.

Vincent Price starred in *The Invisible Man Returns*, playing the original Invisible Man's brother. Accused of a murder he did not commit, Price takes the invisibility potion so he can find the true murderer and clear his name. The catch is, he must do so before the serum drives him mad. Price succeeds and is cured by the end of the movie. The film, which also features Cedric Hardwicke and Alan Napier, is a lot of fun and led to three more invisibility movies.

The first of those was released that same year and was Universal's initial outright horror-comedy, though the comedy elements were first and foremost. *The Invisible Woman* (1940) starred Virginia Bruce and John Barrymore and did not fit in with the continuing saga of the Griffin family. Bruce plays a fashion model who volunteers for a dotty scientist's experiment to turn a human being invisible. Gangsters find out and attempt to steal the secret. Lighthearted and fun, the film is pure fluff and unlike the rest of the series.

In 1941, Bud and Lou had their first starring roles in the service comedy *Buck Privates*. Not fully trusting the boys to carry the picture themselves, the studio made the film a musical comedy, with most of the songs being performed by the Andrews Sisters. (Their most popular song, "The Boogie Woogie Bugle Boy of Company B," appeared here for the first time.) The boys did their drill routine, the dice routine, and the "Go-Ahead-and-Sing" routine, among others, and the film was a smash hit. It was so big that it saved Universal from bankruptcy. Abbott and Costello were, in an incredibly short amount of time, movie stars. Paddy Costello commented on the speed in which the duo became famous: "They had been working individually before and they had been putting in their time, so to speak. But I think, too, it was the times. It was around World War II and it was just the right time for that kind of humor. Abbott and Costello did a lot for the morale, got everybody laughing. They were just off and running."[9]

But Universal still did not trust them in a film without musical interludes, so the Andrews Sisters appeared in their next two films.

Even though the horror-comedy *Hold That Ghost* was already completed, the tremendous raves for *Buck Privates* caused Universal to rush another service comedy into production. *In The Navy* (1941) was released as the duo's next film and was similar to their earlier army adventure — consisting of Abbott and Costello routines strung together by a nominal plot with musical interludes. The story deals with a singing star (Dick Powell) hiding out in the Navy while being pursued by a beautiful reporter (Claire Dodd) who falls in love with him (and vice versa).

When *Hold That Ghost* was finally released in 1941, it did fantastically at the box office. Equally frightful and funny, it was the first time audiences were exposed to Costello's scared routines. The story dealt with the boys inheriting a haunted hotel from a gangster and getting trapped there one stormy night with fellow travelers and crooks looking for hidden loot. Also appearing were the Andrews Sisters, Ted Lewis, Richard Carlson, Joan Davis, and Evelyn Ankers (who was about to become Universal's primary horror heroine and the greatest of the forties' scream queens).

The film was so popular that Universal insisted their next picture, another service comedy called *Keep 'Em Flying*, include a scene where

Costello does his scared schtick. So, a carnival funhouse scene was inserted in which Costello is frightened by ghost props and an ape. The rest of the film featured hilarious routines that saw Abbott and Costello take to the sky in an airplane and bits with Martha Raye playing twin sisters who fall for the boys. Paddy Costello confided that *Keep 'Em Flying* was one of her favorites as a child. "When I was a kid, they told me I wore out a print of *Keep 'Em Flying*. Well, I had earaches when I was little and I'd have to stay in bed or something. We had a projector cause you didn't have video then. And over and over and over and over, I'd watch *Keep 'Em Flying* and I just wore out this 16mm print."[10]

On the horror side, Universal released two films promoting their newest horror star. *Man Made Monster* (1941), directed by George Waggner, featured Lionel Atwill in another of his mad scientist roles and Lon Chaney, Jr., making his first appearance in a Universal horror film. Lon was the son of the great silent film star Lon Chaney, dubbed "the Man of a Thousand Faces." Lon, Sr., played masochistic roles in which he contorted and pulled his body out of shape or hid his face under grotesque and often painful makeup — such as with his two most famous roles, *The Hunchback of Notre Dame* (1923) and *The Phantom of the Opera* (1925). Chaney was supposed to play Dracula in the 1931 film but died of cancer just before the film was to go into production.

Lon always forbade his son to make a career out of film, but Lon, Jr., was bitten by the acting bug and decided to try his luck in movies. Under his real name, Creighton Chaney, he had a few roles here and there but nothing worth noting. Studio executives ultimately convinced him to adopt his famous father's name. Finally, Lon had the greatest success of his career when he played Lenny in the stage and film adaptations of John Steinbeck's *Of Mice and Men* (1939). Many of the roles he played later would contain elements of his brilliant Lenny character.

Lon was signed with Universal and billed as the screen's "newest character creator." Producer/director George Waggner cast him in the role that would become Lon's most popular. He played Larry Talbot in *The Wolf Man* (1941) with a cast that included Evelyn Ankers, Claude Rains, Bela Lugosi, Ralph Bellamy, and Maria Ouspenskaya. The film finally gave the Universal pantheon of monsters a popular werewolf thanks to both Chaney's sympathetic portrayal of a man cursed to become a wolf when the moon is full and Jack Pierce's fantastic makeup.

The next year saw more horror films and more Abbott and Costello comedies. Lon Chaney, Jr., was cast as every monster Universal offered over the course of their series' sequels. He played the Monster in *The Ghost of Frankenstein* (1942), with Bela Lugosi repeating his role as the demented shepherd Ygor. Though Chaney's portrayal was not as subtle or sympathetic as Karloff's, the film is still enjoyable.

Chaney also played Kharis in the next Mummy sequel, *The Mummy's Tomb* (1942). This was Chaney's least favorite role because of its limitations. After all, the Mummy just shambled around choking people, and the makeup prevented any actor from giving the Mummy any personality. The film also killed off the Dick Foran and Wallace Ford characters from the previous picture while at the same time moving the action to America as the Mummy is shipped overseas.

The Invisible Man series continued in 1942 with *Invisible Agent*, a comedy–spy thriller. Jon Hall played a relative of the Invisible Man who has inherited the secret of the invisibility serum. After Japanese and Nazi spies attempt to steal it, he offers his services to America but only if he is the one to take the serum and cross enemy lines. It might sound corny but the film is highly enjoyable and marked by a superb performance from Peter Lorre as a Japanese spy.

Nineteen forty-two was also the year of the first Universal Sherlock Holmes film. Basil Rathbone and Nigel Bruce played the detective and his bumbling sidekick Dr. Watson in one of the most popular film series in history. The first two entries (*The Hound of the Baskervilles* and *The Adventures of Sherlock Holmes*— both 1939) had been done by 20th Century–Fox before the series was sold to Universal. That studio continued making Sherlock Holmes features until 1946 when Rathbone tired of the role. Many of the films bordered on horror and are often included in studies of the genre. The films include: *Sherlock Holmes and the Voice of Terror* (1942), *Sherlock Holmes and the Secret Weapon* (1942), *Sherlock Holmes in Washington* (1943), *Sherlock Holmes Faces Death* (1943), *The Spider Woman* (1944), *The Scarlet Claw* (1944), *Pearl of Death* (1944), *House of Fear* (1945), *The Woman in Green* (1945), *Pursuit to Algiers* (1945), *Terror by Night* (1946), and *Dressed to Kill* (1946).

Abbott and Costello made three pictures for Universal in 1942. *Ride 'Em Cowboy* was a routine western spoof with a great climactic chase. The supporting cast included Dick Foran, Anne Gwynne, Douglas Dumbrille, and Ella Fitzgerald.

Pardon My Sarong is very funny and features horror star Lionel Atwill as the villain. The boys get shipwrecked on a tropical island where Lou is declared the "chosen" hero and forced to brave a haunted temple.

Who Done It?, one of the duo's funniest pictures, is a murder mystery set in a radio station. Bud and Lou work as soda jerks but aspire to be radio writers. When the head of the network is killed, the boys decide to solve the murder themselves so they can get jobs as mystery writers. In the course of events, they are chased by both the police and the killer, and Lou ends up performing with acrobats and winning $10,000 on a wheel of fortune show. Although the clues to solving the mystery are never that clear, the absence of musical numbers helps keep the pace moving and the laughs abundant.

Universal loaned Abbott and Costello to MGM on a year-to-year basis, and their fourth film of 1942 was their first feature for that studio. *Rio Rita* was the second film adaptation of the musical stageplay produced by Flo Ziegfeld in 1927. MGM updated the story to include Nazi spies and dropped all but two of the original songs. Abbott and Costello play two bumblers hired as house detectives at the Hotel Vista del Rio, run by the beautiful Rita. They defeat the enemy agents who are using the hotel as a base of operations.

Nineteen forty-three saw two Abbott and Costello releases. The first was *It Ain't Hay*, based on a Damon Runyan story and set in the world of horse racing. This is the only Universal Abbott and Costello film not currently available on video due to a dispute over musical rights.[11]

Hit the Ice was the other 1943 release. With Sheldon Leonard, Patric Knowles, and Ginny Simms offering support, the film has Abbott and Costello chasing bank robbers all the way to the ski slopes of Sun Valley. Although the musical numbers are even cornier than usual, there are enough great Abbott and Costello scenes to make the film worth watching.

Universal offered a nice selection of horror features that same year. One of them proved to be a genius of marketing. The studio decided that if one monster made a lot of money, then two monsters would make even more. Supposedly, writer Curt Siodmak had jokingly suggested teaming up Frankenstein's Monster with the Wolf Man for a film called "Frankenstein Wolfs the Meat Man." The producers took him seriously and commissioned him to write *Frankenstein Meets the Wolf Man*. Lon Chaney, Jr., was originally supposed to play both monsters but logistics made this impossible (especially since ads promised "The Battle of the Century"). Bela Lugosi was cast as the Monster. This was a low blow to the actor who had originally turned down the role in 1931. But typecasting kept him from getting good parts and he was hard up for work. His performance is considered to be the worst out of the actors who played the Monster, but it was not all his fault. The Monster, with Ygor's brain transplanted into his head in *The Ghost of Frankenstein,* was supposed to be blind so Lugosi played him that way. He also talked. But when the producers heard the Monster speaking with Bela's Hungarian accent, they cut out all his dialogue and all references to the Monster being blind. The result was the stumbling, oafish Monster seen in the film.

The plot deals with Talbot reviving and returning from the grave, still cursed as a lycanthrope. He searches for a way to die and finally be at peace. Maleva the gypsy (again played by Maria Ouspenskaya) takes him to see Dr. Frankenstein but they discover the doctor is long since dead. Talbot finds the Monster who shows him where Frankenstein's notebooks are hidden. Talbot's young doctor (Patric Knowles) reads the notebooks and decides to bring the Monster to full power. In the end, werewolf and monster battle until frightened villagers blow up a dam and wash away the creatures. The film definitely has its faults, but Chaney's performance is one of his best. The picture's opening scenes are classic, an example of Universal at its creepiest. (*Frankenstein Meets the Wolf Man* appeared on a double bill with *It Ain't Hay,* foreshadowing *Abbott and Costello Meet Frankenstein*[12]).

Chaney was soon cast as Dracula in *Son of Dracula* playing Anthony Alucard. Critics still debate whether or not he was an appropriate choice for the role. He certainly brought a different interpretation to the character, at times making the aristocratic vampire more of a thug.

Chaney also appeared in the first of the Inner Sanctum Mysteries, *Calling Dr. Death.* Based on the radio program, these films were borderline horror mysteries designed as vehicles for Chaney. Insanity, murder, and false accusations were the main themes of the series which ran until 1945 and included: *Weird Woman* (1944), *Dead Man's Eyes* (1944), *The Frozen Ghost* (1945), *Strange Confession* (1945), and *Pillow of Death* (1945). For years, these were the most difficult Universal horror films to see but they were recently released on video as part of the Universal Horror Classics series.

Chaney probably hoped to play the role his father had made famous when Universal remade *Phantom of the Opera* in 1943, but Claude Rains was cast instead. The film displayed more opera than horror and was not nearly as good as its silent predecessor.

The Mad Ghoul had George Zucco as a mad scientist who turns

David Bruce into the title character, a creature forced to consume human hearts, in order to steal the boy's fiancée Evelyn Ankers. A bit different from most Universal horror films, the film unfortunately did not start its own series.

Captive Wild Woman did. John Carradine stars as a mad scientist who turns a gorilla into Paula, a beautiful and exotic woman. But jealousy over a man causes Paula to revert back to her simian state. Paula was woodenly played by the studio's latest discovery, Acquanetta, an actress of very minor talent.

Nineteen forty-four saw the continuation of the Invisible Man franchise with *The Invisible Man's Revenge*. Jon Hall returned as the Invisible One but there was no connection to previous films in the series. Here, an unhinged crook uses scientist John Carradine's invisibility serum to take revenge on a family who wronged him.

Jungle Woman (1944) continued the adventures of Paula the ape woman. Unfortunately, 75 percent of the picture was made up of flashbacks to the first film, making this a very dull excursion.

The Mummy series was wrapped up (pun intended) that year with *The Mummy's Ghost* and *The Mummy's Curse*, both starring Lon Chaney, Jr. The plots were the same, with the Mummy being revived and killing at the command of an Egyptian priest before being destroyed by townspeople. John Carradine and Martin Kosleck played the Mummy's evil controllers, respectively, while Virginia Christine provided an effective turn as the reincarnation of Princess Ananka in *Curse*. The scene in which she emerges from a swamp is both creepy and atmospheric, possibly the best moment in the Mummy series. Curiously, when Abbott and Costello later met the Mummy in 1955, it was not Kharis they met but a new mummy named Klaris.

Ghost Catchers was a comedy-horror film featuring Ole Olson and Chic Johnson, Universal's other comedy team who were never as popular as Abbott and Costello. The two own a nightclub next to a haunted house. The new residents ask their help in exorcising the spirit, and the pair soon discovers that gangsters have been using the house for illegal activities. A strange mishmash of music, comedy, and scares, the film is only for genre buffs looking for something odd. After all, any film casting Andy Devine as the "horse" and Lon Chaney, Jr., as the "bear" is bound to be weird.

Since *Frankenstein Meets the Wolf Man* was a success, Universal decided to really give the audience a treat. *House of Frankenstein* was advertised as featuring five monsters: Dracula, the Frankenstein Monster, the Wolf Man, the mad doctor, and the hunchback. Actually, the film consists of two stories. Boris Karloff is a mad doctor who escapes from prison with his homicidal hunchback assistant J. Carrol Naish. They murder George Zucco, the proprietor of a "Circus of Horrors" which features the skeleton of Dracula. Dracula materializes as John Carradine and kills one of Karloff's old enemies before being destroyed by sunlight. The second story has Karloff and Naish allowing a gypsy girl Naish has fallen in love with to accompany them on a trek to Karloff's home village. On the way, Karloff discovers Talbot and the Monster (Lon Chaney, Jr., and former western actor Glenn Strange) frozen in ice. Karloff promises to cure Talbot but is more interested in using the Monster to wreak vengeance on more of his enemies. In the end, the gypsy girl shoots Talbot with a silver bullet, the Monster kills Naish, and villagers force the Monster (carrying Karloff) into the swamp where both drown in quicksand.

For Abbott and Costello, 1944 was a tragic year. Lou came down with rheumatic fever on his thirty-seventh birthday which kept him from working for many months. His recovery was helped along by his infant son Butch, of whom he was very proud. But in November of 1944, on the day Butch was to hear his father on the radio for the first time, the child drowned in the family's swimming pool. Lou was heartbroken but went on the air anyway, hoping his son would still hear no matter where he was. Many say Lou never fully recovered from the loss and, as a result, lost his youthful spirit. He became indifferent toward his work, less patient on the set, and less friendly.[13] *In Society* was the only Universal Abbott and Costello film to appear in 1944. But, they did do a film for MGM, *Lost in a Harem*, one of their less memorable pictures.

By 1945, neither the horror pictures nor the Abbott and Costello films were doing well at the box office. The overexposure of the horror product[14] was one reason for the decline in that genre's popularity, while the Abbott and Costello pictures just could not recapture the magic of their earlier works. Three of the duo's films were released that year, two from Universal and one from MGM.

Here Come the Co-Eds featured the boys as caretakers of a girls college. Lon Chaney, Jr., also appeared with them and wrestles with Lou in one of the scenes. Although just an average film, it did have a good climax with Lou in drag playing basketball with the school's team.

The Naughty Nineties was a period piece that proved much funnier.

It is the only film in which Bud and Lou performed "Who's on First?" in its entirety. They do lots of other bits, too. In fact, the plot, about crooked gamblers taking over the riverboat where Bud and Lou work (Bud as a famous actor, Lou as ... well, Lou), is just an excuse to get from bit to bit. They must have been hard up for material, however, because many of the bits are taken from other comedians. For example, Lou bakes a cake not knowing an oven mitt is inside the batter, and soon a room full of gamblers are coughing up feathers. This was a routine used time and again by the Three Stooges. They also lift the mirror routine from the Marx Brothers with Lou mimicking villain Joe Sawyer as he tries to shave.

MGM's release was *Abbott and Costello in Hollywood*, the first film to feature the comedians' names in the title. They play barbers in Hollywood who hope to become big name talent agents by representing an up and coming singer. The film featured cameos by Lucille Ball and Rags Ragland and is probably the best of the MGM Abbott and Costello films.

Besides the Inner Sanctum and Sherlock Holmes mysteries, the horror output from Universal in 1945 consisted of *House of Dracula* and *Jungle Captive*. *House of Dracula* was another teaming of the three monsters along with a mad scientist and a hunchback, although this time the hunchback was a female nurse. Also different this round was more interaction between the characters. Talbot met Dracula for the first time, though not in his werewolf form.

The plot has Dracula (again played by John Carradine), coming to scientist Dr. Edelmann (Onslow Stevens), seeking a cure for his vampirism. The doctor agrees to help even though the vampire sets his sights on Edelmann's beautiful assistant (Martha O'Driscoll). Meanwhile, Larry Talbot (who else but Lon Chaney, Jr.) is arrested and held at the local jail. Edelmann joins the local police in watching Talbot transform into the Wolf Man and agrees to also take on his case. But Talbot cannot wait and tries to commit suicide by jumping off a cliff into the ocean. He is found by the doctor in a seaside cavern where the remains of the Frankenstein Monster (Glenn Strange) have washed up from the previous film. Dracula has second thoughts about being cured and, unbeknownst to the doctor, gives Edelmann his own tainted blood. Edelmann destroys Dracula but goes mad, killing a villager and making plans to revive the Monster. In a rare moment of lucidity, he expands Talbot's cranium and cures him of being a werewolf. As villagers storm the house, Talbot kills Edelmann and the Monster. He even gets the girl!

By this time, the Frankenstein Monster had become nothing more than a prop, spending most of the film lying on a table. Still, the film is enjoyable. Dracula plays a more significant role and the mad scientist is a Jekyll-Hyde type of fiend. Talbot does not kill anyone in his wolf state and survives at the film's conclusion. (His cure would not last long. He turns up in *Abbott and Costello Meet Frankenstein* still cursed as a werewolf, with no explanation given as to why!)

Jungle Captive wrapped up the jungle woman series with Vicky Lane replacing Acquanetta as Paula the ape woman and Otto Kruger playing the obligatory mad scientist. Also in the cast was Rondo Hatton, Universal's newest horror "star." Hatton suffered from acromegaly, a disease of the pituitary gland causing abnormal growth in the hands and face. Because he was overly large and deformed, studio publicity made a big deal of the fact that Hatton played his roles without any makeup. He appeared in *The Spider Woman Strikes Back* (1946) and in the Sherlock Holmes thriller *Pearl of Death*, which was the first time he played the Creeper, an insane killer who breaks his victims' backs.

The Creeper would appear in two more films in 1946. *House of Horrors* featured Martin Kosleck as a sculptor unable to find favor with the critics. After saving the Creeper's life, he uses the creature to kill the critics who mocked his work.

The Brute Man was a prequel to that film, telling the origin of how the Creeper came to be. By now, Universal was totally exploiting Hatton, who had no acting talent whatsoever. Embarrassed by the film, they refused to release it, instead selling it to a poverty row studio (PRC) who did not share Universal's qualms in presenting the film. Hatton died that same year. So did the Universal horror film.

Again having money problems, Universal merged in 1946 with International Pictures, becoming Universal-International. William Goetz and Leo Spitz took charge of the studio's productions while Nate Blumberg became chairman of the board. With Basil Rathbone walking away from the Sherlock Holmes series and the public seemingly disinterested in the classic monsters, the horror films ceased production. Goetz also had no use for Abbott and Costello, but he realized they still had some power at the box office. So, Abbott and Costello films continued to appear.

Nineteen forty-six saw the comedians experimenting with a new format. *Little Giant* featured Abbott and Costello playing separate characters and not working as a team. Costello is a farm boy with dreams of being a successful salesman. Abbott plays two roles as brothers working for a vacuum cleaner company. The film did not go over very well even though they did perform one bit, "13 x 7 = 28," in which Costello proves through multiplication, division, and addition that seven, thirteen times over, is twenty-eight.

The Time of Their Lives is a much better film with the two again working separately. It features Lou and Marjorie Reynolds as Revolutionary war ghosts falsely branded as traitors and cursed to haunt a plantation until their innocence is proven. Abbott again plays two roles, the evil servant who frames Costello and the servant's modern day descendant who helps the ghosts gain their entrance to Heaven.

These two experiments failed because audiences wanted to see the boys working as a team. So, in 1947, they attempted to boost their box office by returning to the property that made them stars in the first place. *Buck Privates Come Home* was the only sequel they ever appeared in as they continued their adventures as Slicker Smith and Herbie Brown. There were no musical interludes this time around as the boys attempted to adjust to civilian life by finding jobs and caring for a French orphan girl.

This was followed by the great western spoof *The Wistful Widow of Wagon Gap* which also featured popular Universal star Marjorie Main (star of the Ma and Pa Kettle series). Hilariously funny, the story has Lou mistakenly believing he has killed a man in a gunfight. An obscure town law states the murderer of a man must care for that man's wife and family. So, Lou inherits the feisty widow and her bratty brood. Lou eventually becomes sheriff, cleaning up the town because no one has the guts to shoot him and take on the widow.

Although they were still making good films, Abbott and Costello's careers were at an all-time low. In 1948, Abbott and Costello made their last film for MGM, *The Noose Hangs High*, a jumbled film about gangsters that does contain some good bits. Meanwhile, at Universal, studio execs searched for a good property that would fit the two comics.

That was when someone had the great idea of bringing back the classic monsters for one more blaze of glory while, at the same time, inserting Abbott and Costello. Combining Abbott and Costello with Dracula, the Wolf Man, and the Frankenstein Monster was a risky idea. Would it work? Would it be funny?

The answer turned out to be "yes" for both questions. *Meet Frankenstein*, today considered by most to be the greatest horror-comedy ever made, was so successful it influenced the majority of the Abbott and Costello films to come, resulting in them teaming up with a multitude of fictional characters.

That same year saw the release of *Mexican Hayride* with Lou again cast as the victim of con man Bud. The highlight of this film was a comic bullfight with Costello as matador, but otherwise the picture did not have much to offer.

Starting in 1949, the team decided to produce one independent feature a year and they sought a deal with an outside studio.[15] *Africa Screams* was the first of these, done for the Nassour Brothers. The plot has Abbott and Costello on safari in Africa looking for priceless diamonds. Costello's character is deathly afraid of animals which allowed him to do his scared routine with a gorilla. The supporting cast was incredible, and included Hillary Brooke, Max Baer, Buddy Baer, Frank Buck, Clyde Beatty, Shemp Howard, and Joe Besser.

Meanwhile, over at Universal, the duo appeared in the first film directly inspired by *Meet Frankenstein*. Teaming with one of the all time great horror stars, *Abbott and Costello Meet the Killer, Boris Karloff* was more of a murder mystery spoof than a horror-comedy.

The duo's next three films were also done at Universal. *Abbott and Costello in the Foreign Legion* (1950) has a pretty self-explanatory title. In some ways it was a remake of *Lost in a Harem* but had the boys play wrestling promoters chasing after one of their star wrestlers and winding up as soldiers in the French Foreign Legion. *Abbott and Costello Meet the Invisible Man* (1951) featured Arthur Franz and William Frawley and was one of the team's last great films. Highlighting the antics was a boxing match with Lou being helped by the Invisible Man while in the ring. That same year saw the release of one of the team's worst pictures, *Comin' Round the Mountain*. Here, Lou discovered he was actually a member of the McCoy hillbilly clan and in line to inherit a fortune in gold. The film was marred by a bad script and poor acting but did have a standout scene with Lou matching wits with Margaret Hamilton (playing her typical witch character).

Meanwhile, Universal attempted to bring back the horror picture with two Gothic costume dramas. *The Strange Door* (1951) starred Boris Karloff and an over-the-top Charles Laughton and told the story of a French nobleman obsessed with tormenting and torturing his brother and niece. Nineteen fifty-two's *The Black Castle* also starred Karloff and featured Lon Chaney, Jr., in a small role. Here, a nobleman infiltrated the castle of the sadistic count who murdered his two friends. Neither were overly well received, and neither are more than footnotes in the history of the horror film. Recently, they were released on video as part of the Universal Horror Classics series.

Abbott and Costello appeared in two independent films and one Universal entry in 1952. The Universal film was *Lost in Alaska* which also starred Tom Ewell. With the boys searching for gold in Alaska, the film was reminiscent of Hope and Crosby's *Road to Utopia* (1945) but not nearly as well made.

The two other 1952 pictures, one produced by Costello and the other by Abbott, were both done in color. *Jack and the Beanstalk* had babysitter Costello falling asleep and imagining himself in the title role of the famous fairy tale. Although enjoyable, this film has the worst romantic leads of any Abbott and Costello picture. Neither of the two leads could act at all and were solely cast due to vocal talent. Even there they fail, however, for they are forced to sing sappy songs that ruin the movie.

Abbott and Costello Meet Captain Kidd featured Charles Laughton as the infamous pirate. Laughton took a salary cut to work with the boys because he was a fan of their work and wanted to learn how to do "low" comedy. It is strange but fun to see him doing doubletakes and breaking the fourth wall. Hillary Brooke was also on hand as a female pirate who is inexplicably interested in Lou. At one point, she tells Costello that she first wanted to kill him but now wants to kiss him. Years later, Bruce Campbell would utter a similar line in the very funny Universal production *Army of Darkness* (1991): "First you want to kill me. Now you want to kiss me. Blow."

The horror film had completely died out in the fifties. Prevalent Communist paranoia and fear of atomic war caused the science fiction picture to replace the horror film in the hearts of the movie-going public. The monsters were still there but now they were either space aliens or creatures created by rampant technology. Universal was right there in the forefront. *It Came from Outer Space* (1953), based on a story by Ray Bradbury and directed by Jack Arnold, starred *Hold That Ghost*'s own Richard Carlson as a scientist who discovers aliens are taking over the bodies of his neighbors and using them as slave labor to help repair their spaceship. The film was done in 3-D, a then-popular trend in science fiction, and the trailer featured Carlson explaining the process.

Abbott and Costello's 1953 releases capitalized on the sci-fi craze.

Abbott and Costello Go to Mars put the duo in a rocket and sent them soaring into space. They first thought they had landed on Mars but had really landed in the midst of Mardi Gras. A second take-off takes them to Venus, a planet consisting entirely of women (a popular sci-fi theme in such films as *Cat Women of the Moon* [1953] and *Queen of Outer Space* [1958]). *Abbott and Costello meet Dr. Jekyll and Mr. Hyde* was set in Victorian England but used science as the means necessary to turn meek Henry Jekyll into the vicious werewolf-like Mr. Hyde.

Universal's last monster series was the Creature trilogy which began with *Creature from the Black Lagoon* in 1954. A wonderful film, it starred Richard Carlson, Richard Denning, and Julie Adams as explorers on the Amazon who discover a prehistoric gill-man. He takes a fancy for Miss Adams and kidnaps her after killing many of the ship's crew. Bullets destroy him, but he returned for *Revenge of the Creature* (1955) and *The Creature Walks Among Us* (1956), in which he was given lungs only to become a zombie-like hulk who drowns upon returning to the ocean. The first was the best film of the series, helmed by Jack Arnold and featuring a great score and good underwater photography. The poetic scenes of the Creature swimming beneath Julie Adams are unforgettable. (Bud and Lou would later "meet" the Creature on a segment of *The Colgate Comedy Hour*.)

Other 1955 sci-fi releases included *Cult of the Cobra*, *This Island Earth*, and *Tarantula*, the last of which was inspired by the giant insect subgenre begun by *Them!* in 1954. Abbott and Costello, meanwhile, appeared in their final two films for Universal in 1955. *Abbott and Costello Meet the Keystone Kops* was their homage to silent comedy and featured a cameo by Mack Sennett. *Abbott and Costello Meet the Mummy* was the worst of the "Meet the Monsters" series and will be covered later in the book.

Universal would continue producing science fiction thrillers, including *The Mole People* (1956), *The Monolith Monsters* (1957), *Monster on the Campus* (1958), and *The Leech Woman* (1960), before that genre also died out. *The Monolith Monsters* is a particularly good thriller about a small town endangered by falling rock crystals from space that turn people to stone. The star of that film, Grant Williams, appeared in Universal's most mature science fiction film yet. *The Incredible Shrinking Man* appeared in 1957 and was directed by Jack Arnold. It told the story of an everyday man who, after being exposed to a strange radioactive cloud, starts to shrink in size. Nothing is able to stop the process and he ends up only a few inches tall fighting for his life against the pet cat and a spider in the basement. The uncharacteristic ending was downbeat in that Williams was left for dead by his wife. Yet the message proved upbeat — about to shrink into subatomic worlds, Williams realizes that no matter how small he becomes, he will still be acknowledged by God. His last words: "To God there is no zero; I still exist!"

The horror film came back in to vogue in the late fifties thanks to Britain's Hammer films, which brought back the classic characters of Dracula and Dr. Frankenstein in the guise of new horror stars Christopher Lee and Peter Cushing. Universal would eventually give Hammer permission to remake their old horror pictures, so up sprang new film versions of such characters as *The Mummy* (1959), *Phantom of the Opera* (1962), and the werewolf (*The Curse of the Werewolf* [1961]).

Abbott and Costello, after a short-lived but successful television show and one final film — the atrocious *Dance With Me, Henry* (1956) — finally split up in 1957. Paddy Costello remembers:

> It's too bad. I think that maybe they had just reached the peak and that was it. But I can remember my Dad talking to me maybe a couple of years before he died that he really wanted to do dramatic parts. And the man could sing. He had a beautiful voice.... And there was talk of him being on Broadway doing Fiorello [La Guardia] and he would have made a great Sancho Panza.... He told me, too, about this script that he wanted to work on where he would play a little priest in Italy, something like that. Just the way he described it, it was great. But he never got a chance to do it, which is really sad because I think he would have done very, very well.[16]

Costello did make television appearances on *GE Theater, Wagon Train,* and *The Steve Allen Show* while making plans to appear on the stage. He made one film without Abbott but was very sick during filming. The picture, a sci-fi spoof called *The 30 Foot Bride of Candy Rock* (1959), was simply awful, and Costello died of a heart attack only weeks after filming was completed. He left our world on March 3, 1959, after suffering a previous attack five days before. He was only 52 years old.[17]

Abbott stayed out of the spotlight for some time during which he had more tax troubles with the government. In 1960, he planned a comeback with comedian Candy Candido doing the old routines and bits. This new team lasted only a short time, as they were forced to split when Bud became ill. In 1961, Bud appeared on an episode of *GE Theater* then retired from entertaining for some time.

Interest in Abbott and Costello picked up and Universal released *The World of Abbott and Costello* (1965), a compilation of clips from some of their Universal films. Several of their best routines were left out, however, and an unfunny narration by Jack E. Leonard did not help much.

In 1967, Hanna-Barbera began producing a series of cartoons based on Abbott and Costello. Bud came out of retirement to supply his own voice for the cartoon (Stan Irwin did Lou's voice). One hundred fifty-six cartoons were produced in all.

In 1971, Universal released the Abbott and Costello films in syndication and Bud was able to see the nationwide revival of his film work.

On April 24, 1974, Bud died in his home in Woodland Hills, California, of cancer. He was 78 years old.[18]

Today, through television and video, both the Abbott and Costello films and the Universal Horror Classics are more popular than ever. Generation after generation of fans continue to seek out and enjoy these incredible films. As time goes by, more and more people seriously study them and many books are available on either subject.

Boris Karloff's daughter Sara commented on both the popularity of Abbott and Costello and the monster films. Of the comedy team she said:

"They were geniuses in that field. They made ... the same valuable, unequalled contribution to the comedy genre as the classic horror stars to the classic horror film genre. They were masters of their craft and ... they will go down and have gone down already in the annals of history as one of the finest comedy teams ever."

Of the horror classics she said:

"They were unique at the time they were made. They were groundbreaking or envelope-pushing at the time. I think that they involved the audiences by virtue of their imagination. I think they were suspenseful. I think they were totally different from the films of today where the gore is dumped right in your lap in your own living room. They were supposed to be titillating but terrifying, not revolting."[19]

Part Two

The "Meet the Monsters" Formula

Abbott and Costello Meet Frankenstein

Released: August 20, 1948   *Running time:* 83 minutes
Reissued: March 23, 1956 (with *Abbott and Costello Meet the Killer, Boris Karloff*)

Directed by: Charles T. Barton; *Produced by:* Robert Arthur; *Original Screenplay by:* Robert Lees, Frederic I. Rinaldo, and John Grant; *Music by:* Frank Skinner; *Director of Photography:* Charles Van Enger; *Art Direction:* Bernard Herzbrun, Hilyard Brown; *Film Editor:* Frank Gross; *Set Decorations:* Russell A. Gausman, Oliver Emert; *Sound:* Leslie I. Carey, Robert Pritchard; *Orchestrations:* David Tamkin; *Gowns:* Grace Houston; *Hair Stylist:* Carmen Dirigo; *Makeup:* Bud Westmore; *Special Photography:* David S. Horsley, ASC, Jerome Ash, ASC; *Assistant Director:* Joseph E. Kenny.

Cast: Bud Abbott (Chick Young); Lou Costello (Wilbur Gray); Lon Chaney, Jr. (Lawrence Talbot); Bela Lugosi (Dracula); Glenn Strange (The Monster); Lenore Aubert (Sandra Mornay); Jane Randolph (Joan Raymond); Frank Ferguson (MacDougal); Charles Bradstreet (Prof. Stevens); Howard Negley (Harris); Joe Kirk (Man); Charles Straight (Man in Armor); George Barton (Man); Charles Sklover (Man); Paul Stader (Sergeant); Joe Walls (Man); Bobby Barber (Waiter); Vincent Price (Invisible Man, uncredited).

Bud Abbott and Lou Costello had previously considered teaming up with Universal's three main monsters for a Broadway show and discussed it with makeup man Jack Pierce in 1942. This idea never panned out and the real team-up occurred in the 1948 film. The concept is credited to producer Robert Arthur who said he just came up with the notion while sitting around with Ed Muhl. He supposedly had the idea of putting Costello's brain in the monster's body, as well as adding the characters of Dracula and the Wolf Man to the mix. Muhl gave him the go ahead and writers were brought in to hammer out a script.[20]

According to other sources, however, this was not the way it happened. Writer Oscar Brodney was the first to take a crack at the screenplay and wrote a treatment (which is not in the Universal archives). Next, Bertram Milhauser did a 47 page treatment titled "Abbott and Costello Meet Frankenstein" which was submitted on February 12, 1947. The idea of using Costello's brain in the monster did not appear in this treatment. Instead, the plot from *Sherlock Holmes in Washington* was recycled in a story wherein a villain named Dr. Fell steals a formula from Baroness von Frankenstein that will re-animate the monsters. The plot that follows is ridiculous. The Baroness tells her granddaughter, Jane, who teams up with FBI agent Dan Barlowe, to stop Fell. Fell is arriving in New York by ocean liner and when he learns that Barlowe knows of his plans, he hides the formula (on microfilm) in a matchbook. He then tricks Abbott and Costello, who are working as stewards, into carrying the matchbook off the ship. Most of the story revolves around the comedy duo losing, then recovering, the matchbook over and over.

Abbott and Costello eventually take the matchbook to the museum where Fell works and where the monsters are on exhibit. Jane has Fell escort her to a costume party at the Waldorf Astoria, then leaves him trapped in an elevator while Barlowe searches for the formula. Eventually Fell catches up with Jane and Dan at the museum. While he reads the formula, Abbott and Costello accidentally bring the monsters back to life by using salt and vinegar on the Monster and baked beans (!) on the Wolf Man. They also remove the stake from Dracula's chest. The monsters chase the boys around until the Baroness arrives with the remedy—an atomizer that shrinks the monsters to four inches tall. Fell is arrested and the boys are allowed to use the monsters in a Broadway show.[21]

This ludicrous story was never used. If it had been, it could have brought an early end to the careers of Abbott and Costello. One can only wonder at the atrocity that would have resulted had the studio gone ahead in producing it, although some elements (the museum and costume party) were recycled for use in the final script.

After this, Robert Lees and Frederic Rinaldo started on a new script. Their first treatment was finished by April 21 and had Dracula enlisting Prof. Stevens' help in reviving the monster. There was no Sandra character, Joan was a camp counselor, and there was no plot of wanting to use Costello's brain. Still, the treatment was entitled "The Brain of Frankenstein," a title that was used all the way into the actual production of the film but later discarded.[22] Eventually, as the script was rewritten, it came closer to the final film.

It is well known that Lou hated the script. He was supposedly nervous about using all new material and not being able to rely on any of the duo's patented routines. He read the script and tossed it aside, commenting, "It stinks." He reportedly even made the remark, "My five-year-old daughter can write something better than that!"[23] The only way he could be talked into doing it was by being assured of a profit on his 10 percent interest in the film.[24] Later, he realized he had made the right decision. After the premiere, his mother told him it was the best work he had ever done.[25] (I asked Paddy Costello about this story. "I don't know if that's true or not, to be honest with you," she said. "I can't really envision my grandmother saying that, but I'm sure she enjoyed it a lot."[26])

No one at Universal seemed interested in the film. No executive ever visited the set to see how it was progressing. They just wanted it done quickly so they could release it and make money off of it. Everyone could tell this was the case because an attitude of "anything goes" was prevalent early in the production. Early press releases announced that along with Abbott and Costello and the three monsters, the film would also include Marjorie Main, the Mummy, and Count Alucard, the son of Dracula![27]

The cast signed for the picture was a great one. Lon Chaney, Jr., returned as Lawrence Talbot, the Wolf Man, the part he had always called his "baby." Chaney was at his best when playing simple-minded brutes unable to cope when dramatic events overtook them — as evidenced by his sterling performance as Lenny in *Of Mice and Men* (1939).[28] But it was in the horror genre that he became a star, playing the Wolf Man character in four previous films along with other monster roles such as Kharis the mummy, the Son of Dracula, and the Frankenstein Monster. Chaney had previously appeared with Abbott and Costello in *Here Come the Co-Eds* and commented in his later years that the comedy team ruined the horror genre by making buffoons of the monsters.[29] Sara Karloff agrees with Chaney's assessment. "It did [mark the end of the classic monsters]. Again, that's what my father was saying. Keep them in their own home. Don't make the Monster a foil for someone else's jokes. That isn't how it was intended."[30] Paddy Costello has a different view: "I guess Lon Chaney was looking at it from one perspective. Here he was making serious B films, monster B films, and maybe he did see it that way. But that film [*Abbott and Costello Meet Frankenstein*] has really held up over the years. That's really a classic and it'll just go on and on and on. It's a real kick in the head to watch."[31]

According to writer Don G. Smith, the alcoholic Chaney was hitting the bottle hard, even during filming, though he knew his lines and was one of the most popular people on the set. However, he almost died before the film was released. On the evening of April 22, 1948, Lon took 40 sleeping pills after a fight with his wife. He hid in his truck waiting to die but was found by his son Ron who rushed him to the hospital. The nature of the argument was never made public but Chaney made up with his wife and never attempted suicide again.[32] Chaney died many years later on July 13, 1973, after a long series of illnesses. At the time, Chaney's widow declined to disclose the cause of death.[33] Bela Lugosi, Jr., recalled meeting Lon Chaney on the set of the film. "[He] was a very nice man to me, also. I was a little scared of his get-up. He was a very big man. He was certainly very nice. I had my picture taken with him."[34]

Bela Lugosi was born Bela Blasko in Hungary in 1882. He became a romantic idol on the Hungarian stage but was forced to leave the country due to political upheaval. After taking the role of Dracula on stage, he repeated it in the 1931 film, though Universal was nervous about casting him. He became a star but found himself typecast in horror films for the rest of his life.[35] After turning down the role of the Frankenstein Monster, he was eclipsed in stardom by Boris Karloff. However, Lugosi would outdo Karloff in *Son of Frankenstein* (1939), appearing as the hunchbacked, raspy-voiced Ygor, one of his greatest roles. Bela Lugosi, Jr., summed up the appeal of his father's films:

> He was unique in the way he portrayed different roles, with his voice and his movement based mostly on his theatrical background and training. So I think he brings some unusualness to any role he does. He stands out and there's no two ways about it. And I think that's one reason why he's remembered — not because the role was so great but because his portrayal was.[36]

Lugosi was signed to play Count Dracula in *Abbott and Costello Meet Frankenstein* even though Universal wanted Ian Keith for the role. (Interestingly, Keith was also up for the part in the original 1931 *Dracula*.) Stories say Lugosi's agent, Don Marlowe, pleaded with the studio executives to give Bela the part and they finally did, paying him a small salary. Film historian Gregory William Mank says Bela's former agent gained considerable mileage out of the story about how he won Bela the role. He supposedly stormed into William Goetz's office on the eve of production, waving telegrams showing how much money exhibitors had made showing Dracula. This shamed the president into giving Bela the part. Mank disproves this through studio records which showed Bela cast in the role early on when the film was still being called "The Brain of Frankenstein."[37]

Although famous for the role, this was only the second time the horror great played the vampire Count on screen and it was his last blaze of glory. Most feel this was Bela's last good performance flick. Lugosi was in his sixties when this film was made and makeup man Bud Westmore had to apply a heavy coat of makeup to conceal his age.[38]

Paddy Costello could not recall much about Lugosi. "I can't remember much about him to be honest with you. I think he was probably one who would kind of go off by himself."[39] Unlike Chaney, Lugosi showed no worry over having Abbott and Costello meet the famous monsters. He assured the *New York Times* during preproduction that the film would not ruin the Count's dignity.[40] Lugosi died on August 17, 1956, at the age of 74.

Glenn Strange had played the Frankenstein Monster in *House of Frankenstein* and *House of Dracula*, but in neither film was he given much to do. Here, he had plenty of screen time and was even given the chance to speak. In fact, he was originally supposed to have voiced the Invisible Man's final lines until Vincent Price was brought in to do so.[41] Strange had previously appeared with Abbott and Costello in *The Wistful Widow of Wagon Gap* and would go on to appear in *Comin' Round the Mountain* (probably the duo's worst film). Strange later told interviewers *Abbott and Costello Meet Frankenstein* was the most enjoyable picture he had ever worked on. Of Strange, Bela Lugosi, Jr., said, "Glenn Strange was a very credible Frankenstein and he was a very nice person, very nice to me."[42]

Strange and Lugosi made live stage appearances in costume to promote the movie, with Strange wearing the first in a line of Don Post rubber Frankenstein masks.[43] When doing so, Strange always made sure to thank Boris Karloff, the man who had originally played the Monster in 1931's *Frankenstein*.[44] Oftentimes, shows would advertise Strange appearing as the Monster when another actor was actually filling the role. Strange only later found out about it when members of his family went backstage to see him only to be denied entry.[45]

Rounding out the cast were two beautiful women. The role of Sandra was originally going to go to Patricia Morison but was given to Yugoslavian born Lenore Aubert. Aubert would also appear in *Abbott and Costello Meet the Killer, Boris Karloff* (1949). Bela Lugosi, Jr., recalled Aubert as "very beautiful and a good actress."[46] Jane Randolph played Joan Raymond. She was no stranger to horror films, having appeared in two of the classic Val Lewton films, *Cat People* (1942) and *Curse of the Cat People* (1944). In the former, she was the woman menaced in the swimming pool by the panther.

Director Charles T. Barton helmed *Abbott and Costello Meet Frankenstein*. He had previously done *The Time of Their Lives*, a ghostly Abbott and Costello film in which the two did not appear as a team. The supernatural scenes in that picture were also played straight, including a slightly chilling seance sequence.

As mentioned before, makeup was done by Bud Westmore, who replaced the great Jack Pierce at Universal. Pierce was considered too old and his techniques too old-fashioned to be of use to the studio. For the Wolf Man and the Monster, Westmore had special foam rubber and latex masks made which streamlined the makeup and made things easier overall.[47] Westmore also made subtle changes in the Frankenstein Monster's look. He made the forehead scar more jagged, made the hair longer and combed it back, placed the electrodes higher on the neck, and changed the Monster's color from blue-gray to a silvery-gray.[48]

With Frank Skinner composing an original (and marvelous) score and David Horsley and Jerome Ash signed for special effects, the film was soon on its way. And from all accounts, life on the set was pretty wild.

At first, Bud and Lou had a chip on their shoulders because neither of them wanted to do the movie. One story, related by Chris Costello in *Lou's on First*, said Bud and Lou were going to do the "Pack/Unpack" skit in the film. Barton thought the joke was old and that they had done it in too many movies already. He had writer John Grant come up with a new skit. Bud and Lou were given the scripts and they said, "What the hell is this crap?" They insisted on doing the old routine. While they did, Barton just watched, refusing to say "Cut." Lou finally stopped and asked Barton what he was doing. Barton replied, "I'm waiting for something funny." Bud and Lou walked off the set and did not return for three days. On the fourth day, they came back with the new routine down pat.[49] This story is odd in that there is no place in the film where "Pack/Unpack" might fit in. More likely, the events of this story happened during the filming of *Mexican Hayride* (1948), which Barton also directed. It seems a more likely place for that scene to have occurred. (Although Stephen Cox and John Lofflin repeat the anecdote in their book, they are only retelling Chris Costello's story.[50])

The boys did constantly fight with Barton. He once commented that "all three of the monsters were the nicest. The real monsters were Abbott and Costello."[51] But once the duo finally settled in, they were up to their old tricks.

Lou's best friend, Bobby Barber, was paid to hang around the set and be the team's target for practical jokes and mayhem. One day, they locked him in the pillory while everyone went to lunch.[52] But Barber also initiated many of the pranks. Every day there were pie fights and seltzer water battles. In fact, the total bill for pies was a rumored $3,800 to $4,800.[53] Lon Chaney would often join in the fun but Glenn Strange was declared off limits due to his makeup.[54] Lugosi reportedly steered clear of the antics. However, a still exists which shows Lugosi joining Abbott and Costello as they dump water on Barber. Lugosi's then-wife Lillian said Bela took all the jokes graciously.[55]

Bela Lugosi, Jr., talked of being on the set and seeing all the antics:

> There was a lot of cutting up going on between takes, and I was also impressed by how much time is wasted or just how much time it takes to set scenes up, too. And how many people it takes ... to screw in a lightbulb.[56]

He did feel Lugosi enjoyed his time making the film:

> I think he did [enjoy it] other than the part where other people would screw up the scene and it would have to be done over and over again, not because of him but because of others. Other than that, I think he really enjoyed himself on the set, seemed to anyway. He was happy to have me there.[57]

Paddy Costello was on the set a lot, too:

Other than *The Time of Their Lives*, *Meet Frankenstein* would be my favorite among those. And the others, I enjoy, too. But I, fortunately, was able to be on the set a lot when I was growing up. With me being the oldest kid, you know, I have a fairly good memory of it. My sister, Chris, she was only 11 when Dad passed away and she spent some time on the set but my sister Carole and I were there, really, for a lot of the earlier films and stuff.... The funniest thing would be, I think, when you see these people made up as Frankenstein, as Dracula, whoever, and then when you see them in between takes, sitting in a chair smoking a cigarette, reading a paper, drinking a cup of coffee.... It brings you right back into reality, you know.... I was able to see quite a bit of the filming there [on *Meet Frankenstein*]. One day, my mother brought my sister to the set and I think she was only about 3 years old. Glenn Strange, who played the Monster, was a very sweet man — very, very sweet and giving — and, of course, he wanted to come over and he made a big fuss over Chris. He wanted to hold her and Chris took one look at this guy and wailed. She wouldn't shut up and my father had to get my mother to take her home.[58]

One day, Lenore Aubert put a leash on Strange in his monster makeup and walked him around the studio lot with Lon Chaney (also in makeup) and Abbott and Costello.[59] Strange also lunched one day, in full makeup, with Ann Blyth who was made up as the title mermaid for the production of *Mr. Peabody and the Mermaid* (1948).[60] A tourist turned the corner, shrieked, and walloped Strange before running away.[61] Stills exist of Strange carrying Blyth.

Lou, notorious for stealing props from the sets of his films, was no different here. He took the antique clock from the mantle in Dracula's castle. They still needed the clock for continuity purposes so Barton was forced to make a deal with Lou. If Lou brought the clock back, he could keep it after the film was in the can. Lou agreed to the bargain.[62] Paddy Costello confirmed this trait of her father's: "He'd take anything he could probably get away with. He was a real character that way."[63]

Supposedly, Bud was spending his afternoons on the set drinking heavily in fear of his chronic epilepsy. He suggested to Barton that he film what he could before four o'clock.[64] The truthfulness behind this is questionable and sounds more like Hollywood apocrypha since a similar story was told about Lon Chaney, Jr., in his later years.

Abbott and Costello Meet Frankenstein opens with a cartoon that sets the tone for the film by having a humorous scene give way to a darker one. The Frankenstein Monster knocks on two coffins and out pop two skeleton versions of A&C who scream and run into each other. The bones mix up and drop down to spell the title. This is followed by a parade of monsters in silhouette with the actor's name written under the monster he is playing. The caricatures are frightening (in fact, they gave me chills as a kid) and accurately portray the powers of each monster. The Wolf Man is a slobbering canine, Dracula flies up in the air with bat wings, and the Monster flexes and gives off electricity. All three monsters are followed by an animated Lenore Aubert, whose place with the monsters gives away her role as a villain in the film. She stops for a moment and rubs her hips. With this, the film is already equating excessive sexuality with monstrousness. (David J. Hogan stated that the animation was most likely the work of Grim Natwick or James "Shamus" Culhane, since the studio's most famous animator, Walter Lantz, had severed his ties with Universal in 1947.[65])

The music heard during the credits is fantastic. In fact, the score throughout the film is one of Universal's best. Alternately frightening, whimsical, and humorous, the music is always appropriate and well matches each scene. It was recycled in most of the "Abbott and Costello Meet..." movies to come.

The action proper opens in London. A worried Lawrence Talbot looks out over the city at night before making a call to the express office in La Mirada, Florida. (This opening — from here all the way to the beginning of the wax museum sequence — is often cut from TV prints.)

At the express office, Abbott and Costello are introduced with their well-established roles intact — slick Bud is bossing stupid Lou around. Bud plays Chick Young and Lou plays Wilbur Gray. Wilbur is, of course, childlike and effeminate while Bud is impatient and stiff. He always expects too much of Lou — as he does here when he orders him to answer the phone and the customer bell at the same time. Wilbur puts the caller on hold and goes out to the truck to get a woman's bag — pausing for a moment to bark at the woman's mink (an ad-libbed move more appropriate for Curly Howard of the Three Stooges). In a classic Costello bit, he finds the lady's grip at the bottom of the truck, pulls it out, and brings the rest of the luggage down on his head. With a classic Abbott line, Chick admonishes him for trying to ruin the lady's baggage.

European Sandra Mornay (Aubert), whom we later learn is a doctor, suddenly appears concerned about Wilbur's head. She gives away her medical training when she checks his cranium. Finding it okay, she tells Wilbur that if anything happened to him she wouldn't know what she would do. As incredible as it might seem, Sandra is sweet on Lou, which makes Chick extremely jealous. "Frankly, I don't get it," he says. Sandra replies, "And frankly, you never will." By today's standard, we would interpret that line as possessing strong sexual content. Wilbur is getting "it" but Chick is not.

Chick wonders why "a classy dish" like Sandra would fall for Wilbur. Wilbur doesn't see why she wouldn't, so Chick tells him to look in a mirror sometime. Wilbur asks why he should hurt his own feelings. This joke was originally used in *Lost in a Harem*.

Wilbur answers the phone and shows a not unusual frugality when he asks the operator if the call from London is collect. Talbot asks about two crates that are to be delivered to MacDougal's House of Horrors. Wilbur assumes Talbot is MacDougal himself. Talbot tries to tell him not to deliver the crates but the call is interrupted by Talbot's transformation into the Wolf Man. This is strange, for at the end of Universal's last horror film in the series, *House of Dracula*, Talbot was cured of his affliction. In a classic scene, Talbot growls into the phone and Wilbur, thinking first that MacDougal is gargling and then that he's talking to a dog, barks back. In the original script, Talbot said "MacDougal" before changing which would better explain Wilbur's confusion.[66] But the scene ends with Wilbur hanging up and the Wolf Man tearing apart a chair. For once, we see the savagery of the werewolf as stuffing from the chair flies into the air. Later in the film, he will rip open a man's throat and although we do not see it, we recall the first scene when imagining the second. It is here we first get a feel for the real power of the film — the monsters are going to play it straight.

Wilbur returns to the desk and meets up with the real MacDougal, played by character actor Frank Ferguson. Wilbur is confused by the constantly grouchy MacDougal's sudden appearance and asks if they shot him out of a cannon from England. MacDougal demands his two crates. In a great ad-lib, Wilbur asks him how long he's been there. When MacDougal replies five minutes, Wilbur says he's been there five years and he's not yelling or screaming.

Wilbur calls Chick over and Chick examines the paperwork, surprised to find the crates insured for $10,000. Sandra returns but jealous Chick quickly drags Wilbur back to work.

MacDougal tries to impress Sandra by telling her he has in the crates the remains of Count Dracula and the Frankenstein Monster. In a great bit of detail, he tells her that a European agent picked his name out of thin air and sent them to him dirt-cheap. A strange reference follows. MacDougal says the combination of Dracula and the Monster is "enough to scare the pants — [he looks at Sandra] I mean the shirt — right off your back." But Sandra is unimpressed. She foreshadows her role by saying she doesn't scare easy and coolly blows off the obnoxious MacDougal.

Sandra approaches Wilbur and breaks their date. Wilbur asks if it is another man. Sandra says it is not — but it *is*, because Sandra, learning Dracula has arrived, now plans to meet with the infamous vampire. She calls Wilbur a silly boy, reinforcing the theme of Costello's childishness.

Wilbur says he is floating on a cloud of love. In a line that always gets a laugh, Chick calls him a little blimp. (A blooper exists where Lou says he is floating on a cloud of crap.[67]) Chick speaks to the camera, saying, "Boy, is this kid lost." But Wilbur takes no notice. He is so happy he reaches out and tickles Chick's chin. Wilbur has no problem acting effeminate but Chick slaps his hand away. The clown being seen displaying feminine tendencies is a common strategy used by comedians to get laughs.

A very strange scene follows. The two find the crate and Chick makes Wilbur get on top of it with a rope. Wilbur ties the rope, then Chick pulls down the crate — with Wilbur still standing on top of it! As Wilbur screams and rides the swaying crate, MacDougal complains about the treatment of his exhibits. Typically, no one cares about Wilbur, not even Chick. The only time Chick cares what happens to Wilbur is when someone else (i.e., the monsters) is endangering him. Wilbur safely rides the crate to the floor with a smile and offers to wrap it.

Most of the scene that follows is ad-libbed from the original script.[68] MacDougal demands the boys deliver the crates to his House of Horrors so that an insurance agent can inspect the crates upon delivery. Wilbur says he is a union man and works 16 hours a day. MacDougal reminds him that a union man works only 8 hours a day, but Wilbur replies that he belongs to two unions — a chestnut of a joke. Wilbur mocks MacDougal's angry face, a move many who work serving the general public wish they could emulate.

The scene switches to night and the exterior of the MacDougal House of Horrors, the start of the film's most famous sequence. Chick and Wilbur arrive with the crates, accompanied by a sudden thunderstorm that aptly adds to the atmosphere.

The doors are unlocked and some convenient lightning illuminates the ghoulish museum for Wilbur. Costello stares into the House of Horrors with great trepidation. Wilbur is not stupid; we can tell from his face he knows he is in for trouble.

The duo take the first crate inside. Typical of Abbott, Chick berates Wilbur for not doing his share of the work when Wilbur is the one who is usually breaking a sweat. "Pull it! Do you want me to do all the work?" asks Chick as they pass by the museum's exhibits. Wilbur is frightened by the re-creations and backs into a dummy with an axe. Chick turns on the lights and tells Wilbur to see what he is afraid of — a simple wax dummy. "Sandra should see you now," says Chick, who cannot stop wondering why a beautiful woman like Sandra would be interested in Wilbur.

The scene highlights some typical Abbott and Costello wordplay and also features some of their famous ad-libbing. For example, Chick tells Wilbur that the wax figure is only a dummy. "Dummy, nothing, it was smart enough to scare me." Wax dummies of Dillinger, Bluebeard, and the ape from *Murders in the Rue Morgue* were originally supposed to be featured in this scene.[69]

Chick leaves Wilbur to open the first crate while he brings in the second one. Wilbur is scared to be left alone and tells Chick to hurry back. Here, the duo seem to be taking on the roles of older and younger brothers.

Chick answers the ringing phone and learns MacDougal is on his way. After the call, the storm knocks out the lights and Wilbur is left alone in the dark. Like the child he is, Wilbur is scared of the dark, so Chick returns to light a candle.

The duo discover that the first crate contains Dracula's coffin. Amazingly enough, Chick recognizes Dracula's crest yet later tells Wilbur that Dracula was a fictional creature who never existed. Chick wants to open the coffin and see what is inside, but Wilbur (who might have seen the opening scene of *Frankenstein Meets the Wolf Man*) begs Chick not to do so.

When Chick leaves to fetch the other crate, he tells Wilbur that if he needs him, Wilbur should holler, "Oh, Chick!" Wilbur does so immediately (before Chick has a chance to exit the room), then asks him what took so long. This is reminiscent of a similar scene in *Hold That Ghost* when Costello was to holler, "Oh, Chuck!" At the same time, this sets up a variation of the duo's famous "Moving Candle" skit.

Wilbur is supposed to fold up the canvas but he is distracted by a display card which has the legend of Dracula written on it. The legend scares Wilbur as he reads it, but he cannot stop himself from reading. As easily as he is scared, Wilbur still enjoys the thrill of it all and reads on.

As he reads, the coffin opens and Dracula's hand appears. Wilbur hears the creaking and yells for Chick. The "Moving Candle" scene follows a few minutes later.

The premise of this bit is Lou witnessing some sort of supernatural phenomenon. He yells frantically for Abbott but whenever Abbott enters the scene, the ghostly goings-on stop and Abbott angrily chastises Lou for making up stories. The humor comes from Lou's frightened reactions, Abbott's growing frustration with Lou, Lou's expression when he realizes the phenomenon has stopped, and the eventual climax to the scene when the menace appears in all its glory. The duo used this bit most explicitly in *Hold That Ghost* and were masters of it to the point that *Abbott and Costello Meet Frankenstein* designed its entire concept around the bit. Wilbur repeatedly sees the monsters but Chick never does. In fact, one running gag has Lou repeating, "I saw what I saw when I saw it!"

Here, Wilbur hears the coffin creaking as it opens. He even sees Dracula's hand. He calls for Chick, but when Chick comes in the creaking has stopped, the coffin has closed, and the hand has disappeared. Chick tries to tell Wilbur that the writing on the card is "phony baloney to fool MacDougal's customers." But Wilbur knows better, for every time he reads the card, Dracula makes his presence known. Strangely, a similar scene had occurred a few years earlier in *Spooks Run Wild* (1941), a poverty row East Side Kids horror spoof. In that picture, a gas station attendant reads about the vampire's legend in a book—then finds himself face to face with Bela Lugosi.

Wilbur's reading of the card is also an opportunity to throw in some exposition on the powers of the vampire. In this film there is no Van Helsing–type figure to explain what vampires do, so that information is written on the card which Costello reads aloud. We learn that Dracula drinks blood, can change at will into a vampire bat, and must sleep in his coffin during the day (at which time he is helpless). All this information is used by the characters later in the film.

The "Moving Candle" routine continues. Wilbur returns to reading the card and crouches by the candle he has placed on the coffin. As he reads, Dracula opens the coffin and the candle moves. Wilbur becomes so frightened he cannot speak or whistle. Finally, he calls for Chick, but every time Chick comes in, the candle has returned to its original place. This happens several times until Wilbur loses it and screams for Chick to come back. While Wilbur's attention is focused outside, Dracula emerges from the coffin and silently stalks Wilbur. When he hears Chick entering, the Count hides among the wax statues. (Ironically, a few moments later, Wilbur will also pretend to be a statue.) Oddly, Dracula approaches Wilbur as if he were going to simply tap him on the shoulder. One wonders what he would have done had not Chick interrupted.

Bela Lugosi's performance as Dracula is superb. Bela Lugosi, Jr., said: "He was playing Dracula by that name, the second time in a Universal film, a number of years later, and later in his life. So, he was quite a mature person by that time. His performance on virtually every scene was first take and good, although there were a lot of takes because there's a lot of cutting up on the set. As far as his own work was concerned, he had his lines down cold and was a very professional portrayer."[70] Lugosi, Jr., did not feel his father's performance here was better than in the 1931 *Dracula*. "There wasn't as much meat to the character of Dracula in *Abbott and Costello Meet Frankenstein* as there was in the original. He was the star in the other and the lead, so it made a big difference."[71]

Chick brings in the other crate. He proves to Wilbur the coffin is empty by opening it. (A blooper exists showing Abbott opening the coffin only to find Bobby Barber inside.[72]) Chick tells Wilbur not to believe what he reads on the card. "That's the bunk," says Chick. Wilbur replies, "That's what I'm trying to tell you — that's his bunk!"

The two start to open the other crate. Chick finds a card with the legend of Frankenstein's Monster written on it and proceeds to read it to Wilbur even though Wilbur begs him not to. Chick reads that the monster may not be dead, just dormant. When Wilbur hears this, he says, "Uh-oh." He knows he is in for more trouble.

While this goes on, Dracula flings open his cape and poses, though neither Chick nor Wilbur can see him. It's curious that Lugosi was directed to — or chose to — do this, for it seems awkward and foolish. Nevertheless, Dracula returns to his coffin, causing the hinges to squeak. Wilbur is frightened by the squeaks but Chick thinks the noise is Wilbur pulling out the second crate's nails. Chick always has a rational explanation for whatever is bothering Wilbur.

The crate is finally opened and Chick tells Wilbur to take out the packing. Wilbur uncovers just the head of the Monster, foreshadowing the interest in his own brain and an overall thematic interest in brains, faces, and heads. Wilbur screams and covers up the frightening face. Chick does not understand and pushes Wilbur, who falls into the guillotine, causing it to chop off a wax dummy's head. Again, this foreshadows the operation to cut out Wilbur's brain, thereby cutting off his head.

MacDougal arrives and yells, "Hey! What are you doing in there with the lights off?" This could be seen by today's standards as a hidden homosexual reference, and it is quite possible that MacDougal might see the boys as homosexuals.

Chick tells Wilbur to hide the wax head while he talks to MacDougal. Wilbur opens the coffin to place it inside and comes face to face with Dracula. The funny thing here (which most people don't notice) is that the coffin is a bad hiding place to begin with — MacDougal would have found the head when he opened the casket later! Dracula puts Wilbur in a trance (the hypnosis is conveyed by some wonderful close-ups of Lugosi's eyes, the actor's most often used feature and the center of his fame as Dracula). Before turning his attention to the Monster, Dracula pokes Wilbur in the stomach like some gigantic Pillsbury doughboy. The motion is almost playful and foreshadows some of the homosexual overtones of the Dracula-Wilbur relationship.

Dracula uses his ring to revive the Monster with a jolt of electricity (which is portrayed through animation). This is a never-before-seen power that Dracula has developed and would be used in later films such as the grade-Z *Dracula vs. Frankenstein* (1971). (Lugosi's Dracula ring is now in the collection of Forrest J Ackerman.[73]) The Monster then speaks for the first time since *Ghost of Frankenstein* and says, "Master?" Dracula answers "yes" in a coolly evil manner, and the Monster bursts out of the crate, a scene which shows just how strong the Monster really is.

Wilbur comes out of the trance as the Monster is breaking out. He makes a crying face, then pretends to still be in a trance. Dracula leads the Monster past Wilbur. But when the Monster sees Wilbur, he is frightened. Dracula assures him he has nothing to fear from the fat man. This seems to be the first of only two times any of the Monsters break from their straight portrayal and act buffoonish. The other instance occurs when the Wolf Man attacks Wilbur in the woods.

Dracula and the Monster hide in the back. MacDougal turns the lights back on. He, Harris the insurance inspector, and Chick return, and MacDougal is furious that there are no bodies to be found. In a small continuity error, Chick has to snap Wilbur awake, as if Wilbur had fallen back into a trance. In a hilarious scene, Chick argues with the other two men that there were no bodies in either of the crates. The whole time, a speechless Wilbur tries to pantomime to the others that the monsters are hiding in the back. It takes a few viewings to notice that Wilbur is doing this, for our attention is drawn to the loud arguing of the other men. MacDougal and Harris take the boys to the police and, as they leave, Dracula has the Monster take the coffin out.

The action moves to a very impressive castle on a nearby island. An animated bat flies up and looks in at a laboratory where Prof. Stevens works. At the front door, the bat transforms into Dracula. The transformation occurs many times during the film and always features a real bat, then an animated transformation, then the real Dracula. Ingenious and well done, these transformations are probably the best ever seen in a Universal horror film. Some disagree. Don Glut felt the transformation had not improved,[74] claiming the changes created by Horsley and Ash — as well as the cartoon bat — were unconvincing.[75] As a note of trivia, this is the only film in which Bela Lugosi turns into a bat on-screen.[76]

Dracula knocks and Sandra answers the door. There is some banter between them in which Dracula comes off as a real charmer. We learn the vampire is going under the name "Dr. Lejos" (he was "Baron Latos" in *House of Dracula*) because he does not want to frighten Stevens, Sandra's technical assistant. But Stevens is too engrossed in his work to notice anything and will be out of the castle by the next day. Sandra is worried, though, because he is asking too many questions about the equipment that has been arriving. Dracula promises to take care of it and Sandra gets a wrap to join Dracula at the cove. As she leaves, the vampire seems to be admiring the castle's architecture. He obviously feels at home.

At the cove, Sandra examines the Monster. She is nervous. We learn through Dracula that Sandra had performed illegal operations in Europe that caused her to flee the police. Bela's acting here is fantastic as he casually reminds Sandra of her past. He tells her if she restores the Monster for him, she can have anything she wishes. Sandra says it is dangerous to leave the Monster in his weakened condition and assures Dracula that she has mastered Dr. Frankenstein's notebook (which is the same "Secrets of Life and Death" used throughout the Universal series).

Dracula asks about a brain. He does not want to repeat Frankenstein's mistake by putting an unmanageable brain in the Monster, a reference to the original 1931 *Frankenstein*. "This brain must have no will of its own, no fiendish intellect to oppose its master…" Sandra says she has picked out a perfect brain — simple, pliable, and ready to follow Dracula like a trained puppy. This is a revealing moment, because we realize why she was acting like she loved Wilbur and just what she plans to do to him. Sandra explains that in two days Wilbur will take her to a masquerade ball but she plans to suggest a quiet evening at the castle instead. They can then perform the operation. The Monster is taken inside.

Back at the hotel room, Wilbur is still trying to convince Chick he saw the two monsters. Chick says they were arrested because Wilbur would not shut up about seeing them. They spent a whole day and night in jail until a lady bailed them out. They both assume it was Sandra.

Wilbur imitates Dracula and the Monster for a disgusted Chick. When he impersonates Dracula, Chick pretends to be hypnotized (just as Wilbur had been!), and Wilbur is worried that he has really put his friend in a trance. He begs Chick to be just like he used to be, and Chick slaps him. This is reminiscent of a scene in *Buck Privates* when Lou had to beg Bud to slap him.

Talbot arrives and takes the room across the hall. He meets Chick and Wilbur and explains he was the one who called because he knew the bodies were alive. Wilbur is happy to have someone back up his story, but Chick thinks Talbot is a screwball. Lou had a lot of trouble with this scene and there is a string of bloopers showing him repeatedly forgetting his lines.[77]

Talbot says he has followed Dracula all across Europe because he knows the vampire is planning to revive the Monster. (Watch Costello's face here as he is first sad, then frightened.) Chick tells him to go to the police but Talbot cannot because he would have to tell them who he is and how he knows what he knows. The moon will soon rise, and he asks the boys to lock him in his room. Wilbur agrees to do it, telling Chick, "He's scared, too."

Talbot says to Lou, "Remember! No matter what you hear or what happens, don't let me out!" Two minutes later, Wilbur will show how stupid he is by going back inside!

Back in the room, Chick makes fun of Talbot. Wilbur trips over Talbot's suitcase and decides to take it over for him. Wilbur goes inside the room where, unseen by him, the Wolf Man emerges (a frightening appearance by Chaney). Wilbur leaves a note and, after looking both left and right to see if anyone is watching, takes an orange. The Wolf Man pounces twice but misses the oblivious Wilbur each time. Wilbur locks the door. He almost goes back inside again, wondering if Talbot had counted the oranges, then changes his mind and returns to his room. According to the script, Wilbur was originally going to have his coat ripped by the Wolf Man.[78]

At the insurance company, MacDougal complains that Chick and Wilbur were let out of jail. Joan Raymond, an insurance investigator from the home office, explains that she arranged it. She thinks she can persuade "the chubby, little fellow" to lead her to the missing exhibits. This scene was not in the original screenplay and was added later.

In the hotel room the next morning, Chick complains about the nightmares he had all night about dead bodies. Sandra arrives saying she just heard about the boys going to jail. Chick thanks her for bailing them out, but she says she was not the one who posted it. She asks Wilbur if he has been unfaithful, and she seems amused by the idea he may have found another woman. Wilbur asks, "How can you look me in the face and say that?" Chick adds, "How can you look him in the face, period?" Again, an emphasis on the face appears.

Sandra reminds Wilbur about the masquerade ball and tells him to pick her up at sunset — alone. Chick asks Sandra what Wilbur has that he does not. She replies, "A brain," giving another hint about the overall plan.

After Sandra leaves, there is a knock at the door and Wilbur thinks Sandra forgot to kiss him good-bye. But Joan sticks her head in and kisses him. Wilbur is shocked and Chick demands to know who this new woman is. Joan introduces herself, and Wilbur breaks the fourth wall by repeating to the audience, "She's Joan Raymond." Joan reveals she was the one who bailed them out due to love at first sight. Chick arrogantly assumes she is referring to him, but she runs over to Wilbur. Chick is even more confused than before and even more jealous.

Joan asks Wilbur what they are doing that night. Chick answers for him, getting more laugh lines than Costello in this sequence. "He's going to a masquerade ball, but I'm not doing anything," says Chick. Joan replies, "In that case, you'll be awful lonesome."

Joan invites herself to the ball and Wilbur accepts the second date. Chick angrily pulls Wilbur aside to "get a good look at him in the light."

Chick says he still does not get it, which could again be seen as a sexual reference.

Joan leaves to get her things before shopping for a costume, and Chick demands Wilbur give him one of his dates. He even calls Wilbur a bigamist. Wilbur cannot decide which one to give up because they both "send" him. Chick raises a fist and says he'll send him, but Wilbur replies that Chick does not even appeal to him (another hint of homosexuality in Wilbur's childish character).

On their way out, they remember Talbot and use his key to go inside Larry's room. The place is a mess due to the Wolf Man's rampage, but the boys think Talbot was simply on a bender. Talbot awakens and explains he is a werewolf. Immediately, Wilbur looks worried, a cute comic touch (as if Wilbur has read the script and knows he will have to deal with this). Soon, however, Wilbur is wisecracking and he tells Talbot, "I'm kind of a wolf myself." Watch Abbott in this scene when Wilbur cracks the joke. He smiles and motions as if to say, "Oh, you kidder." Talbot does not take the comment so humorously and grabs Wilbur, shaking him violently. "You have seen the living dead," says Talbot as he tells Wilbur he must help him to destroy Dracula. But Wilbur is more worried about being stuck with two dates. Talbot tells him he has a date with destiny. Interestingly, "Destiny" was going to be the original title for the film *The Wolf Man*. Wilbur says Chick can go with "Destiny"—a good tie-in to the previous jokes.

That night, Wilbur, Chick, and Joan take a boat to the island. On the dock, Wilbur tells Chick and Joan to wait while he gets Sandra. He coyly reminds Chick that "She's mine, too," then wipes his mouth with Chick's tie! Chick stops Wilbur by recalling that the last time Chick had two girls, he gave Wilbur one. Wilbur reminds Chick of how ugly she was. Ad-libbing an ancient joke, Wilbur says, "She had so much bridgework that every time I kissed her I had to pay toll."

Joan asks to go along to the castle and Wilbur says, "Yes, mon amour... (to Chick). That's Spanish."

"That's French!" corrects Chick.

"How do you like that?" says Wilbur. "I speak French, too!"

This entire scene, which ends with Wilbur childishly skipping up to the castle, is different in the film than originally written in the screenplay.[79]

At the door, Chick raps the massive knockers, anticipating the moment in *Young Frankenstein* when Gene Wilder comments, "What knockers!" In the script, Chick is supposed to say, "They're all dead in there," but this was omitted.[80] Stevens answers the door and lets them in.

Joan and Stevens are immediately attracted to each other as introductions are made. (Ironically, Joan pretends to have fallen in love "at first sight" with Wilbur only to have it actually happen to her when she meets Stevens). Sandra comes down as the boys and Joan wait in the library. She is suspicious of Joan even though Wilbur says she is Chick's date (Joan, of course, has been told that Sandra will be Chick's date). She wants to get rid of both Joan and Chick but when she greets the two she is uncharacteristically pleasant to Chick.

Sandra and Joan play cat and mouse with each other in a scene that the two actresses do not quite pull off. Soon, they leave to powder their noses. Chick is furious — he wants one of the girls. He asks Wilbur what he would do if yet a third girl, named Mary, fell in love with him. Wilbur asks if she is pretty and Chick says yes. Wilbur, becoming more and more arrogant, says, "Of course. She'd have to be." Chick offers to take one of the three girls off his hands and asks which one. Wilbur replies, with perfect timing, "You take Mary."

The phone rings and Chick makes Wilbur answer it. It is Talbot looking for Dr. Lejos. Talbot recognizes Wilbur's voice and tells him he has a line on Dracula and the Monster. Dr. Lejos has been receiving electrical equipment that could be used to revive the Monster. Starting to sweat, the now-nervous Wilbur answers, "So what? I'm way out on an island!" Talbot tells him he may be in the house of Dracula — a sly reference to a previous film. That's enough to send Wilbur racing for the door.

Chick stops Wilbur, who informs him of Talbot's phone call. Chick tries to tell off Talbot but he has already hung up, so Chick decides to search the place in order to prove to Wilbur that Talbot is crazy. But Wilbur reminds Chick that Dracula will soon be wanting breakfast, and since he is the fatter, he is therefore the more preferable choice.

Wilbur tries to vacate the premises by using the old joke of "I'll search outside, you search in here." When Chick says no, Wilbur replies, "OK, you search in here and I'll search the outside." Chick agrees and Wilbur again breaks the fourth wall to tell us, "It worked!" Chick grabs him and they start searching.

Each take a door. Because the audience constantly focuses on Costello, it is very easy to miss a joke here. Chick opens the door to the broom closet and pulls out a broom. Wilbur opens the door to the basement and finds a creepy dock. He quickly closes the door. When Chick asks him what is behind the door, Wilbur replies, "Broom closet!" Chick looks back at the other door with confusion, knowing Wilbur is lying.

They go down to the cellar, and here we see another example of the great sets created for the film. Wilbur tries to sneak out but the door slams and Wilbur holds on to Chick with fear. Chick pushes Wilbur away, asserting his own masculinity (again seemingly threatened by Wilbur's homosexual overtones). This scene originally had more dialogue but, as shot, it relies on quick pantomime.[81]

While Chick looks around, Wilbur leans on a secret passage and falls into a hidden room. Unknowingly, he sits down in the lap of the Frankenstein Monster. In one of the funniest scenes in the movie, Wilbur slowly realizes he is in great danger. A blooper exists showing Glenn Strange cracking up during this scene.[82] Strange himself reported he had trouble keeping a straight face and they had to do many re-takes (much to Costello's growing impatience). Lou, himself, actually thought the scene would not work and did not want to include it.[83]

The Monster stands and chases Wilbur who runs right into Dracula. The vampire again hides his face with a cloak. It is important to note that every time Wilbur sees Dracula, the vampire hides his face with his cloak. Later, when they meet face to face, Wilbur will not recognize Dr. Lejos as Dracula.

Wilbur escapes through the secret passage and tries to tell Chick what happened. He is so excited he is unable to speak. He drags Chick through the secret passage. If you listen carefully, you can hear Costello accidentally call Abbott by his real name instead of "Chick."

As the boys go through the passage, Dracula, the Monster, and Dracula's coffin appear on the other side of the revolving door. Chick gets angry when no monsters are to be found. Wilbur whistles for them. Chick says he will look around, but if he does not find anything he will "beat Wilbur's ears off." Wilbur, of course, ends up on the other side of the wall and is menaced by the monsters once more. They try to corner him but he gets through the passage in the nick of time. Watch carefully and you will notice that Glenn Strange seems to stumble just before the scene cuts back to Chick and Wilbur.

Wilbur grabs Chick and they return to the basement as Dracula, the Monster, and the coffin are swung back around to the hidden room. (This part of the film appears rather hokey because the monsters move so fast and are able to take the coffin back and forth seemingly at warp speed.) In essence, this sequence is simply a re-working of the "Changing Room" skit which Abbott and Costello used so effectively in *Hold That Ghost*. The changing room scene is another aspect of the comic idea behind the "Moving Candle" routine.

Chick yells at Wilbur and threatens him. In a running gag, the comedians do imitations of the monsters with Wilbur correcting Chick's renditions. Before leaving, notice that Wilbur quickly glances down toward the water to make sure the monsters are not hiding down there. In the script, Bud explains the presence of the secret room as a hiding place for bootleg liquor during prohibition,[84] another aspect reminiscent of *Hold That Ghost*.

Upstairs, in the bedroom, Joan and Sandra get ready for the party. Joan lies and tells Sandra that she and Wilbur are old friends. While Sandra is busy, Joan looks through her bureau and finds Dr. Frankenstein's notebook. Sandra sees her and goes through Joan's purse, discovering her insurance investigator ID card. They leave, each knowing the truth about the other.

Below, the boys wait. Chick threatens to take Wilbur to a doctor to have him examined. When the girls come down, Wilbur blurts out to Sandra that he was in the basement. He still trusts Sandra and is ready to tell her everything. Chick covers up and says Wilbur fell down the stairs. Dracula appears in a handsome smoking jacket and tells Wilbur he should be more careful. They are all introduced and "Dr. Lejos" says he approves highly of Sandra's choice. Lugosi is given some great lines here. He says, "Ah, Wilbur. I've heard so much about you that I feel as if we have already met!" and "I approve of your choice very highly ... what we need today is young blood — and brains." At this point, bashful Wilbur actually snuggles on Dracula's arm! (A blooper exists showing Dracula descending the stairs followed by stooge Bobby Barber in a cape.[85])

Stevens comes in and wants to ask Lejos some questions. He tells Stevens to save his questions and go along to the masquerade ball. "Ah, you young people, making the most of life — while it lasts," says Lugosi while glancing knowingly at Costello. Stevens decides to go, asking Joan if she would mind. She makes it clear she is interested in him. Wilbur is jealous, but Chick gets a laugh out of it.

Dracula tries to fix it so Wilbur and Sandra will end up alone at the castle, but Sandra says she will not go to the party because she has a splitting headache. Notice that she uses the classic excuse for a woman who does not want to have sex, reinforcing the connection between those who are sexually active and those threatened by monsters (to be discussed later). Dracula is worried and pursues her, but he is polite enough to say, "Pardon me," to the others. Wilbur informs Chick that he just lost his date.

Upstairs, Dracula confronts Sandra, who explains why she does not want to go forward with the plans. Dracula refuses to jeopardize the success of the operation and tells Sandra he has "ways of securing her cooperation." She replies that her will is as strong as his — but she is wrong. Dracula hypnotizes her and then bites her. This scene aggravates all horror fans due to a glaring mistake — Dracula's reflection can be seen in the mirror! It's interesting, though, to watch Sandra's reaction to the bite. Her face is pure ecstasy, showing the true pleasure of the vampire's bite and the erotic force of Dracula, a concept that came to the forefront in such modern vampire films as *Bram Stoker's Dracula* (1992) and *Interview with the Vampire* (1994). (According to Gregory William Mank, Charles T. Barton said Bela Lugosi was helpful to Lenore Aubert in this scene. He tried to help her look as if she were really hypnotized.[86])

At the party, Wilbur tells Joan that he and Chick are going inside to put on their costumes. Stevens whisks Joan onto the dance floor. When Wilbur realizes what has happened, he tries to dance with Chick, who will have none of Wilbur's "homosexual" antics.

The duo run into MacDougal, dressed as a devil. Demanding to know where his exhibits are, he throws Wilbur around. Chick wants to have him arrested for assault but has trouble finding a witness. He makes MacDougal throw Wilbur around again, but the witness, dressed as a knight, misses it because his faceplate falls down. The script originally had Wilbur say, "I'm a ba-ad boy," for old times sake.[87] The scene was also to have included a photographer. But when the shutterbug tries to take a picture of MacDougal beating on Wilbur, his flash goes dead.[88]

In the locker room, Talbot asks a waiter if he has seen Chick and Wilbur. The cocky waiter — played by Bobby Barber in one of his many bits — says he doesn't even know them. Chick and Wilbur enter and Talbot asks if they found anything at the castle. Chick tells him to leave them alone, saying, "You and Wilbur are just trying to scare me, but it won't work." Wilbur, in costume as Mr. Hyde, appears, scaring Chick. (In the script, Wilbur was supposed to first scare himself in the mirror;

luckily, this was thrown out, for the gag works better as is.⁸⁹) Interestingly, Wilbur calls Chick a sissy when he is the one who is always acting effeminate.

Chick puts on his mask, a wolf's head. This upsets Talbot, who explains that he turns into a wolf when the moon rises. Wilbur replies with the most often quoted line from the film: "You and twenty million other guys."

Talbot angrily shoves Wilbur, saying he could tear him limb from limb. "Is that serious?" asks Wilbur. "He'll murder ya!" says Chick. "Oh, that's serious," says Wilbur. A similar joke was used in *Hold That Ghost*.

Talbot asks them to lock him in his room later that night. Chick says he should hire himself a keeper.

At the dock, Dracula and the now-vampiric Sandra arrive. A scene was cut here in which Talbot, Chick, and Wilbur watch them get off the boat.⁹⁰ Dracula gives Sandra instructions to get Wilbur to the island while he takes care of Joan.

The five characters meet, and when Talbot accuses "Lejos" of being Dracula, the vampire tells him he is hallucinating. A blooper exists showing the actors screwing up this scene and Lou smiling for the camera.⁹¹

Joan and Stevens finish their dance and rejoin the others. Talbot warns Joan that Lejos really is Dracula and Joan is suddenly interested in talking to Talbot. But the ever-charming Dracula steps in and offers to tell Joan the whole story while they dance. A scene was omitted showing Dracula and Joan dancing,⁹² and it is a shame. It would have been wonderful to see Lugosi as Dracula on the dance floor.

Sandra asks Wilbur to join her for a walk in the woods and Wilbur rubs this in Chick's face by saying, "Toodle-oo." Chick asks, "Perfesser [sic], do you understand women?" to which Stevens replies, "I don't even try."

In the woods, Wilbur picks a rose but childishly holds on to it instead of giving it to Sandra. They sit on a bench and Wilbur notices something strange about Sandra. She says she wants him to go to the island. "I want to be the only one in your life. I want to be a part of you. I want to be in your blood." Wilbur immediately grasps the situation and understands what has happened to Sandra. Because he read the legend in the wax museum, he knows Sandra is a vampire. He recognizes the symptoms and shows his understanding when Sandra says, "You're so full-blooded, so round, so firm," and he replies, "So fully-packed." In the Warner Bros. Foghorn Leghorn cartoon *Walky Talky Hawky*,

Henery Hawk uses this exact line to describe the dog he thinks is a chicken.

Lou pricks himself on a thorn and Sandra eyes the cut, a reference to the scene in *Dracula* when Renfield cuts himself on a paper clip. Wilbur takes the cut away preferring to suck the blood himself, commenting, "There's not enough there for two." This scene could symbolize Wilbur's reaction to Sandra's pushy sexual urgings. He would rather do it himself (masturbate) than have her do it for him (but this may be pushing it a bit and does not fit into later interpretations).

Sandra has Wilbur look into her eyes just as Dracula had her look into his eyes. Wilbur sees bats flying in her pupils. "Don't you know what happens now?" she asks. "I'll bite," answers Wilbur. "No, I will," states Sandra. At the time, this exchange might have received big laughs, but since the phrase "I'll bite" has passed out of common usage, the exchange has now lost some humor.

Sandra is about to bite Wilbur when Chick and Talbot interrupt. Sandra runs away. Chick tells Wilbur that Joan is missing. Talbot is sure Dracula got her. Wilbur, not seeing the big picture and still naively worried about who gets which girl, tells Chick that he can have Sandra.

The three search for Joan in the woods and split up. Wilbur, not realizing Chick has gone a different direction, stops to rest. Meanwhile, the full moon rises and Talbot transforms into the Wolf Man. (The transformation scene is framed within some logs and looks very unrealistic.) The Wolf Man goes after Wilbur, but Wilbur assumes the creature is Chick wearing his mask. Klutzy and overly buffoonish, the Wolf Man trips over vines, falls over, and gets stuck in his attempts to slaughter Wilbur. At one point, Wilbur actually punches the Wolf Man in the nose! This scene is a variation of the "Bear Routine."[93] In this routine, Abbott and Costello try to pull the wool over someone's eyes by having Abbott dress up as a wild animal (such as a bear). Costello will then do his part to tame the beast, knowing Abbott is impersonating the animal. But a real bear always shows up and scares off Abbott, leaving Costello to find out on his own that the animal is real. This routine appears in both *The Naughty Nineties* and *Africa Screams* (1949) and here substitutes the Wolf Man for the animal.

When Wilbur finally sees that the Wolf Man is trying to kill him, he runs off. He never realizes an actual werewolf was menacing him because he later accuses Chick of trying to take a bite out of him. The Wolf Man picks up the scent of an easier target and attacks MacDougal (providing payback for beating on Wilbur). MacDougal's cries for help attract a crowd and Stevens examines him. Stevens declares that, "another half inch would have severed the jugular vein," then proceeds to have MacDougal stand up and talk! This incident brings into question Stevens' medical training.

Chick arrives with his mask and MacDougal accuses Chick of trying to kill him. When Wilbur shows up, MacDougal accuses him, too. Bud and Lou split up and high-tail it into the woods, with a crowd in hot pursuit. It is very ironic, but very typical, that with three frightening monsters loose in the area, the angry mob decides to chase Abbott and Costello! Also of interest is the fact that since MacDougal was bitten by a werewolf and survived, then he too should become a werewolf — which is, after all, what happened to Lawrence Talbot in *The Wolf Man*.[94]

In the woods, Wilbur loses the mob but finds Dracula. The vampire turns into a bat (another impressive animated transformation) and chases Wilbur to the boat, where he finds Joan in a trance. Chick arrives and watches the bat change back into Dracula. Finally realizing Wilbur has been telling the truth, Chick faints. Wilbur also faints, and Dracula takes the boat back to the island. This scene is creepy and funny at the same time, with the animated bat, the reactions of the boys, and the evocative music choreographed to fit each action appropriately.

The next morning, Talbot awakens and finds an armed mob hunting Chick. Talbot wants to turn himself in to clear Chick, but Chick, who now believes Talbot's story, stops him by telling him Dracula took Wilbur back to the castle. Chick even uses the line, "I saw what I saw when I saw it." Oddly, Chick, who never before seemed to care about Wilbur's well-being, now is intent on rescuing his pal. Talbot, who has surely had experience eluding the authorities, helps Chick escape from the mob and the dogs. Chick is eager to get to the castle, but Talbot tells him they have to hide until nightfall. Chick is concerned, but Talbot assures him that Dracula will sleep all day. This is a strange bit of logic. Wouldn't it be better to go during the day so they wouldn't have to deal with a wide-awake and powerful vampire? Why tempt fate? But Chick follows Talbot's advice and waits until nightfall.

At this point, a scene was excised which had Stevens finding the hypnotized Joan.[95] Instead, the film cuts to Wilbur held in wooden stocks (in the script he's supposed to be in chains[96]) trying to talk to zombie Sandra, who stands ready by Dracula's coffin. Wilbur asks the Monster for help, calling him, "Junior." This reinforces the theme of the Monster being a "son" of Dr. Frankenstein. This idea popped up again and again in the series. In *Son of Frankenstein*, Ygor says Frankenstein was the monster's father, but his mother was electricity.

Dracula emerges from his coffin. Wilbur does not want to look and he covers his eyes. But his body betrays him and he peeks, only to see Dracula and Sandra check on the Monster. Dracula uses his ring to recharge the brute. The Monster is weak but will respond to the operation if the generators are kept running.

Sandra tells Wilbur that instead of being short and chubby, he will soon be big and tall and "strong as an ox." Stupid Wilbur thinks Sandra still loves him until he finds out that his brain is going to be transplanted into the Monster's head. The brain transplant ideas stem from earlier films in the series such as *The Ghost of Frankenstein* and *House of Frankenstein* and were the "brainchild" of Universal writer Curt Siodmak, who seemed obsessed with the idea. Siodmak's most famous work is his novel *Donovan's Brain*.

In the lab, Dracula gets the equipment running. It is classic Universal horror lab equipment with plenty of sparking electricity worthy of Kenneth Strickfaden. Stevens enters, very angry because he found both Joan and Frankenstein's notes. While he raves impotently about how he will go to the police, Sandra sneaks up behind him and knocks him out. "Excellent!" says Dracula. He decides to dispose of all the bodies at once.

Chick and Talbot arrive at the dock. In one of the worst lines in the film, Talbot points and says, "That must be the entrance to the castle!" No kidding, Larry.

Dracula and Sandra wheel the Monster up to the lab. Wilbur tells "Frankie" that getting his brain is a bad deal. "Ask me how much one and one is — I don't know."

Chick and Talbot wait for Dracula to leave, then rush in to help. Talbot wakes up Stevens while Chick tries to get Wilbur out of the stocks. He uses a rock on the lock, then sets the stone on Wilbur's fingers, getting big laughs. Chick sets Wilbur free and tells him to run. "Not that way — to the left!" yells Chick when Wilbur heads the wrong way. Wilbur runs smack dab into a wall. "No door," he tells Chick, and a frustrated Chick grabs him by the ass and leads him out.

In the lab, the Monster is hooked up to the electrodes. Outside, Stevens tells the men they have to go back inside and rescue Joan. Wilbur is left behind to get the boat ready. "I've got too much of what they want—" he says, "brains."

When Dracula and Sandra find Wilbur missing, Dracula personally handles the situation. Outside, he hypnotically commands Wilbur to come back. Wilbur cannot resist the vampire's sway and skips happily back to the villain. Originally, Wilbur was to have tried to run away but he would have been drawn back. The effect would have been achieved with a treadmill buried in the sand, but budget limitations killed the idea.[97] Nevertheless, Dracula's control over Wilbur hints at a possible homosexual connection while reinforcing Costello's childlike character.

Chick, Talbot, and Stevens return with a dazed Joan and find Wilbur gone. Lights in the lab show that the operation is starting. Stevens stays with Joan while Chick and Talbot go back to rescue Wilbur.

Wilbur is strapped to the operating table. Sandra is about to cut open his head with the scalpel. Wilbur begs for some ether but Sandra says coldly, "You won't need it. You won't feel a thing." Subtly horrific, this is the most disturbing and chilling scene in the picture.

Chick and Talbot invade the lab and Talbot throws Sandra to the ground. Then he tries to free Wilbur. (Interestingly, *Here Come the Co-Eds* featured a scene in which Lon Chaney tied Costello down to an operating table.) In an easy-to-miss moment, Dracula chases Chick, who fends him off with a chair. Behind him, Sandra rises and is about to stab Chick with the scalpel! Chick swings the chair back, unknowingly knocking out Sandra, and throws it at Dracula. Then he runs off with Dracula in pursuit.

While freeing Wilbur, Talbot notices the full moon has risen and he transforms into the Wolf Man. He is about to kill Wilbur, but Wilbur begins to shake uncontrollably and, with his foot, kicks the table away from the wall. The Wolf Man is knocked over. He falls on the electrical equipment, causing it to overcharge and revive the Monster. Dracula enters and he and the Wolf Man engage in a tug-of-war with Wilbur's table. The Wolf Man suddenly becomes focused on destroying the vampire and becomes the good guy!

Dracula is not strong enough to keep up the struggle and runs off, pursued by the werewolf. They leave Wilbur spinning in circles. Chick comes back and frees him while the Monster breaks loose from his bonds. "Do you believe me now?" asks Wilbur, the end of that running gag.

Sandra revives and orders the Monster to halt. The Monster unexpectedly turns against Sandra and, in a brutal scene, throws her out the window (much like he threw Daniel the hunchback out a window in *House of Frankenstein*). Glenn Strange accidentally fractured his ankle in this scene. He threw stuntwoman Helen Thurston at the breakaway window but she rolled back and bowled him over. She got some of the candy glass in her eye and Strange hurt his ankle when he lunged to catch her. Lon Chaney put on the makeup and finished the scene. Strange completed his scenes with a cast hidden under his costume.[98]

In one of Abbott and Costello's funniest sequences, the Monster pursues the boys through the castle. In one room, they barricade the door with a bed. But the monster opens the door outward and gets inside. The boys run out but, as a last gesture, Wilbur covers the Monster with blankets from the bed.

They run across the hall and hide in another room only to find Dracula and the Wolf Man battling it out. In the next room, the Monster is waiting for them. In the room after that, the other two monsters are fighting again. Running out, they see the Monster at the end of the hall. Wilbur pulls a tablecloth out from under some candlesticks and dishes — then looks at the audience proudly as if to say, "I did it!" He uses the cloth as a cape and masquerades as Dracula, telling the Monster to move "Back ... back...." Wilbur pulls off the scam because he has been imitating Dracula through the entire picture, but he ruins it by dropping the cape and telling Chick, "He thinks I'm Dracula." The Monster snarls, Costello throws the cape over the creature's head, and the boys hide once more.

The Monster starts opening doors as if playing a game of hide-and-seek. The boys sneak up and push him in a room, locking the door. They stand against the door and Wilbur says, "Well, we got him!" The Monster's fist then smashes through the door and they run off. Costello actually missed his mark in this scene and was hit by Strange's fist. But Barton liked the scene and they printed it, never doing a second take.[99]

Dracula and the Wolf Man battle savagely and the vampire tries to escape. He changes into a bat and almost flies away but the Wolf Man takes a running jump and grabs the bat so that both fall to the rocky rapids below. Some critics say that neither monster should have been killed by this stunt and that Universal was keeping things open for a sequel. But in vampire lore, running water can trap a vampire forever. Either way, the effect is well done and quite exciting.

Joan wakes up from her trance as MacDougal and a friend arrive at the dock by rowboat. Wilbur and Chick are chased out of the castle with Wilbur screaming like a girl. They run into MacDougal and ask him if he still wants his exhibits. "Here comes one of them now!" says Wilbur. As the Monster lumbers down the dock, the frightened Mac-Dougal and friend jump into the moat and swim away. According to the original script, the friend is a police sergeant (though this is never mentioned in the film).[100]

Wilbur and Chick jump in the rowboat and try to row away but Wilbur will not untie the boat even though Chick keeps ordering him to do so. The Monster throws barrels from the dock at the duo, narrowly missing them each time. Meanwhile, Stevens and Joan fill buckets with gasoline and set the dock on fire. Wilbur finally unties the boat and they begin to row away. The Monster senses he is trapped and inexplicably walks into the flames, almost as if he is committing suicide. The burning figure falls through the dock and drops into the water.

Wilbur tells Chick, "And another thing, Mr. Chick Young. The next time I tell you I saw something, you believe me that I saw it!"

Chick: "Oh, relax; now that we've seen the last of Dracula, the Wolf Man, and the Monster, there's nobody to frighten us anymore."

A cigarette mysteriously lights itself and floats in the air while a voice says, "That's too bad, I was hoping to get in on the fun."

Chick: "Who said that?"

Voice: "Allow me to introduce myself, I'm the Invisible Man!" (Actually, it is the voice of Vincent Price, making an uncredited appearance — sort of.)

As the voice laughs maniacally, there is a jump cut to the duo's stunt doubles as they leap from the boat and swim away. It is a great ending to a great film.

The final budget for *Abbott and Costello Meet Frankenstein* was $759,524,[101] and the film was a box office sensation, revitalizing the careers of Abbott and Costello and raking in big bucks for Universal. In some countries, however, the horror scenes were felt to be too intense. The censor board in British Columbia banned the film completely. Universal appealed their decision and the board gave in — only after most of the Wolf Man's scenes were deleted. Australia's censor cut out almost every scene with a monster, making the film a jumbled mess.[102]

Universal bribed Boris Karloff (who refused to see the movie — as explained in a later chapter) into posing for publicity pictures outside a New York theater showing the film by paying his hotel bill.[103]

Portions of the film were used in such films as *The World of Abbott and Costello* (1965), *Sweet Charity* (1969), *Il Vicino di Casa* (1969), *Dr. Strange* (1978), the remake of *The Getaway* (1994), and the Universal 8 home movie compilation, *The Best of Abbott and Costello*, part one. Clips were also used in the *Hey, Hey, Hey — It's Fat Albert* TV special as well as *Wayne and Shuster Take an Affectionate Look at Monsters, The Wolf Men, The Horror Show*[104] and A&E's *It's Alive: The True Story of Frankenstein*. There was even a Mexican remake of the film —*El Castillo de los Monstruos* (1957), featuring German Robles as Dracula.

A story adaptation appeared in *Movie Story*, July 1948, using photographs from the film as illustrations.[105] A filmbook appeared in issue 105 of *Famous Monsters of Filmland*.[106]

The film played all around the world but often under varying titles: Belgium —*Abbott et Costello et les Monstres*; England —*Abbott and Costello Meet the Ghosts* and *Meet the Ghosts*; France —*Abbott et Costello contre Frankenstein* and *Deux Nigauds contre Frankenstein* ("Two Simpletons vs. Frankenstein"); Germany —*Mein Gott, Frankenstein* ("My God, Frankenstein"); and Spain —*Abbott y Costello contra los Fantasmas* ("Abbott and Costello vs. the Phantoms").[107]

The picture is a classic for many reasons. First, it looks good. It was made with care and boasts finely crafted sets, a great score, and excellent acting. In fact, the film is technically superior to most of Universal's horror output. Paddy Costello recalls being amazed by the sets: "I was always fascinated by the scenery and by the sets. By the staircase, for example. I can remember those people coming down the staircase, seeing Lenore Aubert and Jane Randolph all dressed up in their evening clothes. It was neat."[108]

Second, the film is a rare example of a horror spoof that works. The comedy and horror elements flow perfectly, and there is a simple reason for this. The horror elements are played straight. The monsters are treated with respect and affection and are not expected to be funny or campy. If one was to take out the comic elements, as Donald Glut often points out, a serious horror story remains.[109] Third, the film does not expect the audience to have a deep knowledge of the preceding horror pictures (unlike *Young Frankenstein*).[110]

Amazingly, the film was long considered a blasphemy. As mentioned before, even Lon Chaney blamed A&C for the downfall of the horror genre. Although reviews were good and most authors today recognize the film as a classic, critics for a long time pointed to the picture as an example of how far both the monster series and the Abbott and

Costello series had fallen.[111] They obviously missed the magic of the film, as well as some of the picture's more serious undertones.

There are two plots in the film: the comic plot in which Wilbur is pursued by two beautiful women (which makes Chick very jealous) and the horror plot in which Dracula wants to put Wilbur's brain into the Monster. When combined in the movie, these two storylines create new themes and a confrontation. Before exploring the themes, it is necessary to look at the film's nine major characters — who can all be split into three separate categories:

A. *Those Who See The Monsters*	B. *Those Who Don't See The Monsters*	C. *Those Who Are The Monsters*
Wilbur	Chick	Dracula
Sandra	Prof. Stevens	The Wolf Man
Joan	MacDougal	The Monster

While all the characters in list B eventually do become aware of the monsters' presence, they do so only later in the film, within the last 15 to 20 minutes. Those in list A all somehow encounter or become endangered by the monsters earlier in the picture.

Now another listing can be made: those who are sexually (or romantically) active in the film and those who are not. Those who are active correspond to those in list A. Wilbur is pursued by two girls (prompting Chick to call him a bigamist). Sandra and Joan are the two girls. Sandra woos Wilbur, constantly kissing and caressing him. Joan does the same while also making advances towards Stevens.

Those who are not sexually active are the same characters as in list B. Chick is frequently frustrated in his attempt to take away one of Wilbur's dates. When he says to Sandra, "Frankly, I don't get it," she replies, "And frankly, you never will." A sexual connotation can be inferred. Stevens, while immediately attracted to Joan when they meet, is "too engrossed in his work" to make a serious move. In fact, he is quite impotent. While he does whisk Joan onto the dance floor, she is immediately "stolen" by Dracula, prompting Chick to ask, "Perfesser, do you understand women?" Stevens replies, "I don't even try." Later, he is again shown to be impotent when he threatens Dracula in the lab. While going on and on about how he will go to the police, Stevens is quickly incapacitated when Sandra sneaks up behind him and knocks him out. Finally, MacDougal is also inactive. He tries to impress Sandra in the baggage room — even showing his cards by saying, "That combination's enough to scare the pants — I mean, the shirt — right off your back." Sandra, however, is unimpressed and blows him off, giving him a textbook example of the cold shoulder.

It is hardly a coincidence these two lists match. Since those sexually active are menaced by the monsters, the theme here could be that those who are active in this way need to be punished. Sandra is certainly punished — with death! Joan and Wilbur are almost punished but they escape, yet we know their lives will never be the same. Perhaps subliminally, the message warns the audience not to be sexually aggressive, for this type of aggression will only lead to trouble. If so, then *Abbott and Costello Meet Frankenstein* is way ahead of its time, since only in the modern horror films would this theme become prevalent and obvious (i.e., the slasher movie, in which young people are shown being killed after they have had sex — as if they are being punished).

At the same time, the film warns (in the same way) against using sex to manipulate people since the result could be dire punishment (or reverse manipulation). Sandra and Joan both use sex to manipulate Wilbur. Wilbur, on the other hand, uses his newfound potency to impress and frustrate Chick. At the same time, the possibility of getting one of Wilbur's dates allows Wilbur some control over his partner. Again, all three seem to be punished for these acts. They are all controlled by Dracula at one point in the film, reinforcing the retribution warning. David J. Hogan points out in *Dark Romance: Sexuality in the Horror Film* (1986):

> The full force of Dracula's sexual power is levied against Lou. Costello's persona was that of an outrageously vulnerable waif. The impact of Dracula's easy manipulation of him is no less powerful or sexually potent than if Dracula's primary victim had been a woman. The relationship becomes a perversely funny variant on that of Svengali and Trilby. Costello is so trusting it hurts. Dracula pretends to regard Lou as a protege in order to get his brain. The relationship is strictly physical.[112]

The manipulation by Dracula also points to still another thematic warning. Those who are sexually active leave themselves open to attacking outsiders. In other words, being sexually active makes one weak. Sandra warns Dracula not to attempt to hypnotize her. "My will is as strong as yours," she says. But it is not. She and Joan end up under his hypnotic control. Wilbur is also entranced, once in the wax museum and again during his escape attempt. None of the three have the energy to resist Dracula, for they have spent too much of it on romantic activity. Notably, all three of the manipulated "weaklings" can be classified as feminine. Sandra and Joan are beautiful women while Wilbur displays many feminine (if not homosexual) tendencies: he skips, flirts with Chick, and, at one point, even dances with Chick to make Joan jealous. Perhaps this is acceptable because one of the comic strategies is to make the stooge come off as gay. It is funny for the same reason men in drag are funny.

One final interpretation is the idea that sexuality is the equivalent of monstrousness, that sexual aggression in women is unnatural. Those who are sexually active are existing in the same world as the monsters, since they continually see — and are menaced by — the three creatures. They, in fact, become monstrous (Sandra becomes a vampire, Joan is a zombie under Dracula's control, and Wilbur is slated to become the Frankenstein Monster). In this interpretation, the three in list A are not being punished but are just following a logical path into the unnatural monstrousness they brought upon themselves by daring to be sexually aggressive.

None of these themes would be possible without the comic Abbott and Costello plot (which leads to the sexual activity) or the straight horror plot (which yields the punishment and monstrousness). With both the comic world and the horror world trying to coexist within the framework, a confrontation is bound to occur. And it does — in the famous, wild climax that targets horror fans while at the same time producing big laughs. Symbolically, the battle is between the comic world and the horror world. In the end, the monsters are all destroyed, and Chick and Wilbur survive to prove that the light and happy comic world will always defeat the frightening, bleak horror world (something found to be untrue in *Abbott and Costello Meet Dr. Jekyll and Mr. Hyde*). However, in a strange twist, the horror world becomes comic with the film's final seconds when the Invisible Man shows up and frightens away the comedians. They swim away as the two worlds combine into a bit of black comedy.

Cox and Lofflin, however, find a completely different message within the film:

> [*Abbott and Costello Meet Frankenstein*] carries a barely veiled anti–Nazi message to an audience that had learned the hard way to fear

authoritarian societies. The mad scientist here is a woman with a heavy German accent by way, naturally, of Transylvania. Lenore Aubert, playing the role of Dr. Frankenstein's former medical assistant, is the mastermind of a project to resurrect the Frankenstein Monster. As she and Count Dracula kneel over the inert creature in a foggy wood, Dracula says, "This time the monster must have no will of his own, no fiendish intellect to oppose his master." She counters that once "the chubby little fellow's brain ... has been transplanted into the monster's crop he will obey you like a trained dog." The super-race overtones could not have been lost on postwar audiences.[113]

The film received rave reviews from *Variety, The Hollywood Reporter, The Los Angeles Examiner, The New York Daily Mirror,* and *The New York Star.* The *Los Angeles Times* said teens and youngsters "shrieked with that fusion of terror and glee which only a motion picture of this sort can inspire," adding that the film was "put together with enormous ingenuity."[114] Other periodicals, such as the *New York Times, The New York Sun,* and *The Chicago Sun-Times,* panned the picture[115]; but these reviews meant nothing, for audiences loved it. The film made 3.2 million dollars worldwide in 1948 and was Universal's biggest box office draw in three years,[116] saving Universal from bankruptcy yet again.[117] Abbott and Costello returned to the *Motion Picture Herald*'s Top 10 Box Office Attractions.[118]

Today, the film is seen as Abbott and Costello's best picture and is considered to be the most successful Frankenstein film since the original 1931 release. Donald F. Glut calls it "the best spoof of the horror genre ever made with top production values and good performances throughout,"[119] while Jim Mulholland said it was "the best satire on horror movies ever made."[120]

The Encyclopedia of Horror Movies called it "Abbott and Costello's first and best flirtation with horror ... made with care and looking good."[121] In *Living in Fear,* Les Daniels wrote: "Sometimes very funny and never as bad as purists might imagine ... the popular comedy team of Abbott and Costello made expository scenes more entertaining than many more serious performers had been able to do."[122] Michael R. Pitts simply labeled it "a fitting close for the genre in that decade."[123]

Leonard Maltin, in his *Movie and Video Guide,* calls the film the "all-time great horror-comedy,"[124] while *VideoHound* says it is one of Abbott and Costello's "best efforts."[125] Martin and Porter's *Video Movie Guide* says: "Whenever someone writes about the Universal horror classics, they always cite this film as evidence of how the series fell into decline. Likewise, screen historians call it the beginning of the end for the comedy team. It deserves neither rap."[126]

In his in-depth essay on the film, David J. Hogan particularly praises the screenplay, saying it is a model of construction, time compression, and narrative economy and logic. He urged aspiring screenwriters to look at the film to pick up on its nearly subliminal pacing.[127]

The film has never been forgotten. In 1950, fans cheered when Lugosi, Chaney, and Strange joined Abbott and Costello on television for an episode of *The Colgate Comedy Hour* to re-enact scenes from the film.[128] Homages and references to it are still made. Recently, catching a bit of the film *Attack of the 60 Foot Centerfold* (1995) on cable, I was delighted when a character asked a passerby if he had seen two giant fighting women terrorizing Hollywood. "Seen them?" replied the man. "I don't even know them."

The film has also had some famous fans over the years. According to one of the King's fans, Elvis Presley was a big fan of the film, seeing it for the first time when he was 13. Although it was reported he was a bit scared by the picture, the movie helped bring about his love for comedy and films in general.[129] Another rock and roll icon who loved the picture was the Grateful Dead's Jerry Garcia. When asked on AMC's *The Movie That Changed My Life* what movie changed his life, Garcia picked *Abbott and Costello Meet Frankenstein*. He said his fascination with the bizarre could be traced directly to that film.[130] Years later, hotshot director Quentin Tarantino expressed his love for the film, admiring the mixture of horror and comedy as "two great tastes that taste great together."[131]

The Invisible Man's line at the close of the film was quite prophetic. At the end of the very successful preview, Robert Arthur turned to the writers and said, "There's your next picture."[132] Universal picked up on the success and made plans to cash in. The duo would go on to meet the Invisible Man, Dr. Jekyll and Mr. Hyde, and the Mummy (along with non-horror icons such as Captain Kidd and the Keystone Kops). But each subsequent horror spoof declined in quality and popularity and eventually the fad and the fun died out. But for aficionados, *Abbott and Costello Meet Frankenstein* remains the best hybrid of the two opposing genres and a film that certainly deserves classic status.

Abbott and Costello Meet the Invisible Man

Released: March 19, 1951   *Running time:* 82 minutes

Directed by: Charles Lamont; *Produced by:* Howard Christie; *Screenplay by:* Robert Lees, Frederic I. Rinaldo, and John Grant; *Original Story by:* Hugh Wedlock, Jr., and Howard Snyder; *Suggested by:* H.G. Wells' *The Invisible Man*; *Director of Photography:* George Robinson, ASC; *Art Direction:* Bernard Herzbrun, Richard Riedel; *Musical Direction:* Joseph Gershenson; *Song "Good Old DDT" by:* Frederick Herbert, Milton Rosen, and Joseph Gershenson; *Film Editor:* Virgil Vogel; *Sound:* Leslie I. Carey, Robert Pritchard; *Set Decorations:* Russell A. Gausman, John Austin; *Hair Stylist:* Joan St. Oegger; *Makeup:* Bud Westmore; *Special Photography:* David S. Horsley, ASC.

Cast: Bud Abbott (Bud Alexander); Lou Costello (Lou Francis); Nancy Guild (Helen Gray); Arthur Franz (Tommy Nelson); Adele Jergens (Boots Marsden); Sheldon Leonard (Morgan); William Frawley (Det. Roberts); Gavin Muir (Dr. Philip Gray); Sam Balter (Radio Announcer); John Day (Rocky Hanlon); George J. Lewis (Torpedo); Frankie Van (Referee); Bobby Barber (Sneeky); Carl Sklover (Lou's Handler); Charles Perry (Rocky's Handler); Paul Maxey (Dr. Turner); Ed Gargan (Milt); Herbert Vigran (Stillwell); Milt Bronson (Fight Announcer); Donald Kerr (Ice Cream Vendor).

After *Abbott and Costello Meet Frankenstein*, the next "Abbott and Costello Meet..." picture was *Abbott and Costello Meet the Killer, Boris Karloff* in 1949. Although many reference works consider this a horror film, it is not a true horror-comedy. (Nevertheless, it will be covered in this book's third section.) The next true horror spoof was this one, in which Bud and Lou met up with another Universal monster stalwart, the Invisible Man. The character first appeared in James Whale's *The Invisible Man* (1933), a masterpiece of black comedy based on the novel by H.G. Wells. The role made Claude Rains a star even though he was seen only briefly during the epilogue. A string of sequels followed: *The Invisible Man Returns* (1940), *The Invisible Woman* (1940, itself a spoof), *Invisible Agent* (1942), and *The Invisible Man's Revenge* (1944).

Robert Arthur was resigning as producer for the comedy team who had just come off *Abbott and Costello in the Foreign Legion* (1950). He suggested Howard "Red" Christie as his successor, and Bud and Lou agreed. *Abbott and Costello Meet the Invisible Man* was one of the projects Arthur had already had in development for the duo.[133]

Early in 1948, Hugh Wedlock and Howard Snyder wrote a straight sequel to the last Invisible Man film entitled *The Invisible Man Strikes Back*. This screenplay was going to be used as the basis for the A&C comedy until Russell Rouse and Clarence Green created a new script. Robert Lees and Fred Rinaldo were brought in to rework the screenplay that was eventually used. They began with the concept of the Invisible Man as the third man in a boxing ring and went from there.[134] As it turned out, the film became a re-working of Lester K. Cole and Curt Siodmak's *The Invisible Man Returns*. In fact, lengthy passages from that script were lifted verbatim.[135] The director this time around was Charles Lamont, a comedy veteran who had directed, among others, the Three Stooges. (He would go on to direct all the remaining Bud and Lou horror-comedies.) Lamont stuck closely to the script as was his habit. Only the money-changing scene was added in during shooting, though the scene in which Tommy returns to visibility was expanded.[136]

The film was budgeted at $697,000, with Bud and Lou receiving $150,000 plus 10 percent of the profits. Production was scheduled for 34 days with 16 days for trick unit photography, even though several stock effects by John Fulton were lifted from previous Invisible Man films. The picture finished four days early and was $70,000 under budget.[137]

In all of the Invisible Man films, the title character is a different one from the film before, and little or no connection exists between them. In both *The Invisible Man Returns* and *The Invisible Agent*, the invisibility formula was handed down from Dr. John Griffin, the first Invisible Man, to his descendants. The same occurs in this film, with the formula passed on to Dr. Philip Gray, played by Gavin Muir, with mention being made of original creator John Griffin. Playing the role of Tommy Nelson, the boxer accused of murder who becomes the new Invisible Man, was Arthur Franz. Born in 1920, Franz had only appeared in a few films (most notably *Sands of Iwo Jima* [1949]) before working with Abbott and Costello.[138] He became a regular in many fifties' sci-fi films, including *Monster on the Campus* (1958) and *The Atomic Submarine* (1959). This was his first time in the fantasy genre, though he appears only briefly. (Stills for the film feature the Invisible Man drawn in.) He read most of his lines off-camera, but did appear in the scenes where he is wrapped in gauze. To help alleviate the heat from the bandages, a flat flask filled with ice water was strapped to his waist and equipped with a long straw that reached up to his mouth.[139] Franz did not attend the preview of the film but did take part in a big party at Bud's house when the duo paid off the IRS, which had been troubling them around that time.[140] Franz also attended parties at Lou Costello's house, as related by Paddy Costello (who seemed to have a crush on the young actor):

> Everybody would come to [my father's parties]. That was a kick in the head. And Arthur Franz came. My Dad was always remodeling the house, and he brought Arthur Franz up and he wanted to show him the wallpaper and stuff. I was just looking at this guy — I was about 14 or 15 — and (gasps) "He touched my wallpaper! He touched my wallpaper! My wallpaper's sacred!"[141]

Also in the cast were Nancy Guild, Lou's best friend Bobby Barber, and two Abbott and Costello veterans, William Frawley and Sheldon Leonard. Frawley had appeared in Bud and Lou's first film, *One Night in the Tropics,* and was only a few months away from playing his most famous role of all, Fred Mertz on *I Love Lucy.* (Frawley's role was originally meant for Jesse White.) Leonard, cast as the gangster villain, had played a similar role in *Hit the Ice* and was Lamont's favorite heavy.[142] Jack Dempsey was originally slated to play the fight referee but Frankie Van played the part instead.[143]

For Bud and Lou, this was a traumatic time in their professional relationship. Supposedly, they were constantly arguing in the dressing room, and every time Bud gave Lou a slap, it was more like a blow. Lou would get very angry but he was quoted as saying, "If I ever hit Bud, it'll be the end of our relationship."[144] Paddy Costello had this to say about the stories regarding Bud and Lou's relationship:

> You have to understand, I was a very small child then, and even as an adult, I never saw anything. I never saw them argue or not get along. We were raised together — their kids and my sisters and I — and we always referred to Bud and Betty as Uncle Bud and Aunt Betty. Always, always, we were always very close. Whatever differences they had, they never let spill over into their private lives, ever, ever. And Bud was a great guy.... He was the mild mannered person of the two. My father could be volatile and not bad or anything like that — but I mean where Bud was more "bend with the breeze" type of thing. I never saw any dissension. And that's the truth.[145]

If there was a strain, it does not show in the film, which stands as a fairly good horror romp.

Although they officially "met" the Invisible Man at the end of *Abbott and Costello Meet Frankenstein*, the beginning of this film does not continue from the end of that one. It begins with opening credits that feature cartoon drawings of Bud and Lou enacting scenes from the movie to follow. The accompanying music is reminiscent of the score from *Abbott and Costello Meet Frankenstein*. Abbott and Costello portray Bud Alexander and Lou Francis (their real middle names) who are just graduating from the Dugan's Detective Training School (Graduation Class of 1951)—an opening very similar to the Bowery Boys' *Spook Busters* (1946). A low angle shot shows the procession walking along. When a pair of legs stumble on the carpet, they are immediately recognizable as Costello's. To give the film a sense of closure, the ending also features Lou having trouble walking (much like he does in the procession scenes of *Buck Privates* and *Buck Privates Come Home*).

As soon as the boys take their seats on the stage, Lou immediately falls off of it. He also realizes he is wearing the wrong hat. From this point of their film careers on, the boys often seem to be preoccupied with their hats (a schtick usually reserved for Laurel and Hardy, who themselves had long started using material similar to Abbott and Costello's). Lou takes his place, wearing his graduation cap, and cries as the alma mater plays. Bud has a great line here. Lou wonders how he ever graduated and Bud tells him he slipped the instructor twenty bucks. Bud's con man personality is already coming through, as is Lou's innocent, bumbling child character.

Dugan delivers his graduation speech, mentioning that most of the students have studied extra hard. Bud shoots Lou a reproachful glare and Lou looks embarrassed. Dugan then hands out the Dugan Detective Training Diploma (DDT Diploma) and calls up Bud. Bud will receive a trial run with the McQuillian Agency in the Fort Building. Lou is given his diploma and sent to the same place.

The scene cuts immediately to the agency where the boys are working the night shift. Lou hangs his diploma on the wall. He is dressed like Sherlock Holmes—complete with hat, pipe, and magnifying glass. Bud even tells him he has been watching too many Sherlock Holmes movies, a series that had been produced by Universal in the forties. Lou, the man-child, shows off by sucking on his magnifying glass like it is a lollipop. Bud is more interested in business and turns on the radio to listen to the police calls. He hopes they will get a call and solve a murder so they can become famous detectives. His hopes for glory are similar to the ones he had in *Who Done It?* when the boys actually tried to solve a murder by masquerading as detectives.

The music in the next sequence, straight from *Abbott and Costello Meet Frankenstein*, is wonderful. As the police radio warns of the escape of suspected murderer Tommy Nelson, Nelson himself enters the office. Tommy uses the phone and Lou, listening to the police description over the radio, tags the stranger as Nelson. Bud is not even paying attention, showing in this scene that Lou is the better detective! The radio says Nelson, a professional boxer, is wanted for the murder of his manager after his last fight.

Bud writes down the description as Tommy uses the phone. Lou crawls under the desk and stares at Tommy through the magnifying glass. Tommy glares at him, his face magnified by the glass. It is a frightening moment, one that always gave me the chills as a kid. Lou tells Bud the stranger is Tommy Nelson but Bud scoffs. Lou says, "If it's not Tommy Nelson, then it's Frankenstein … FRANKENSTEIN!"—a nice little reference to the previous film.

Tommy calls his girlfriend Helen. He wants to see Dr. Gray and even offers money. She tells him to come to Maple Street. In a good moment, the clock chimes and Tommy takes a fighter's stance. There is now no doubt in Lou's mind that this is Tommy Nelson.

Tommy hires Bud and Lou and they all go to 823 Maple Street. Lou is already frightened. Tommy heads into the house and Lou shines his flashlight on the wall. He sees a silhouette of a bat, a reminder of Dracula's amazing transformations in the previous horror spoof. Bud quickly points out that the shadow is just a moth on the edge of the flashlight. A similar gag was used in Roland West's *The Bat* (1930) in a sequence that also inspired the Bat-signal in DC's *Batman* comic books.

Inside, Helen hugs Tommy, who insists on seeing the doctor. Bud and Lou wait in the library where Lou accidentally slaps Bud (just as he did in *Abbott and Costello Meet Frankenstein*). Lou overhears Helen call Tommy by name but Bud still does not believe they have been hired by Tommy Nelson. What would an escaped killer want with two private detectives, Bud wonders. "So he could catch himself," offers Lou.

Helen's uncle, Philip Gray, is the doctor Tommy is referring to, and he tells Tommy it was unwise to come to the house. Tommy demands the special serum Gray promised him while in jail. In a scene right out of *The Invisible Man Returns*, Tommy becomes paranoid and wonders if Helen and Philip think he actually killed O'Hara, his fight manager. To prove his trust, Gray shows Tommy the special serum, an invisibility potion. He tests it on a guinea pig, which immediately fades from view. The footage here was taken from *The Invisible Man Returns*.

Tommy wants the formula. If he could turn himself invisible, he could hide from the cops and prove his innocence. But the doctor warns of the serum's side effect — within a week Tommy would become a raving maniac. He tells the story of how this happened to the serum's original creator, Dr. John Griffin. He points to Griffin's picture on the wall, and fans will delight in seeing a portrait of Claude Rains, the original *Invisible Man*.

Contradicting previous films, Gray reveals that Griffin willed him his serum. Gray vowed never to use it until he had found a safe reagent. Tommy still wants to take the chance. He has no choice — if he doesn't clear himself he'll get the chair.

In the meantime, Bud and Lou are in the library watching a football game. This shows their incompetence as detectives. Instead of trying to figure out what is going on, they watch TV. Bud tells Lou that a "halfback ran around his own end." Lou replies, "Some trick." This could be seen as a bit of foreshadowing of the film's final moments. Costello is also up to his old trick of delivering some of his punchlines to the audience, breaking the fourth wall as he has done before.

A bulletin airs on the television showing a picture of Tommy and offering a $5,000 reward for the boxer. Bud, realizing Tommy is in their midst, plans to catch him and claim the reward. Lou shows some scruples when he tells Bud they cannot turn Tommy in because they are working for him. Bud replies that Tommy is a rat for not mentioning the reward.

Meanwhile, the doctor still refuses to inject Tommy with the serum. Outside, the police surround the house. Bud and Lou start to sneak out, then remember they are detectives, not crooks. "Am I a crook?" asks Bud. Lou would say yes. However, their behavior is not surprising considering how many times they have been in trouble with the law in past films.

Tommy tells Helen and the doctor to stall the police while he sneaks out the back. But when they leave, he injects himself with the serum.

Detective Roberts has his men take their positions. He has a warrant to search the house. Bud and Lou watch the proceedings while the doctor and Helen lead the police upstairs.

Bud tells Lou they must get Tommy before the police do. He makes Lou wait in the room while he watches the hall. Lou is nervous about being left alone, so Bud says, "In that case, I'll watch the hall and you wait here." This is the same trick Lou attempted to pull on Bud in *Abbott and Costello Meet Frankenstein*. This time it works.

Tommy enters the room and Bud locks him in with Lou. He has no problem leaving Lou with a suspected murder when money is at stake. Lou approaches the preoccupied Tommy and tells him he does not care about the reward. He wants to shake hands and, as he does, Tommy's hand fades away. Lou does his patented scared routine as Tommy completely turns invisible. Laughing maniacally, all that is left of the boxer for a second is his teeth. Then he is gone. As usual in an Invisible Man flick, the title character does a striptease only to reveal nothing beneath the clothes. This is always a frightening image. (What might be even more frightening is the fact Tommy Nelson is not wearing any underwear when he takes his clothes off![146]) And as is always the case in an Abbott and Costello monster picture, Lou is the first to see the title monster. When he tries to tell Bud what he saw, he is disbelieved.

Bud brings in Roberts, telling him Lou has Tommy covered. (In truth, nothing is covering Tommy!) "That boy is always on his toes!" says Bud, but when he opens the door, Lou (having fainted) falls out. He is revived with smelling salts which make his hat pop off. The emphasis on the boys' hats would continue into *Abbott and Costello Meet Dr. Jekyll and Mr. Hyde*.

Lou tells Roberts that Tommy disappeared in installments. "He did a Gypsy Rose Lee." The script listed a less funnier alternative for that line: "He did a striptease."[147] An amusing fact to remember is that the Invisible Man is always running around naked. "What was he wearing the last time you saw him?" Roberts asks, and Lou replies, "Air!" Dr. Gray and Helen realize what Tommy has done, but the police think Lou is crazy and take him downtown.

Before leaving, Bud kicks Lou for letting Tommy get away. Tommy kicks Bud and calls him a double-crosser. A dumbfounded Bud blames Lou. Bud is kicked again. Roberts breaks up the two and they all depart. Abbott had taken abuse from an unseen person before. In *The Time of Their Lives*, Costello, playing a ghost from the Revolutionary War era, delights in tormenting Abbott. Many fans were happy to see Bud get his comeuppance in scenes like these.

Before leaving, Tommy pauses to smoke a cigarette. The scene is reminiscent of the conclusion of *Abbott and Costello Meet Frankenstein* when the Invisible Man enjoyed a smoke while frightening the boys out of their boat.

At the police station, city psychiatrist James C. Turner has Lou tell his story. Unlike in *Abbott and Costello Meet Frankenstein*, Bud's threat of taking Lou to a doctor to be examined finally comes true. The doctor asks Lou if he ever saw someone disappear before. Lou says he saw his brother disappear — down a manhole.

Turner is frustrated by Lou's stupid answers to his questions. He has Lou lie down on the sofa, but somehow Lou reverses their roles and the doctor is answering Lou's questions. Finally, Turner decides to hypnotize Lou, but his attempts backfire. He has Lou stare at a dangling watch, but soon Turner is asleep instead of Lou. As seen in *Abbott and Costello Meet the Killer, Boris Karloff*, it is quite impossible to hypnotize Lou. Only Dracula was able to do so!

Lou is frantic; he wants the doctor to snap out of it (just like he wanted Chick to "be just like you used to be" in the previous monster meeting — these scenes continually repeat themselves). Roberts sends in a cop to find out what is taking so long. Soon, Lou has a whole room full of people asleep, including cops and cleaning women. Roberts and Bud finally investigate for themselves. They wake up Turner who throws the boys out. This is a humorous scene but it is buttoned badly by having the doctor repeat verbatim Lou's joke about his brother falling down a manhole. This awkward conclusion adds nothing funny or new to the scene.

Back at the agency, Bud yells at Lou for messing up the case. Helen is waiting for them with a message. Tommy wants them to prove his innocence and he has sent a $500 retainer. They are to take a grip full of clothes to the south end of the park and leave it there. Bud now believes Tommy may be invisible but is not shocked or surprised by this knowledge. After Helen leaves, they do their money-exchanging routine in which Lou continually takes the bill back from Abbott. The two are quite adept at performing this very funny routine which they used in *The Naughty Nineties* and on their TV show. After straightening out the money problem, Bud surreptitiously calls the cops.

At the designated spot, Bud sends Lou into the woods with the grip. Tommy's presence is made known with the use of footage lifted from *The Invisible Man Returns*. (The script even makes reference to these shots: "The grip must match the grip used in *The Invisible Man Returns*.[148]) Frightened, Lou leaves the grip and runs away. Tommy gets dressed. Lou returns to Bud, who now believes Tommy is *not* invisible. Lou tells Bud the empty woods are full of Tommy Nelson.

Tommy emerges in the traditional guise of the Invisible Man — suit, bandages, and goggles. At the sight of him, Lou's hat pops off a second time. He crawls under the car and emerges on the other side. Bud plays up to Tommy and says they can be trusted. Just as Tommy is ready to shake on it, the police arrive.

Tommy and Lou jump in the car while Roberts talks to Bud. Tommy peels off the bandages while Lou tells him not to lose his head. When Lou sees the "headless" Nelson, he faints again.

When only Lou is found in the car, Roberts yells at the boys for wasting his time. The police leave and Bud again berates Lou. Tommy kicks Bud and pulls his hat down around his ears. Bud is ready to beat up Lou but Tommy threatens Bud and calls him a double-crosser. (In a marvelous bit of effects work, Bud's coat moves back and forth as if Tommy was yanking it.) Bud now believes Tommy is invisible and asks Lou for help. (A portion of the script was cut here as Bud realizes Tommy Nelson is invisible.) Lou pulls out a watch and chain and swings it back and forth — a nod to the earlier hypnosis scene. Lou says, "Go to sleep, go to sleep." Bud says, "Stop it! Tommy Nelson's here I tell you!"[149]

Tommy tells the boys that if they double-cross him again, he'll kill them. He has them get in the back seat of the car while he drives. As they leave, Bud yells at Lou for letting Tommy beat on him. Lou says he did not see a thing. Lou's facial expressions in this scene are appropriately anxious, as he is extremely nervous riding in the "driverless" car.

Tommy drives like a madman, forcing a truck off the road. (This scene suspiciously resembles a similar moment in Stanley Kubrick's *A Clockwork Orange* [1971]). The serum is already taking effect. Bud apologizes to Tommy for double-crossing him and Tommy tells them his story. He stepped out of the shower after the fight only to find O'Hara on the floor beaten to death. The evidence all pointed to him, but he was framed. Bud then gives Tommy Helen's message. Without the re-agent, he will become a raving lunatic with an uncontrollable urge to kill. Now that's comforting!

A motorcycle cop pulls up alongside the car and orders the boys to pull over. Lou tells the cop to speak to the driver. When the cop sees that no one is driving the car, he's so astounded *he* has to pull off the road. Later, he is hypnotized by the psychiatrist. Detective Roberts is baffled by repeated reports of an invisible man.

Bud, Lou, and Tommy head for the gym. Lou asks a man in a rowing machine why he is rowing so fast. The man says he has to be in Staten Island in twenty minutes. Typical of the boys, they pay no attention to the lunatic before them. Their whole universe is insane and they are so used to it that nothing like this affects them. In the script, Lou does recognize that the man is insane and pulls out the watch and chain, once again referencing the hypnosis scene.[150]

Announcer Stillwell proclaims that Rocky Hanlon is about to fight Young Malloy. Rocky is the boxer Tommy fought the night he was framed. Someone in the crowd yells out that Rocky could not beat Nelson, which angers Rocky.

As Bud and Lou watch the fight, Tommy fills them in. O'Hara had made a deal with a gambler named Morgan for Tommy to take a dive during his fight with Rocky. But instead, Tommy knocked out Rocky.

Tommy tells Bud to ask Stillwell if Lou can train at the gym. Naturally, Lou is the one who has to play the role of the boxer and be put in danger. Ironically, before becoming a comic, Costello was an amateur boxer fighting under the name Lou King. He fought twelve times, with eleven wins and one draw. His career came to an end when his father discovered what he was doing. Nevertheless, his experience must have helped him in this film's boxing scenes and the hilarious bout he fights in *Buck Privates*.

Bud is confident he can convince Stillwell since he is a con man by nature. Stillwell agrees to let Lou train but says Lou does not look like a fighter. Bud asks Stillwell to give Lou a bout. But Lou wants "a bout" twenty minutes to get out of town. (He should have taken the rowboat to Staten Island.)

Meanwhile, the trainer tells Morgan that Malloy will take a dive in the sixth round. The fight will put them all in the clear. Tommy listens in on the conversation.

Lou acts like he is pummeling the punching bag and soon Tommy is punching it for him with remarkable speed. Lou pretends to be a skilled fighter, attracting the attention of everyone in the gym. Even though Lou is occasionally hit in the face by the bag, the reporters come over and begin taking his picture. Rocky is infuriated by the loss of attention. Although funny, this scene is ridiculous, for it is fairly obvious Lou's fists are not coming anywhere near the bag. Still, a good touch is added when a reporter comments that Lou hits the bag just like Tommy Nelson. (By the way, in the script the promoter of the upcoming Hanlon-Malloy fight is introduced as Colonel Duffle.[151])

Rocky demands the reporters pay attention to him so Bud antagonizes him even further. He accuses Rocky of taking dives. Bud orders Lou to take a punch at Rocky but Lou is too afraid. Rocky tries to punch Lou but Tommy stops the fist and knocks him out. The reporters are amazed because they "didn't even see the guy move." When they ask Lou what kind of punch he threw, he replies, "A half Nelson." Lou is christened "Louie the Looper."

Lou makes up stories about past fictional fights while Bud tells the press Lou would like a shot at Hanlon. The reporters assure them when the stories see print the public will be demanding that fight instead of the Malloy-Hanlon bout.

Soon, a sports announcer is telling the public to keep a close eye on Louie the Looper, saying his style is half Tony Galento and half Benny Leonard.

In a high-class hotel room, Tommy beats Bud and Lou at poker. With the aid of remarkably good special effects, the Invisible Man cuts and deals the cards, then holds up his hand. He also catches Lou cheating. (This scene is an in-joke, since Abbott and Costello were famous for the high stakes poker games they played in between takes on the set.)

Tommy says Morgan will think Bud and Lou are a couple of free spenders and make a contract with them. They will lead him on. On the night of the fight, Lou will go in the ring with Tommy at his side. When Lou doesn't take the dive, they will catch Morgan.

Helen shows up and Bud and Lou leave the two alone. Tommy wears a robe. Helen is worried that Tommy will be caught. She also fears that his mind might become infected by the drug, but Tommy says he has never felt better. Helen urges him to be careful and leaves. In private, she asks Bud and Lou to call her if Tommy should start acting strangely.

Tommy hands the boys their hats, telling them they are going to the Bubble Room (a ritzy nightclub). Before they can leave, Roberts shows up. Lou disguises Tommy as a table. Just like in *Abbott and Costello Meet Frankenstein*, Lou pulls out a tablecloth while leaving the dishes on the table (only this time he does not mug to the camera). Actually, the fact Lou even tries to hide Tommy is ridiculous since the man is invisible!

Roberts claims he is checking up on Lou's hallucinations, but he also wants information. The boys say they have not seen Tommy since last night — one of many gags based on the fact that no one can see Tommy. Roberts thinks Tommy is disguised as the table, but when he pulls away the sheet, no one is there. Roberts departs disgusted.

At the Bubble Room, Bud and Lou try to keep Tommy from becoming too intoxicated from champagne. Lou pretends he is drinking the alcohol, confusing a waiter. Tommy then causes trouble when they try to order dinner. Lou tries to order spaghetti but Tommy interrupts with his order, a steak. Lou finally tells the waiter he wants both entrees.

Bud asks if he could have the swell looking "dish" across the bar as a side order. It is Boots Marsden. Morgan notices the boys looking at Boots and tells her to work her magic.

Bud thinks he has caught Boots' eye when she approaches them, but she completely ignores him and goes for Lou. In a rare bit of risqué humor, she says she has two good reasons for wanting to meet Lou — then takes off her jacket, drawing attention to her breasts. She says that when she saw Lou she thought, "There's a man." Lou says that is the first time anyone ever said that about him. As always, Lou is portrayed as a boy.

Bud offers Boots a drink but she says she would prefer some privacy. With all the sexual innuendo she can muster, she tells Lou to come see her at the Carlton Towers. After telling off Bud, Boots departs, leaving Lou repeating over and over again, "Boots ... Boots..."

"Shut up," says Bud, "you sound like Gunga Din." Bud is allowed his fair share of good cracks in this film.

At this time, the picture presents a situation common to the "Abbott and Costello Meet Monsters" films. A beautiful woman, in cahoots with the villain, pretends to be attracted to Lou in order to manipulate him. Bud, of course, becomes jealous. In fact, in this scene, Lou's cries of "Boots ... Boots..." even mimic his outspoken love of Sandra in *Abbott and Costello Meet Frankenstein*. This device is practical and gets the plot rolling. It is also a wonderful comic touch. If Bud knew what the various women had planned for Lou he would never be jealous but instead very relieved!

Tommy says it will soon be time to make their first move. Meanwhile, the food arrives. In a patented Costello bit, he reaches right for Abbott's food only to have his hand slapped away as if he were a naughty boy. This bit of business can be seen in *Hold That Ghost*, *The Naughty Nineties*, and *The Wistful Widow of Wagon Gap*.

Decent special effects allow Lou and Tommy to eat a string of spaghetti at the same time. Lou is forced to clip it with his fingers rather than suffer an embarrassing variation of the famous scene in *Lady and the Tramp* (1955).

Bud and Lou arrive at Boots' room sans Tommy. Nervous Lou carries flowers with a "recording machine" hidden inside. Lou is let in by the seductive Boots but, being the bashful boy that he is, tries to leave. Bud makes him go back in. Bud then peeks in the keyhole to watch the proceedings. But this time Lou gets one up on him. He squirts Bud in the eye through the keyhole with a squirt gun. "I'm a little squirt," Lou says, delivering a line that could today be interpreted as possessing a sexual meaning. In later years, on their television program, Lou would constantly play with a cap gun.

Lou begins recording the conversation. Boots uses her wiles to urge Lou to throw the fight. She kisses him. Naughty Lou asks her how many rounds she can last. She says she will talk to a nice man who will pay him to take a fall. "Remember, this is all off the record," she says. Lou takes the record out and hides it in the back of his pants.

Boots says they must return to the Bubble Room but Lou wants to kiss some more. Boots throws him down, sits on his lap, and breaks the record. Lou's facial expression here is wonderful.

Later, Helen calls Tommy at the Bubble Room while Bud listens in. The drunken Tommy tells her he likes being invisible. Bud takes the phone and tells Helen that Tommy is drunk, to which Tommy adds that he is drunk with power. Bud shows what a good actor he is in this scene. His worried expressions as Tommy rants and raves are quite good, as is the moment when Bud must pretend to be a crazy drunk so the waiter will not discover Tommy's presence. Tommy says he will be "the ruler of an invisible empire — loyal subjects [he] will reward, enemies [he] will destroy." This dialogue is lifted directly from *The Invisible Man Returns* and is quite chilling. The waiter begins to notice the commotion and Bud pretends to be drunk by quoting Shakespeare. He makes the waiter pour two drinks, saying he is a two-fisted drinker.

Boots and Lou show up. Photographers want pictures of Lou drinking champagne from her shoe. Lou ends up pouring champagne all over a bystander. The man almost beats up Lou but chickens out when Boots tells him Lou is the now-famous Louie the Looper.

Boots leaves Lou to get the moneyman. The tough guy tells Lou that Rocky will cream him. Lou reports to Bud and Tommy, explaining that he broke the record. Tommy (finally!) complains that he thought he was hiring good detectives. Lou tries to make up for it by saying they are good friends. Again using dialogue from *The Invisible Man Returns*, Tommy says he does not want friends, but instead wants worshippers and followers who will obey him.

Lou tells Tommy that Boots is contacting Morgan, which makes Tommy happy. He celebrates by drinking more. Lou warns him that every time he goes into a saloon, the devil goes in with him. Tommy says, "If he does, he pays for his own drink!" Bud and Lou previously used this joke in *Keep 'Em Flying*.

In a private room, nervous gangsters agree to do things Morgan's way. When Boots enters, Morgan knocks off "Sneeky's" hat because he did not take it off in the presence of a lady. Sneeky is played by Lou's best friend Bobby Barber, who appeared as a waiter in *Abbott and Costello Meet Frankenstein*. Rocky insists he can handle Louie the Looper, saying the previous knockout was just a lucky punch. But Morgan says Lou will have to take a dive or else he will get the same treatment Tommy Nelson got.

Back in the bar, Tommy drinks the tough guy's drink, letting Lou get caught with the glass. The tough guy tries to punch Lou but Tommy knocks him out. The bartender warns Lou to save his punches for the ring. Tommy wants another drink but Lou threatens to cut him off. In defiance, Tommy drinks from the glasses of everyone at the bar. This time Bud gets into a fight, thinking Tommy will cover for him. But Tommy lets Bud take the punch. Bud reverses earlier sentiments and calls Tommy a double-crosser.

Lou starts a fight with the man who punched Bud. The bartender pulls out a mallet and knocks out Lou. Tommy punches the bartender, then tries to revive Lou with seltzer. Bud and Tommy are forced to carry the unconscious Lou out. This a great scene with the Invisible Man lifting Lou's legs and shocking the bartender.

Detective Roberts enters through the bar's revolving door and knocks out Tommy. Lou comes to and he and Bud carry Tommy out. The two comedians show here that they are also adept at pantomime as they carry out Tommy's "body." Roberts watches, then heads straight to the psychiatrist to tell him what he saw. This is a good capper to the running gag.

Back at the lab, Tommy comes to, hung over and strapped to a table. Dr. Gray is still having difficulty finding a reagent. Helen is given a good line here when she tells Tommy it is good to *see* him.

Tommy says he plans to double-cross Morgan in the ring by knocking out Rocky. Lou is scared to go in the ring and scared Morgan will bump off Bud and blame it on him. Tommy says he will be in the ring with Lou the whole time. To make sure Lou can tell he is there, Lou sprays him with perfume. They leave with Helen.

In a unique scene, Tommy discovers he is tied down. The cover slips down, revealing straps that move as the invisible Tommy struggles. The doctor plans to keep him there until a cure is found. This reveals to the audience that the doctor and Helen have actually double-crossed Bud and Lou! Tommy accuses the doctor of being afraid of what the medical community will say when word gets out that the invisibility serum has been used. He is right, for Gray is ashamed.

Announcer Sam Balter makes a prediction about the upcoming fight. The wise money has switched over to Rocky when the photos of Lou's night on the town hit the papers. Since both men have a strong offense, Sam promises this will be the most *offensive* fight of the year.

A nervous Lou and Bud wait for Tommy to arrive in the dressing room. Bud is confident he will show. Lou thinks he hears Tommy scratching at the window, but he is soon scared by a black cat (Lou had previously been scared by a cat in *Africa Screams*). Extremely worried, Lou takes Bud's cigar and puffs smoke, hoping to see Tommy's outline. The only result of this effort is a coughing fit for Lou. (Offscreen, Lou was never seen without his trademark cigar.)

Sneeky arrives with a box for Bud and Lou, saying, "Compliments of a friend." Inside the box are flowers with a note that reads, "You can smell them or wear them." Under the flowers is the money promised to the boys. Bud now wants to keep the money. He starts planning to double-cross Tommy, not knowing Tommy has just entered the room. Tommy makes his presence known, saying he broke the straps. He threatens the boys if they do not follow the plan.

The boys get the word that Lou's bout is next. Bud tells Lou to keep his stomach in, an exchange reminiscent of the "Throw out your chest!" portion of the drill routine in *Buck Privates*.

In the ring, contender Rocky is introduced, followed by Louie the Looper. Lou sees Morgan in the audience. Morgan motions for Lou to take the dive in the fifth round. Lou wants to lay down and Bud is willing to go along with it, but Tommy orders Lou into the ring.

The bout begins, refereed by Frankie Van. It is a well-choreographed scene, definitely the high point of the film and almost the equal of the fight scene in *Buck Privates*. In the audience, Morgan tells Boots that all the syndicate's money is on Rocky, who refuses to shake hands with Lou in the ring.

Tommy gives Lou instructions and the fight begins. Rocky swings and misses, but Lou falls down anyway. Tommy yells at him and Lou gets up, taking a punch from Rocky. Lou falls again. Tommy tells him, in a frightening and disturbing bit of dialogue, that if he plans to throw the fight, he will hold Lou up and let Rocky cut him to ribbons! Rocky swings again. This time, Tommy blocks the punch and hits Rocky back. Lou does not even move, but Rocky hits the canvas. Amazingly, most of the shots in this scene were achieved in one take.[152]

Lou is told to go to his corner but instead he hangs around as the ref counts over Rocky. Bud sweats due to Morgan's increasing anger. Rocky gets back on his feet, only to be pummeled by more of Tommy's punches. Rocky soon hits the canvas again.

When Rocky is back on his feet, Lou asks Tommy if he can finish him off. Lou swings but Rocky ducks, and Lou knocks out Tommy by mistake. What follows is an extended routine in which Lou and Rocky repeatedly trip over Tommy's body as Lou tries to bring Tommy around by spitting water in his face.

Tommy revives, and the first round ends with Rocky taking another one of his punches. Bud yells at Lou for not throwing the fight, but Tommy says the situation is under control. In the other corner, Sneeky listens as Rocky complains that he feels like he is fighting two men. Sneeky reports to Morgan, who senses that something about the fight is phony. He sends for "Torpedo." Morgan's character is shown here to be very smart. Unlike other Abbott and Costello villains, Morgan should be considered very dangerous.

Unknown to Lou, Tommy has left the ring to listen in on Morgan and Sneeky. The round begins and Lou takes a beating. He is hit and falls, then sniffs around for Tommy. The ref stops the count and asks him what he is doing. "I'm smelling," says Lou. The ref replies, "It's poor English, but you sure do."

Lou is hit again and again, which makes Bud happy. Lou asks Bud to throw in the towel but Bud says it is too dirty.

Meanwhile, Morgan orders Torpedo to put Milt into a police uniform so they can give Bud and Lou the same treatment they gave Tommy and O'Hara.

Tommy rings the bell to end the round and keep Lou from getting killed. Lou is given smelling salts, which causes the ice bag to pop off his head. This is the end of the running gag of having things pop off Lou's head.

When the next round begins, Tommy carries Lou into the ring, moving him out of the way of Rocky's punches. Tommy then knocks out Rocky. Lou is declared the winner.

Morgan and his men head for the dressing room while Tommy tells Bud and Lou he will see them later. Morgan tells Milt not to let anyone but Bud and Lou in the dressing room. Milt comments, in reference to his police get-up, "I hope my muddah don't see me."

Bud and Lou meet up with Helen and Dr. Gray who are looking for Tommy because Gray has finally found the reagent. Detective Roberts shows up and stops Gray and Helen. "If you think I think Louie the Looper knocked out Rocky Hanlon, you must think I'm a fool," he says, to which Gray replies, "Again you have the correct answer."

Bud and Lou, worried about what Morgan might do, tell Milt they are glad to have police protection. They enter the dressing room thinking they are safe. Milt keeps Helen, Gray, and Roberts from entering, and when he back talks the detective, Roberts becomes suspicious.

Inside, Bud tells Lou they are one step ahead of Morgan because he does not know they are detectives, not realizing Morgan and his henchman are waiting in the room. Morgan confronts them, but Tommy suddenly beats up the henchman. "This is the pay-off," Tommy tells the confused Morgan.

Morgan now realizes what is going on and draws a gun. Tommy knocks the gun out of his hands and it falls in the water cooler. He grabs Morgan from behind and orders him to confess.

Lou tries to get the gun but can't hold on to it because he is still wearing his boxing gloves. When he tries to shoot it, water spills out. He tries again but this time hits the radiator, causing steam to fill the room.

One of Abbott and Costello's trademarks is having Lou interpret everything Bud says literally. In this case, Bud tells Lou to let Morgan have it and Lou childishly hands Morgan the gun. Morgan takes the opportunity to hold Bud hostage. Tommy taunts Morgan, who continually tries to shoot the invisible man. Unfortunately, Lou keeps getting in the way. One bullet hits the radio, turning it on to an opera singer belting out a tune. Lou hits the radio and the singer falters and trails off, a distinctly surreal touch.

Bud, finally proving his worth to the team, knocks the gun from Morgan's hand. Tommy catches it. Bud then takes great delight in punching out Morgan. Ironically, Tommy is now "in the clear" two ways. He is cleared of O'Hara's murder and he is also visible as he stands in the steam.

The henchman wakes up and throws his switchblade at Tommy's outline. Tommy is hit near the heart. Lou, in a rare case of heroics, beats up the henchman. All the business of handling the gun, the water cooler, and the radio does not appear in the script. The scene is much shorter; all the comic business was added later.[153]

Outside, Roberts orders Milt's arrest. The police, Helen, and Gray burst into the room. Bud tells Roberts what has happened. Morgan and his goon are taken away. Gray orders Tommy taken to the hospital.

At the hospital, Gray gives Tommy a blood transfusion, explaining that the new blood will give him the strength to stand the reagent. Bud tells blood donor Lou he was lucky he had the same blood type as Tommy. "Why can't you be lucky some time?" asks Lou.

Tommy becomes visible as he awakens. He and Helen kiss. Meanwhile, Lou starts to fade away. Gray explains that some of Tommy's blood must have backed up during the transfusion.

Lou revels in his invisibility, thinking he will become the world's greatest detective. He leaves the room with Bud in pursuit. They get in an elevator with a group of beautiful nurses. Lou then does exactly what each one of us would do if we were invisible — take advantage of it. He begins by pinching each one of the women. Naturally, they blame Bud and take turns slapping him.

Realizing he missed one nurse, Lou takes her in his arms and kisses her. As he does he becomes halfway visible. The nurse faints as Lou realizes he is naked. He grabs a towel and wears it like a diaper, emphasizing his childish character. Roberts shows up and watches as Lou reappears — only Lou's feet are on backwards! Roberts checks his pulse and calls for a doctor. Bud also sees what has happened. He does a great double take, then (as usual) immediately starts yelling at Lou. "That's just like you," he says. "You get everything backwards."

Lou starts running — only in reverse — and crashes through a glass door. This final sequence is both funny and disturbing at the same time. One can only wonder how Lou would possibly get back to normal. The endings of the monster spoofs are usually twists and conclude the film not with a straightforward ending but rather in the middle of action. *Abbott and Costello Meet Frankenstein* has the Invisible Man frightening the boys; this film has Lou caught in a scientific impossibility; and *Meet Dr. Jekyll* will have the boys facing a roomful of monsters.

In the script, the film was to end with Lou looking down at his backward legs and saying, "I never expected the end to be like this."[154]

Abbott and Costello Meet the Invisible Man was released on March 19, 1951, and was well received. In fact, it almost spun off a series of sports-themed Abbott and Costello films. Their next project was to be "Two Bums with the Yankees." Lou would have met a scientist who had invented an atomic ring that grants the wearer incredible power. Lou would use to it to excel at baseball.[155]

The world premiere of the film was a gala benefit for the *Los Angeles Examiner*'s Fund for Wounded Veterans of the Korean War. The stage show accompanying the picture included Bud, Lou, Martin and Lewis, Danny Thomas, Lena Horne, Jerry Colona, Allan Jones, Janis Paige, and Nat Young's Orchestra.[156] At the show, Lou said this was the best film the team had done since *Buck Privates*.[157]

Overall, the horror elements in *Abbott and Costello Meet the Invisible Man* are not very strong. The film is more of a science fiction spoof. (In fact, *The Invisible Man* and its sequels are more often considered to be sci-fi, even though the title character can be quite frightening when done right.) Yet the movie's trailer makes *Abbott and Costello Meet the Invisible Man* look like a horror fan's delight, promising "chills and chuckles" and warning, "Don't look unless you dare."[158]

In truth, the picture is primarily a gangster-spoof set in the world of boxing. Yet many feel the film is not even a typical Abbott and Costello comedy. In an article on the "Abbott and Costello Meet…" movies, James L. Neibaur stated the film is more mature than their earlier World War II films, and the boys show more restraint here than usual.[159] He goes on to say that "it was almost as if the boys had stumbled into a Boston Blackie film and felt as though they had to behave while Chester Morris was away."[160]

Still, elements from *Abbott and Costello Meet Frankenstein* can be found throughout the picture (and the future monster spoofs as well). Although a friend of Abbott and Costello, the titular monster menace is played straight. Though Tommy cracks a few jokes while drunk, the audience is never allowed to forget Tommy is standing on the brink of insanity thanks to the serum he ingested. As usual, Lou is the first to "meet" the film's monster; and when he tries to tell people what he has seen, he is never believed, especially by Bud.

Also common to these monster spoofs is a complex plot enacted by the film's villains. In the previous picture, Dracula planned to put Lou's brain in the body of the Frankenstein Monster in order to take over the world. Here, gangster Morgan plans for Lou to take a fall so that his gambling debts will be cleared. Otherwise, he will kill Bud and frame Lou for the murder. Included in the villains' plots are moments when an attractive female has to come on to Costello and feign love interest. Lou never understands the strange attraction he has over these beautiful women — and neither does Bud. Invariably, Bud will become jealous, not knowing Lou has been chosen because his simple mind is easier to manipulate.

In each film, Bud and Lou stumble onto the plot, never really initiating any of the action. And these films are always capped by a wild chase or fight, climaxing with the disposal of the monsters. (*Abbott and Costello Meet the Invisible Man* is the only monster spoof in which the monster menace lives, due, of course, to the fact Tommy is innocent and is a friend to the boys.)

One other interesting feature in the spoofs is that at one point in the film either Bud or Lou "become" the monster. For example, in *Abbott and Costello Meet Frankenstein*, Bud is thought by the townspeople to be the Wolf Man and is even chased by a mob. Lou, during the wild chase at the finale, momentarily drapes himself in a makeshift cape and fools the Monster into thinking he is Dracula. In *Meet the Invisible Man*, invisibility serum backs up into Costello's blood during the transfusion and Lou becomes the Invisible Man during the film's final moments. Though this usually occurs for the sake of laughs (with mistaken identity being a common staple of classic comedy), it might actually be Abbott and Costello following the old adage, "To defeat your enemy, you must think like [and become] your enemy."

After so establishing the fact that *Abbott and Costello Meet the Invisible Man* is a valid part of the monster spoof cycle, the next question that comes up is: what is this film trying to say? While *Abbott and Costello Meet Frankenstein* can be seen as possessing a significant sexual subtext, this film plays on the classic theme of appearance versus reality — in this case, the ability to see not only what is not there but to see the truth underneath the false front. The characters we are supposed to like and root for can do both of these, whereas the characters we do not side with cannot.

For example, Bud and Lou know that Tommy is invisible and

nearby, even though the police and the gangsters cannot see him. Furthermore, they and Helen see Tommy as a good man. They are able to see and believe in his innocence even though the police think he is guilty. Tommy sees Bud and Lou as both good detectives and as his one hope for survival despite Bud's sometimes traitorous actions and Lou's buffoonery. These are all characters we like and side with during the film.

Morgan (and his gang—which includes Boots), Roberts, and Gray are unable to see beyond the surface. Although Morgan at times suspects things are not what they seem to be, he does not realize until the end that Bud and Lou are undercover detectives and that Tommy Nelson is an invisible man. Roberts does not see Tommy's innocence nor does he notice his presence. He tries to use psychoanalysis to explain the unexplainable. Finally, Gray, though on Tommy's side, does not see the good the invisibility serum can do for Tommy in clearing his name. These characters we do not side with—Morgan because he is the villain, Roberts because he is constantly an obstacle for the heroes, and Gray because of his doubts, his whining, and his reluctance to help.

One fact no one in the film sees is that, at one point or another, each character is a double-crosser. Bud tries numerous times to double-cross his client Tommy Nelson. Bud and Lou double-cross Morgan by taking the money but not taking the dive during the fight. Tommy double-crosses Bud by letting him take a punch when Bud thinks Tommy will block it. Helen and Gray double-cross Bud and Lou (and Tommy) by strapping down Tommy and keeping him from the big fight, leaving the boys' lives endangered. Boots double-crosses Lou by pretending to be in love with him when she is really working for Morgan. Morgan is a double-crosser by fixing fights so he can win at gambling. And Roberts seems to be on the verge of double-crossing Bud and Lou when he shows up at the hotel. He says he wants to check on Lou's mental health, but he is actually looking for Tommy Nelson. Again, the appearance versus reality theme comes into play, for each character is working behind the scenes, lying to and double-crossing other characters. The constant presence and threat of betrayal also adds a minor noirish touch to the film.

The theme of betrayal is even more relevant when applied to Abbott and Costello's real-life troubles. As mentioned before, as the film finished up, the boys were paying off the back taxes they owed to the IRS. Due to their dishonest business manager, they owed quite a lot of money in income taxes. The government decided to make an example out of

Abbott and Costello to the Hollywood community and harassed the comedians until they paid up. They lost a lot of what they owned but finally cleared their debt with the government. But the boys felt betrayed, especially since they had helped to raise millions of dollars worth of war bonds during World War II, more than any other actor or personality. In effect, they had been "double-crossed" by the United States. Lou even makes a joke about it during the film. When counting out and dividing the money brought in by Sneeky, he makes a pile for himself, a pile for Bud, and a third pile for an imaginary person called "him." That third pile is bigger than the other two, prompting Bud to ask who "him" stands for. Lou says "him" is the income tax man.

To go even further, though Tommy Nelson is the Invisible Man of the title (for obvious reasons), many of the other characters are at times metaphorically invisible. This mostly applies to Morgan, for he is equally as invisible as Tommy. Morgan controls the bouts, deciding who will win and who will take a dive. He is behind the murder of O'Hara and the framing of Tommy. Never is he suspected by the police or the public to be a villain or a gangster. As the hidden manipulator, he is invisible. In fact, it is quite some time before he makes his first screen appearance.

But the other characters are also invisible or unseen at times. Bud and Lou are invisible as detectives (with Lou literally invisible in the film's closing moments). No one, not even Morgan, suspects them of being anything but a boxer and his manager. Only Gray, Helen, and Tommy know the truth. Roberts does too, but the fact Bud and Lou are actually good detectives is lost on him. To Roberts, they are nothing but nuisances. So they are also invisible as heroes.

Roberts himself barely fits into this "invisible" framework, but one could argue that he is invisible as a friend to Bud and Lou and as a lawman interested in the truth. Roberts comes off as a brash, closed-minded machine, interested only in capturing Tommy rather than discovering the real facts. He is constantly an obstacle. Only during the end do we see a broader view of his true nature when he has the gangster impersonating a cop arrested and leads the charge into the room, ordering Morgan's immediate arrest.

Helen, who is in love with Tommy, is invisible to him as a friend and lover. While she continually voices her concern for Tommy's well-being, he continually brushes her off, not seeing her as a valuable part of his plan. Gray is not seen by the police as being an accomplice to

Tommy's escape, even though his invisibility serum allows Tommy to stay one step ahead of the law. Boots is not seen as a manipulator of the femme fatale type. Bud and Lou think her affection for Costello is genuine, while the press clamors to get a photo of her and the Looper. All the characters are manipulating appearance, often unknowingly, to hide the reality and remain invisible.

Reviews at the time of the film's release were mostly favorable. *Variety*, who felt the comedians' routines were wearing thin, said they redeemed themselves with this movie.[161] The *New York Times* said the boys tried hard but the "efforts [were] not always rewarding." They did state the fight scene was one of the funniest bits done by Abbott and Costello in a long time. *The Motion Picture Daily* thought the film to be one of A&C's best all-around comedies in years.[162] The *Los Angeles Examiner* admonished, "You're nuttier than a fruitcake if you miss this mirthquake that would shake anybody out of the blues."[163]

Modern reviews are moderately enthusiastic. Jim Mulholland, in *The Abbott and Costello Book*, calls the film a "pleasant surprise" and surprisingly states the special effects surpass the 1933 original.[164] The effects are good but not that good. After all, many are simply lifted from other films! *Universal Horrors* mentions the movie in passing, saying the duo's antics are tiresome and calling Arthur Franz a limited and unappealing actor.[165] James L. Neibaur, following up on his previous comment about the film, says it has adult appeal.[166] Stephen Cox and John Lofflin, in *The Abbott and Costello Scrapbook*, praise the picture for adequately combining the comedy, horror, and gangster genres into "a tasty gumbo of styles and formulas."[167] Maltin calls it "one of the team's best vehicles" with topnotch effects,[168] and *VideoHound's Golden Movie Retriever* says it is "one of the best from the crazy duo."[169] *VideoHound's Complete Guide to Cult Flicks and Trash Pics* expands on this, saying, "Great special effects and hilarious gags ... are what makes it one of the best."[170] Finally, in his capsule review in the *Creature Features Movie Guide* series, John Stanley sits on the fence in his typical fashion by labeling the film "mildly amusing" and "visibly diverting if not memorable in the mind's eye."[171]

The picture actually holds up very well, standing as the last good Abbott and Costello movie before such muck as *Comin' Round the Mountain* (1951) and *Lost in Alaska* (1952). However, *Abbott and Costello Meet the Invisible Man* will prove a disappointment for horror fans looking for a classic scary send-up.

Abbott and Costello Meet Dr. Jekyll and Mr. Hyde

Released: August 10, 1953   *Running Time:* 76 minutes

Directed by: Charles Lamont; *Produced by:* Howard Christie; *Screenplay by:* Lee Loeb and John Grant; *Based on Stories by:* Sidney Fields and Grant Garrett; *Director of Photography:* George Robinson, ASC; *Art Direction:* Bernard Herzbrun, Eric Orborn; *Set Decorations:* Russell A. Gausman, John Austin; *Sound:* Leslie I. Carey, Robert Pritchard; *Musical Direction:* Joseph Gershenson, ACE; *Dance Director:* Kenny Williams; *Costumes:* Rosemary Odell; *Hair Stylist:* Joan St. Oegger; *Makeup:* Bud Westmore; *Special Photography:* David S. Horsley, ASC; *Assistant Director:* William Holland.

Cast: Bud Abbott (Slim); Lou Costello (Tubby); Boris Karloff (Dr. Jekyll and Mr. Hyde); Helen Westcott (Vicky Edwards); Craig Stevens (Bruce Adams); Reginald Denny (Inspector); John Dierkes (Batley); Patti McKaye, Betty Tyler and Lucille Lamarr (Can-Can Dancers); Carmen De Lavallade (Javanese Dancer); Henry Corden (Javanese Actor); Marjorie Bennett (Militant Woman); Isabelle Dwan (Mrs. Penprase); Arthur Gould-Porter (Bartender); John Rogers (First Drunk); Clyde Cook (Second Drunk); Herbert Deans (Victim); Judith Brian (Woman on Bike); Gil Perkins (Man on Bike); Hilda Plowright (Nursemaid); Keith Hitchcock (Jailer); Betty Fairfax (Suffragette); Donald Kerr (Chimney Sweep).

For a long time, Robert Louis Stevenson's *Dr. Jekyll and Mr. Hyde* had the distinction of being the horror story most often adapted on film. Even today, the basic story is being used in such movies as *Dr. Jekyll and Ms. Hyde* (1995) and the Eddie Murphy remake of *The Nutty Professor* (1996). The three most famous cinematic versions are the 1920 silent film starring John Barrymore; the 1931 picture, which garnered an Oscar for lead Fredric March; and the 1941 adaptation starring Spencer Tracy, Ingrid Bergman, and Lana Turner. The latter two versions were produced (by Paramount and MGM, respectively) to cash in on the lucrative horror market pioneered in two cycles by Universal. Surprisingly, Universal itself never bought the rights to do a serious version of the famous character. Hyde would definitely have found a place in their stable of monsters, which already included Dracula, the Frankenstein

Monster, the Wolf Man, the Mummy, and even the Phantom of the Opera. But Jekyll and Hyde only appeared in one Universal film, *Abbott and Costello Meet Dr. Jekyll and Mr. Hyde,* in which the doctor and his alter ego met the comedy duo amidst another of their monster rallies. Played by Boris Karloff, this was the only time he ever acted the role of Stevenson's creation.

Stories vary about how the script was written. Supposedly, Abbott and Costello were lined up to appear in *Fireman Save My Child* to be produced by Howard Christie. Sid Fields, an old Vaudeville friend of the duo (who would later play their landlord on their television series *The Abbott and Costello Show*) brought a two-page story treatment to Christie in which Abbott and Costello met the infamous Dr. Jekyll. Christie read it and decided to make that the team's next film — even though sets for *Fireman* had been built and some chase scenes had already been shot with Bud and Lou's doubles. Christie had John Grant and Lee Loeb write the finished script for *Abbott and Costello Meet Dr. Jekyll and Mr. Hyde* and replaced Bud and Lou in *Fireman* with Hugh O'Brien and Buddy Hackett, who physically resembled the team. (Hackett would even play Lou in the 1978 television biopic *Bud and Lou.*) *Fireman Save My Child* bombed but *Abbott and Costello Meet Dr. Jekyll and Mr. Hyde* did fine.[172]

Other stories change the details of how the script was produced. Some sources say Robert Arthur received an unsolicited treatment under the same title on December 9, 1949. It bore no resemblance to the finished film but did have a great final gag in which Costello transforms into Abbott. Another story says Christie bought a four-page treatment from Fields entitled "Flowers at Midnight" which barely resembled the final production. Christie chose this project for the team over another treatment entitled "Abbott and Costello in the South Seas."

When Grant and Loeb finished the final script, it was submitted to The Breen Office. They told Universal the actual injection of the hypodermic syringes should be hidden from the audience. They also said there should be nothing offensive about Costello's reactions when he sits on the giant needle.[173]

The cast assembled for the film included one of the greatest horror stars ever. Boris Karloff made his second appearance in an Abbott and Costello film as Dr. Jekyll, a role the studio originally wanted Basil Rathbone to play.[174] Born William Henry Pratt in England in 1887, Karloff started his acting career in Canada. He arrived in Hollywood in

1919 and struggled in minor roles while working odd jobs including a stint as a truck driver.[175] Karloff became a star with his sympathetic portrayal of the Frankenstein Monster in *Frankenstein*, a role he would repeat twice (in *Bride of Frankenstein* and *Son of Frankenstein*). He appeared in a host of other horror films, including *The Mummy* (1932), *The Old Dark House* (1932), *The Mask of Fu Manchu* (1932), *The Black Cat* (1934), *The Raven* (1935), *The Walking Dead* (1936), *The Body Snatcher* (1945), and *Isle of the Dead* (1945), to name a few. *Abbott and Costello Meet Dr. Jekyll and Mr. Hyde* provided Karloff with his first role in monster makeup since playing the Monster in *Son of Frankenstein* fifteen years earlier (in 1939).[176] Interestingly, Karloff had refused to even see *Abbott and Costello Meet Frankenstein*, let alone be in it; but here he was a few years later in his second Abbott and Costello spoof. Sara Karloff explained why she thought her father was so disdainful toward that film:

> I think the reason he had only decided to do the first three Frankenstein films was that he felt strongly that the storyline had gone as far as it could go or should go. And he felt anything further would act as, would mock and make a laughing stock out of the Monster. And my father's portrayal of him had been one of pathos and one which elicited sympathy. And he didn't think of him — at least the character he had portrayed and the way it had been written — as a comedy character or ... the brunt of jokes. I think out of respect for the work he had done and the scripts he had performed in, he just didn't want to take the Monster into a venue where he would be made fun of.[177]

Paddy Costello recalled meeting Karloff. "He was just sitting in a chair minding his own business and he was very nice. [He said] "Hello, Miss Costello," or whatever and then just went about his business."[178]

Playing the romantic leads were Helen Westcott, a former child actress, and Craig Stevens, Lou Costello's neighbor in Sherman Oaks.[179] Stevens was born in 1918 and was known for playing solid, reliable types.[180] He worked in another Universal science fiction flick, *The Deadly Mantis* (1957), and he is amazed at the fan mail he still receives from that film. (His greatest claim to fame would be his portrayal of television gumshoe Peter Gunn.) A stock player at Warner Bros., he was loaned out to Universal to appear in *Meet Dr. Jekyll*.[181] In a 1997 interview, Mr. Stevens admitted to this author that he did not remember too much about the picture:

> That's been an awful long time ago, you know. And I just remember I had a pleasant time. They were both very funny, of course, and Mr. Costello lived near us when I used to live in the valley when I was first married. He used to collect 16mm prints and he, very kindly, used to loan us films. So I used to see him occasionally and he was a very nice person, you know. And he had a nice family, nice children. And I've just naturally lost all contact with them and that's been so long ago, way back in 1946 or '47. So, as I said, I only remember working with him was a pleasant experience and fun on the set, of course. And that's about all I can remember.[182]

Stevens did not know Lou Costello before the film but got to know him when Costello discovered they were neighbors. Then Costello took him under his wing, so to speak. "That was very friendly and nice of him. I was just a contract player at the time and he was, of course, a star, so it was very nice of him."[183]

Paddy Costello also remembered having the Stevenses as neighbors:

> They used to live right up the street from us when we were out in the valley. Carole and I would go up there to visit 'cause Craig and his wife Alexis Smith didn't have any children and our maid was friendly with their maid ... Julia, their maid, would come down and say, "Oh, can I take the kids back up to the house?" So Carole and I—we loved to go up there because Julia would give us cookies, soda pop, everything Mom was trying not to give us. So we liked to visit Julia a lot.[184]

Craig Stevens was not nearly as friendly with Bud Abbott. "Oddly enough," he recalled, "I didn't get to know him very well. His daughter, Betty Abbott, was dialogue director on *Peter Gunn* for many years. She was a very nice person."[185]

Stevens did, however, get to know Boris Karloff:

> Yes, he was a very nice man, too. I got to know him later. He was a very good friend of Robert Douglass, an English actor, and the Karloffs lived very near them. So occasionally we'd drop in and say a hello and I got to know him and he was a very nice, you know, nice English gentleman. Anything but the Monster that he played.[186]

Two prominent character actors lent their talents to the film. Reginald Denny was famous for his role as the stiff-lipped Englishman, having appeared in such films as *Rebecca* (1940), *The Secret Life of Walter Mitty* (1947; along with Karloff), and *Mr. Blandings Builds His Dream*

House (1948).[187] Jekyll's silent assistant, Batley, was played by John Dierkes, who was also in *The Thing* (1951) and appeared in westerns such as *The Left-Handed Gun* (1958).

When mentioning the film's cast, one should include stuntmen Eddie Parker and Vic Parks, who doubled for Boris Karloff and Lou Costello, respectively. They are probably onscreen more than the two actors they are doubling for! Parker played the scenes in which Hyde appeared in makeup while Parks played Costello's scenes both as a mouse and as the Tubby-Hyde. The two went through a lot of pain for the little credit they received. During the rooftop chase, for instance, Parker broke his ankle and Parks pulled a leg muscle.

The film was budgeted at $734,805, a figure that included an allotment for stereophonic sound. Director Charles Lamont had 23 days to shoot the picture but, as was his way, brought it in under time and $10,000 under budget. Supposedly, John Grant was constantly on the set with Lamont trying to finish the script. Neither Bud nor Lou okayed the finished screenplay. They did suggest a few ad-libs here and there which Lamont let them do. But when the picture was being edited, the extra scenes were cut out.[188] Perhaps this is why Lamont is seldom considered one of Abbott and Costello's better directors.

Much of the budget was spent on the transformation scenes. These were accomplished through David Horsley's trick photography, with makeup once again being supplied by Bud Westmore. The Hyde makeup recalls Fredric March's ape-like Hyde in the 1931 *Dr. Jekyll and Mr. Hyde* but with even more beast-like qualities. Lou's makeup as Hyde is similar. Vic Parks said Lou would do the first few stages of the transformation in close-up, then Parks would sit in for the rest. Parks also substituted for Lou in the scene where he is transformed into a giant mouse. Parks was asked if he wanted to keep the stills of him as the mouse but he declined, saying no one would ever believe that it was him under the makeup and not Costello.[189]

Abbott and Costello Meet Dr. Jekyll and Mr. Hyde shows not only the Jekyll-Hyde transformation but also the continuing transformation of Bud and Lou as comedians. They were relying more and more on slapstick. The boys are continually whacking each other on the head, and Bud takes just as many pratfalls as Lou. There is hardly any of the wordplay, verbal humor, or satiric wisecracks that were featured in their earlier films. All in all, the movie and the team are weaker, although we will later see that the film was attempting to be different from the previous horror spoofs.

The picture opens with the titles appearing over a shot of London. There are no cartoons or funny drawings of the boys, their absence already marking a change in tone. Unlike *Abbott and Costello Meet the Invisible Man*, this spoof features more scares. The music, a re-mix of Frank Skinner's *Meet Frankenstein* score, adds to the serious mood.

Stock scenes of London fade into a startling opening scene. A man leaves a pub only to be attacked and viciously murdered by a caped figure, who growls like an animal and chokes the man with hairy hands. The body is found by Bruce Adams, a newspaperman. Searching for identification, Adams discovers the victim is Dr. Stephen J. Poole. The character of Dr. Poole never appeared in Stevenson's story, but the name "Poole" was the name Stevenson assigned to Jekyll's butler.

The next day, the murder, one of many in the Hyde Park area, is all over the headlines. Presumably, this is where Mr. Hyde takes his name. He is never referred to as "Edward" as he is in the book, but Jekyll's ward, Vicky, possesses the last name "Edwards."

In the park, Bruce Adams sees a body in the bushes. Thinking he has found another murder victim, he examines the body only to find the man very much alive. The man accuses Bruce of being a pickpocket but Bruce explains his intentions. The two discuss how the monster murders again and again with no one able to catch him. In fact, the police do not know if the killer is a man or a beast. This expository material comes off as clumsy due to the poorly written dialogue.

Bruce mentions the monster could even be a woman, which does not surprise the man because he claims his wife is a monster. She has joined the suffragettes in the park, campaigning for equal rights for women. Bruce confesses to the man that he does not believe women should have the right to vote. This is an odd stance for the hero of the film to take. One imagines the typical hero would be more sympathetic to such a cause.

Bruce and the man watch as the women in the bandstand play music. Nightclub singer Vicky Edwards gives a speech, urging everyone to support their cause. She is heckled by another man. A militant woman threatens to fight back but Vicky stops her, instead opting to "sing" their message. The women hike up their skirts and sing a song about equal rights. For the first time in an Abbott and Costello horror spoof, the studio inserted musical numbers. Today, these numbers only serve to date these Abbott and Costello comedies that contain them. They bring the action to a screeching halt and bore the modern-day viewer who is basically tuning in to see Abbott and Costello run from the monsters. Of course, these films are not nearly as bad as Universal's Olson and Johnson comedies, which feature more music than Olson and Johnson!

The ladies hand out their petition and Vicky asks Bruce, who is obviously smitten with the beautiful suffragette, to sign. He flirts with her and puts down his address and home phone number. Vicky catches on. He assures her he only wants to write an article on their plight but at the same time offers to interview her over dinner.

A ruffian tells Vicky to go back to the kitchen. Bruce stands up for her and a fight starts. Soon, the men are battling the women in an all-out brawl. Since this is a comedy, the women quickly gain the upper hand. With the situation out of control, London bobbies are sure to arrive to put a stop to the proceedings. Unfortunately, Slim and Tubby arrive on the scene first.

Bud and Lou, of course, play Slim and Tubby, two Americans on the force studying British crime-solving techniques. (In the script, their last names are given as Hawkins and Tweedles.[190]) Making an energetic entrance, they rush headlong into the fight, with Tubby immediately getting hit on the head with his own nightstick by one of the women. He is kicked and falls over a bench. This is the first of many, many scenes in which the replacement of Lou with his stunt double is overly obvious. Slim is also hit on the head and beat up by the suffragettes. By this time in their film careers, Abbott was taking just as much physical abuse as Costello, and this makes the team weaker. In earlier films, Abbott would never let himself get beat up by men, let alone women. This is more a scene for the Three Stooges than it is for Abbott and Costello.

Tubby is beat up by three women and a glass light falls and shatters on his head. He yells at the militant woman who had earlier tried to pick a fight. The woman bops him on the head, which drives Tubby into the ground like a stake. The scene has now become ludicrous. Tubby panics and yells for Slim, establishing early in the film that Tubby is quick to panic and call on Slim for help.

Slim helps Tubby out of the hole and they try to stop the brawl. As more bobbies arrive, the brawlers scatter. Slim falls in the hole and yells for help. The militant woman takes a giant drum and busts it over Slim's head. Tubby tries to arrest her but she hits him with her purse. Tubby finally loses his temper and takes a small bit of revenge by wrecking her hat. Although it is great to see Tubby finally obtain some satisfaction, the moment is short-lived as the woman kicks Tubby and he falls back into the hole. (A bit where Tubby drops a mechanical mouse to frighten a woman about to tear his uniform appears in the script but was dropped during filming.[191])

Later, in jail, the same militant woman pleads to Slim and Tubby for release. A clever reverse zoom shows that Slim and Tubby have also been arrested and placed in jail!

Bail is paid and the women are set free. Vicky and Bruce have been talking quietly between the bars in the back of the cells, obviously falling in love. Bruce says he hates whoever bailed the women out (a bit of foreshadowing). But after Vicky leaves, Bruce finds his bail has also been paid and he rushes to catch up to the singer. When Slim and Tubby ask if they are going to be set free, the jailer simply laughs. Bud says, "I think I asked a silly question." Lou replied, "And you got a silly answer."

A scene was dropped from the script in which Tubby wishes he was out of jail. Inside the cell mattress, he finds a big file, a chisel, and a steel saw. Tubby says, "Look! We gotta show these to the Inspector. If they ever put a desperate criminal in here, he could escape." Slim predicts, "Tubby, this'll get you a medal." The jailer sees them with the devices and yells for help. The bobbies come in with guns drawn (a major mistake — even today the English police are forbidden to carry guns) and herd them out.[192]

Outside, Bruce and Vicky find out that Dr. Jekyll, a prominent physician, had posted bail for Vicky and her friends. Vicky has been Jekyll's ward ever since her father died. Bruce offers to pay his share, and when Vicky realizes he could have gotten out of jail all along, she falls for him even more. Jekyll is jealous and reacts coldly to Bruce when they are introduced. Jekyll tells Vicky he wants to take her to dinner but she has an early show at the music hall. When Jekyll offers to take her for a drive before the show, Bruce invites himself along to the West End on the pretense of visiting a friend. He jumps into the cab and Jekyll is obviously furious. Jekyll climbs aboard the cab, and Karloff delivers one of many superbly sarcastic line readings when he says, "I hope I'm not crowding you."

Back at the station, the Inspector complains about putting two Americans on the force. Bud and Lou are sent into his office. The Inspector tells Tubby he is through and strips him of his stripes. Bud agrees with the Inspector saying, "We can't have men like that on the police force." But the Inspector fires him, too. Bud is stripped of his stripes and Tubby helps by pulling the buttons off Bud's coat. So far, the scenes *without* Bud and Lou have been more interesting. Their sequences are just not funny, and the gags used to button the scenes (so to speak) are weak. Here, Tubby tearing the buttons off Slim's coat makes no sense and gets no laughs. (In the script, the Inspector not only berates them for general incompetence but also for attempting to escape with the tools they found.[193])

In the coach, Jekyll sarcastically asks Bruce if he writes the women's section of the newspaper. Bruce explains he reports crime news, like the murder of Dr. Poole. Jekyll claims to have never heard of Poole, but Vicky remembers the man being brought to their house by Dr. Lanson. Jekyll explains that Lanson is always bringing people over to back his arguments against Jekyll's theories. Bruce then asks Jekyll why men commit violent acts like murder. Jekyll says every man has two sides to his nature, a good side and an evil side. When evil dominates, it brings out the animal in a man and a desire to kill to get what he wants. Most are born with the evil side under control, but some are not. Jekyll wants to find a way to control man's evil side and eliminate bloodshed and war. He quickly adds that this is just a theory, one he has not yet experimented with nor one he wants to see in print. Although this is close to Stevenson's idea, the premise does not fit Jekyll's later actions in the film. Though he sounds sincere, Jekyll later reveals a devious plan to keep Vicky for himself. We also find out that Jekyll is using Hyde to kill men like Lanson and Poole who disagree with him. Quite frankly, Jekyll is evil to begin with!

The coach arrives at Jekyll's home and Jekyll bids goodbye to Vicky. Bruce wants to accompany Vicky to the music hall and tells Jekyll he has decided to visit another friend instead. Jekyll is again blatantly sarcastic when he says, "I'm sure Watkins will be delighted to drive you all around London to see the rest of your friends. Good day, sir." Karloff's delivery of these lines is letter perfect. However, by listening carefully, an echo of the dialogue can be heard on the soundtrack.

Karloff glares at the departing coach, barely able to keep his anger in check. Then he stomps inside his home to a hidden laboratory behind a bookcase. The lab contains rows of test animals in cages, chemicals, containers, and test tubes.

Jekyll hits and yells at Batley, his mute and very ugly assistant, for not giving the animals the proper injections. Batley hands Jekyll the newspaper article about Poole's murder. Jekyll explains that he killed Poole because he laughed at his research. But then he corrects himself, saying, "No, I didn't kill him. Mr. Hyde did." So Hyde is not the dark side to Jekyll's good side, but rather one facet of the multiple personalities making up Jekyll's evil nature.

Jekyll vows to not become Hyde again until he has found the right balance in his serum. Either the transformation lasts too long or not long enough. But he changes his mind, saying he must become Hyde again regardless of the danger. Looking at Vicky's picture, Jekyll explains how he has waited years for Vicky to grow up so she could be his. Now that she has fallen for Bruce, Jekyll must kill his rival. Karloff is very evil here, dripping with menace as he expresses his hatred of Bruce.

Batley watches as Jekyll prepares an injection. He injects himself with the serum and repeats over and over again, "Mr. Hyde will kill him." There is a close-up of Jekyll's hand (and the ring he wears) as hair slowly covers it. The camera pans up to Karloff's face as he changes into Hyde. Knowing stuntman Eddie Parker played all of Hyde's scenes does not ruin the effect; the transformation can be frightening for younger children. This Hyde is closer to Fredric March's Hyde than to Spencer Tracy's or John Barrymore's, almost a cross between March's monster and Lon Chaney, Jr.'s, Wolf Man. This Hyde is also more vicious and animal-like and unable to speak, only growl. Hyde pushes Batley out of the way and runs out.

At the music hall, headliner Vicky performs a number while Bruce watches from backstage. He accompanies her to the dressing room while a man in a dragon suit performs an exotic number onstage.

Vicky changes and the two lovebirds talk. Bruce grabs her and kisses her. She kisses him back. Bruce asks if her guardian would approve. Vicky explains how Jekyll has taken care of her since her father died. Anything that makes her happy also makes him happy. The two kiss again. In an eerie moment, the two break away from their kiss, revealing Hyde at the window. He climbs up to the roof.

Meanwhile, Slim and Tubby are walking down the street bemoaning their fate. By this time, the audience has forgotten that Abbott and Costello are even in the movie! Slim tells Tubby that if they catch the monster they'll be allowed back on the force. This plan is similar to Abbott's plans of becoming a radio writer in *Who Done It?* and a great detective in *Abbott and Costello Meet the Invisible Man*.

Slim says they can find the monster in any dark doorway. A frightening man appears and asks Tubby for a match, scaring him. Costello's character is again nothing but a little kid in a man's body.

Tubby soon sights the monster climbing up the theater (coincidence plays a large role in this film). Tubby thinks Hyde is a burglar and wants to catch him, thinking *that* will get them back on the force. Tubby takes off and Slim follows while Hyde finds a door into the theater.

Slim and Tubby enter the theater but are stopped by the watchman. Slim says they are the new dance act and makes Tubby demonstrate. Tubby does a cute little dance, takes Slim by the arm, and enters the theater. Abbott and Costello always have creative ways of getting into places where they are not supposed to be. (For example, in *Who Done It?* Bud and Lou get past the police into the radio station by walking backwards.) In the script, Slim and Tubby were to a tell a joke to prove they are entertainers:

>SLIM: Why do you call your uncle "Label?"
>TUBBY: Because he's so close to the bottle.[194]

Hyde descends a spiral staircase and hears Vicky tell Bruce she will see him later. Hyde hides in a dressing room while Slim and Tubby look around. Tubby opens the door to the girls' dressing room. They scream and Tubby, like a cute little boy, looks at the camera and says, "Girls."

Slim orders Tubby to check the rest of the rooms while he looks backstage. Tubby chooses the room Hyde is hiding in and enters a curtained closet. Hyde follows him into the closet. Tubby comes out the other side, goes back in, then emerges the way he came. Hyde's hands creep toward Tubby from behind, reaching for his throat. Lou steps away before Hyde can choke him and leaves the room. This scene is reminiscent of the Wolf Man's attack in the hotel room in *Abbott and Costello Meet Frankenstein*.

In the hall, the dancer wearing the dragon suit passes Tubby and enters his dressing room. Tubby thinks it is the monster and calls for Slim. He tells Slim the monster is in the room and, amazingly enough, Slim believes him. (Here the film goes against the series' formula by not having Abbott disbelieve Lou.) Slim sends Tubby inside where the man has taken off the costume.

Tubby asks the dancer if he has seen the monster and the dancer shows him his mask. This scares Tubby and he opens the door to leave. Slim falls inside. He apologizes to the actor for Tubby's behavior when he realizes what has happened. The actor is aghast. Slim tells Tubby to find the burglar by looking for clues. Tubby says he knows where to look for clues—in the "clues closet." This old chestnut was used in *Who Done It?* and *Abbott and Costello Meet the Killer, Boris Karloff*. Slim reacts to the joke by telling Tubby his hat is dirty. When Tubby takes it off, Slim hits him with his own hat. This is a move Alan Hale, Jr., and Bob Denver would make all their own when they played the Skipper and Gilligan on *Gilligan's Island*.

Tubby enters the next room and Hyde again hides. Tubby looks at himself in the mirror and catches glimpses of Hyde peeking out from behind the curtains. He becomes nervous and scared. Costello starts to fall into his frightened schtick, then becomes uncharacteristically brave. He opens the curtain and Hyde attacks, growling ferociously. This scene is frightening. After all the playing around, the audience does not expect Hyde to pop out like this—and neither does Tubby. He runs out of the room.

Tubby holds the door shut and tells Slim he has the monster inside. Abbott is totally in character talking to some chorus girls and attempting to con them. Incredibly, he believes Tubby a second time and rushes to get a club. Meanwhile, Hyde sneaks into the next room.

Slim and Tubby enter the room and Slim searches for Hyde behind the curtain. Tubby sees movement and smashes a chair into the curtains. A dazed Slim emerges. Here, the boys are again acting more like the Three Stooges than Abbott and Costello. In any case, Bud takes more of a beating in this film than any other.

Hyde dresses in the dragon outfit to fool the boys. Slim revives and Tubby tells him the monster is in the next room. Slim says he will chase the monster out and Tubby can hit him with the club. "I'll belt him, just like I belted you, my pal," says Tubby.

Slim asks the dragon if he has seen the monster. Hyde just growls. Slim takes off the dragon head to hear better and is scared by the monster. Slim runs into the next room and gets belted by Tubby. Everyone can see this joke coming a mile away. The only good thing about it is that it foreshadows a similar gag seen during the climactic chase.

Hyde escapes to the roof, frightening the theater workers. Slim and Tubby tell Bruce what has happened. They give chase. Tubby tries to sneak away but Slim grabs him and forces him to go. One of the film's weaknesses is the indecision surrounding Costello's character. Most of the time Tubby is scared, acting like the Costello we know and love; other times he shows uncharacteristic bouts of courage.

Bruce, Slim, and Tubby chase Hyde over the rooftops. It was during this chase that Eddie Parker broke his foot and Vic Parks pulled a leg muscle.[195]

Tubby again tries to sneak away but is frightened by wind blowing through hanging laundry. He shakes his hat on his head in a patented Curly Howard move. Not only are Abbott and Costello relying more on physical comedy, they have a newfound reliance on props. The move away from comic patter may be one of the reasons these later films are not as critically acclaimed as the duo's earlier efforts.

Tubby runs into a clothesline and falls, foreshadowing the conclusion of the climactic chase. The pursuit continues, with more jumping and leaping over rooftops. At one point, Tubby jumps but does not quite make it to the next roof. He is saved from certain death when he falls into a pair of longjohns on a clothesline. Slim yells at him and hauls him back up.

In the meantime, Hyde finds a way to the street by climbing into a wax museum. He tries the front door but is forced to hide when he sees an approaching bobby outside. The wax museum is definitely reminiscent of MacDougal's museum in *Abbott and Costello Meet Frankenstein*. In fact, wax dummies of Dracula and the Frankenstein Monster stand in one corner. The monsters are garbed as the Universal movie versions, yet the film is set in the 1880s! The anachronism can be forgiven because it is such a delight to see these old friends. Both dummies are actually played by actors standing rigid and motionless. The Monster's makeup is the same as in the previous film, but his cheek scar is raised and more severe.[196] Studio publicity claimed Glenn Strange stepped in to play the part, but Strange has denied the story in interviews. Instead, he suggested a bit player or extra actually played the role.[197]

On the rooftops, the chase is resumed once more, but there is no sign of Hyde. The three men split up. Tubby is told to holler if he sees the monster, but he is more interested in finding a way to the street. Sighting the skylight, he climbs down into the wax museum. On the way, he pulls loose an electrical wire and swings to the floor. Scared by the Dracula dummy, he runs into the Frankenstein Monster. Then a cat jumps on his back. Totally frightened, Tubby backs into a decapitation scene. The wax head rolls into his hands. This reminds viewers of the severed head that Wilbur had to hide in *Meet Frankenstein*.

Tubby throws the head and it lands on the cat. The head slides across the floor. Tubby runs up to the George Washington statue and salutes it. (Isn't it strange that a London museum would have a statue of Washington?) Hyde emerges and Tubby runs away from him. He again runs into the Frankenstein Monster but, in a stupid gag, the electrical wire hits the dummy and animates it. It walks forward, frightening Tubby. As originally scripted, other wax figures were supposed to react to this encounter: Dracula and George Washington were to cover their eyes and Buffalo Bill was to reach for his gun.[198]

Tubby mistakes a wax bobby for the real thing and begs for help. Hyde then chases Tubby right into an iron maiden and locks him in.

On the street, Bruce and Slim wonder what has happened to the monster and to Tubby. Bruce decides to check in with the Inspector while Slim searches for Tubby. Slim hears Tubby screaming for help. Hyde hides as Slim breaks into the wax museum and sets Tubby free. Tubby tells him the monster is here. Slim orders him to tie up the monster while he gets the Inspector. Lou finds a rope and spots a jail cell display.

Noticing the shadow of Hyde (who is following him), Tubby tricks the monster into the cell and locks him inside, for once acting rather cleverly. He calls Hyde a bad boy (one of Lou's catchphrases) and rushes out to find Slim. Hyde transforms back to Jekyll.

A proud Tubby brings Slim, Bruce, the Inspector, and some bobbies back to the museum only to find Jekyll locked in the cage. Jekyll explains he was strolling along, heard a noise, investigated, and got shoved in the cell by "moron" Tubby. Tubby calls Jekyll a liar and tells him to show the ring, but Jekyll has taken it off. The Inspector is outraged, but Jekyll will not press charges, feeling Tubby suffers from hallucinations (much like Dracula said of Talbot in *Abbott and Costello Meet Frankenstein*). In another good line reading from Karloff, Jekyll says, "Perhaps he and I should have a talk someday. I might be able to help him." The words drip with menace and are again reminiscent of Dracula in the previous film ("Ah, you young people! Making the most of life ... while it lasts").

Since Jekyll is involved, Bruce promises not to print the story. Meanwhile, the Inspector yells at Tubby for being stupid, only to find himself locked in the cell. The police leave. Slim is angry with Tubby, telling him he does not believe a word of the story. This is certainly odd (and evidence of poor writing), for Slim himself had seen the monster back at the theater.

Slim is stopped by Jekyll, who confesses to being nervous with the monster on the loose. When Slim says he would like to get his hands on the monster, Jekyll says, "If I came face to face with the monster, I don't know what would happen." Costello's facial expressions here are priceless. He is the only one who knows the truth about Dr. Jekyll and Mr. Hyde. But before he can convince Slim, his partner has agreed to walk Jekyll home.

On the way out, Tubby yells and spits at the statue of the bobby. Only this time, the bobby is real and he conks Tubby on the head with his night stick. In the script, the decapitated head with the cat inside was to appear again just before Tubby leaves the wax museum. It would have been the impetus to send Tubby toward the door.[199]

A quick cut shows the boys entering Jekyll's house. (On the video copy, the cut is too quick, and it looks like something was deleted. In the script, this cut was noted as a dissolve,[200] so it's very possible that the dissolving element of the shot was cut.) Jekyll tells the boys he will try to get them back on the force, then asks them to spend the night guarding the house. He offers to pay them five pounds. This delights Slim who, typically, is very interested in extra cash. Tubby again shows himself to be the superior detective by searching through a chest of drawers. Slim yells at him and orders him upstairs. Costello again shows his childlike character by making funny noises and doing a happy dance.

Tubby does not want to stay the night. "I gotta go home," he says. "There's something I forgot to do." "What?" asks Slim. "I forgot to stay there," answers Tubby. This is one of Abbott and Costello's stockpile of jokes that they used again and again. (Mantan Moreland used the same joke in *Charlie Chan in the Secret Service* [1944].)

Jekyll shows them to their room where Tubby tries to convince Slim they are in trouble. Slim explains that two people cannot be one. But he is unable to convince Tubby, who insists Jekyll changes into Hyde. Slim accuses him of having hallucinations.

In the lab, Jekyll tells Batley which room the boys are in. He also has Batley hold the ring. There is unneeded emphasis placed on Jekyll's ring, for it does not turn up again and would not be any kind of proof that Jekyll is Hyde. Nevertheless, Jekyll tells Batley the boys must never leave the house, and that he wants to experiment on Tubby. The comment about experimenting on Tubby foreshadows Tubby's own transformation into a monster and also alludes to *Abbott and Costello Meet Frankenstein*, in which Lou was also to be the subject of a ghoulish experiment. Mad doctors must enjoy using simpletons as guinea pigs.

While Slim sleeps soundly, Tubby sneaks out to investigate. He is followed down the stairs by Batley. Each time Tubby steps on a stair, he hears Batley step on one behind him. This is drawn out until the moment when Tubby finally turns around. Seeing Batley, he yells and falls down the stairs. We never see Tubby fall; instead, the motion is conveyed by watching Batley's expressions. This is a unique capper to the scene. (A similar routine was used in *Hold That Ghost* involving Joan Davis and a ghost. There, the set-up was the same, but the climax differed by having Joan scream and scare away the ghost.)

Tubby tries to escape, but a bulldog at the front door blocks his passage. Instead, he runs into the library where he finds the revolving door leading to the lab. Batley follows Tubby into the laboratory.

In the lab, Tubby finds the caged animals Jekyll uses in his experiments. The doctor has been transforming animals: a rabbit barks like a dog, a dog meows, and a monkey moos. (When I was in junior high school, I would often be a contestant on a local AM radio station's trivia contest. I always chose "old horror movies" as a category and I often won [usually small prizes such as a free pizza or an album]. I will never forget the time I did not get a perfect score of 6 out of 6 because I failed to remember what noise the monkey made.)

Tubby blows into a test tube like a tuba. Batley attacks and chokes him, causing Tubby to knock over some chemicals. They blow up, and Tubby escapes back to the library. The explosion awakens Slim.

Tubby tries to leave the library but runs into Jekyll. Slim arrives and Tubby tells him about the hidden lab and the murderous Batley. Jekyll confesses to having a secret lab and agrees to show it to them. Jekyll enters the secret passage. Slim says, "Follow me," then pushes Tubby ahead of him. This is the start of a running gag.

Batley hides as Jekyll shows the boys around. He explains he has been experimenting with weird drugs for fifteen years (hmmm ... what kind?). He says he can transfer the characteristics of one animal to another. But he denies the existence of Batley. Slim thinks Tubby is hallucinating and tells Jekyll he should throw his partner out in the street (which would probably make Tubby happy).

Jekyll excuses himself. Slim looks for a drink of water while he explains to Tubby that doctors have to experiment in order to find cures. Tubby takes a potion from him and drinks it, thinking it is water. The potion tastes funny, making Tubby want to leave. While Slim is droning on, Tubby sneaks out a back entrance to the street. Slim chases after him. Jekyll, who had been preparing a drug to dispose of them, enters and finds them gone. Angry, he orders Batley to bring them back.

On the street, Tubby feels ill. He worries that Jekyll might have the capability to turn a human being into something else. Slim scoffs and enters a pub for a drink. Tubby, meanwhile, transforms into a mouse. Lou's stunt double plays the mouse, with Lou doing the voice-over. Unfortunately, the makeup is poor and the mouse looks more like a cat. Paddy Costello recalls being around for the transformation: "I was there when they were doing the makeup on him where he changes into a rat. God, that was interesting. I remember that. It was very time consuming. I was really fascinated with the whole process — to watch that change occur."[201]

Tubby joins Slim in the pub, but Slim does not see the change. Batley watches through the window as Tubby frightens a real mouse. Tubby then orders sarsparilla and cheese from the barkeep. When the bartender puts on his glasses and sees Tubby, he screams and runs out. Two drunks see Tubby and decide to harass him. They say they might have to live with mice but they do not have to drink with them. When Tubby speaks to them, they too run out screaming.

Slim finally sees Tubby and faints. He comes to and faints again. Abbott's double takes here are great. Tubby sees his own reflection and faints. He transforms back. As both men awaken, Costello makes the obvious joke: "Slim, am I a man or a mouse?" (In the script, Lou was to end up with a mousetrap on his nose after falling on the floor.[202])

Slim figures out what has happened, and he and Tubby tell the Inspector. The Inspector does not believe the story and accuses the two of being drunk. He throws them out. A scene was cut from the script in which Batley reports to Jekyll that Tubby drank the mouse potion, and that he could not bring the duo back because they went to the police. Jekyll then vows to destroy them.[203]

The next day, Slim and Tubby return to Jekyll's house, bringing along Bruce and Vicky. Vicky refuses to believe their story. Bruce is not so sure, but he promises not to print a story without real proof.

Jekyll welcomes the group into his home and Vicky asks about the laboratory. He says he has never concocted any drug to turn a man into an animal and denies the existence of a hidden lab. Vicky believes him, but Bruce requires proof. Tubby assures Bruce the story is true. He says, "When I say I seen something, I seen something," a variation of his repeated line, "I saw what I saw when I saw it" in *Meet Frankenstein*.

Jekyll takes them behind the library bookcase, but everything has been cleared away. All aspects of the lab have disappeared and a wine cellar stands in its place. Bruce apologizes, shoots the boys a dirty look, and takes Vicky and Jekyll upstairs. In the script, Jekyll suggests to Bruce that Slim and Tubby were drunk. Bruce demands that the pair "say something" to Jekyll. Tubby replies, "Where is the five pounds you were going to give us?" They were also thrown out at this point and had to sneak back into the cellar instead of just being left there.[204]

Slim and Tubby stay behind, determined to find where the magic mouse potion is hidden. If they can turn Tubby back into a mouse, then Bruce will surely believe them.

While searching through the various bottles, Slim finds a bottle of "Moselle" which he thinks will turn Tubby into a mouse. Abbott shows uncharacteristic stupidity here. Still, Tubby drinks himself tipsy.

Upstairs, Bruce again apologizes to Jekyll, who is understanding. Meanwhile, downstairs, Tubby is intoxicated. He imagines that Slim is becoming a mouse. Slim now realizes Tubby is smashed. Tubby tries to take Slim upstairs but stumbles on the steps. He falls into a cage. Now sober, he asks Slim for a piece of cheese. The scene is very weak.

Bruce inquires about the wedding and Jekyll gives his approval. As the two lovers kiss, Jekyll glares at them and breaks the wine glass he holds in his hand (a great touch). Bruce leaves but Jekyll asks Vicky to stay to discuss wedding plans. In private, she asks her guardian what plans he has for her and Bruce. He replies, "None."

Boris is again excellent in the dialogue that follows. He confesses his love for Vicky and tells her she cannot marry Bruce because she belongs to Jekyll. Every plan he ever made, he made for her. He wants to take her to Paris, but she says he is crazy. He becomes forceful. He grabs her and tells her he will not let her marry anyone but him. All the while, Bruce smokes a cigarette out front, unaware of the danger.

Jekyll threatens to transform Bruce into a monster and then kill him. The police will think he was saving his ward. (In the script, Jekyll tells Vicky he loves her and will kill Bruce and frame him as the monster. She calls for help and Jekyll says sinisterly, "I like temper in a woman. But I will tame you and, in time, you will learn to love me."[205])

When Vicky tries to escape, he grabs her and throws her down. With his back to Vicky, the transformation starts to occur in Jekyll without an injection (which is what happens in Stevenson's story and in the previous films as well). Vicky realizes Tubby was right—Jekyll *was* responsible for the creation of the monster. When Jekyll turns around, he has become Hyde. Now Vicky realizes, with horror, that Jekyll *is* the monster. She screams and faints. Bruce hears the scream, as do Slim and Tubby. All three rush to rescue her.

Hyde tries to carry off Vicky, but Bruce barges in. Vicky is put aside while Bruce struggles with Hyde. Slim and Tubby run in and Slim attends to Vicky. Tubby sees Bruce needs help and enters the fray. Now it is Costello who is out of character by running in to help and showing rare bravery. He grabs Hyde, but when the monster spins around and Tubby catches a glimpse of him, Tubby falls onto the sofa. He lands on a needle filled with the Hyde formula. One can easily imagine the pain Tubby feels as he sits on the hypo.

Tubby tries to escape but Batley corners him with a pistol. Hyde grabs Tubby and unknowingly forces him onto the needle again and again. Some might see Tubby's forced thrust onto the hypo as a symbol of homosexual rape. The needle does pierce his behind repeatedly and is quite painful to watch.

Bruce is about to smash a vase over Hyde's head, but Batley holds him at bay with the gun. Slim kicks the gun out of Batley's hand and Bruce catches it. (Again, Abbott shows he is actually good in a fight — just not against women). Bruce puts the gun to Hyde, but Batley grabs him. Bruce shoots the servant while Hyde grabs his hat and cloak and makes his escape. Vicky says she is fine, so the three men pursue Hyde. They each run out and leap over the patio railing. Naturally, Tubby *falls* over it. He follows Slim and Bruce into the street.

Hyde hides in a doorway, a now-ill Tubby falls into another doorway, and Slim and Bruce stop in between the two doorways. Tubby, injected with the serum, transforms into another Hyde creature. Slim and Bruce hear growls coming from both doorways, and each sees a Hyde run off in a different direction. Both yell, "There he goes!" and knock each other over. Bruce follows the Jekyll-Hyde while Slim pursues the Tubby-Hyde. What follows is one of the most exciting chase scenes in all of Abbott and Costello's films.

As a child, I loved the elongated chase sequence and always thought it was one of the better climaxes in their movies. It was not until years later I realized Karloff and Costello are not in the chase at all, that their stuntmen took their places. Still, it is easy to get caught up in the fun.

Vicky calls the Inspector and tells him Hyde is in the neighborhood of Dr. Jekyll's house in the East End. The Inspector sends men to the area and marks the location on his map of the city.

Another women's suffrage campaign is being held in the park. Tubby shows up and scares everyone away. The tough woman from the opening is so scared she falls off her soapbox. In a way, Tubby is having his revenge for his earlier humiliation at the hands of this woman.

Slim has gathered a mob of men to hunt the monster. He warns a nurse to take her baby home. The woman grabs her charge, but when she opens the carriage she finds Tubby inside. Tubby growls and the nurse runs off. Tubby, the man-child, is actually in a very fitting setting — a baby carriage. As his character proves, he is just a big baby.

Slim and the men return and realize the nurse has run off without the carriage. A cowardly man who knows where the child lives offers to return the carriage because he is "not anxious to meet the monster."

The Inspector, meanwhile, receives a call that the monster has been spotted in Hyde Park — the opposite side of London from the first sighting. This both confuses and distresses the inspector.

Some fishermen in the park ask to see the baby the man is carting in the carriage. When the men look inside, they see Tubby, who frightens them so much that they jump into the water and swim away. Tubby climbs out of the carriage and runs off.

Bruce spots the real Hyde frightening a horse. At the same time, the Inspector gets another call. The monster has now been sighted in the vicinity of the wax museum. The harried Inspector sends out more bobbies. The map, now covered with markers, drives him crazy.

Tubby jumps on the back of a buggy and is soon chased by a pack of dogs. Slim and his mob also give chase. When Tubby turns around and snarls at the dogs, they run away whimpering.

The Inspector continues to receive calls. He cannot understand what is happening. Reginald Denny plays these scenes wonderfully as his confusion builds and builds until he finally reaches a breaking point. He orders a patrol wagon to scour an entire section of town where the monster was last seen.

Tubby arrives at the station as the bobbies pile into the police wagon. He jumps in the front of the wagon and takes the reins, now driving his own pursuers. One bobby tells him to slow down. Tubby turns and growls, and the bobbies realize he is the monster. Tubby jumps from his seat and lands between a husband and wife on a three-seated bicycle. Although improbable, in the Abbott and Costello comedy universe an action like this is normal. (The real anomaly of this scene is that the couple rides a three-seated bike. Wouldn't they just get a two-seater?) Anyway, the man tells Tubby, "You have your nerve." But when he sees

Tubby is a monster he falls off the bike. The wife tells her now-missing husband he is peddling too fast. She, too, sees Tubby and promptly falls off the bike.

Tubby grabs a ladder and mounts a fire escape, climbing to the roof of the building. Slim orders his mob to surround the building while he goes up after the monster (a brave action for Slim). By coincidence, the real Hyde also arrives at the same building, and he also climbs to the roof. He is followed by Bruce.

On the roof, each of the four characters takes a place alongside the walls of a square box-like structure. None of them know anyone else is around the box. The geography is something like this:

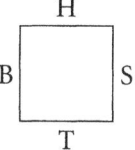

H = Hyde, B = Bruce, S = Slim, and T = Tubby

The four move around the block at the same time, never seeing the other, only suspecting someone is along the next wall. They even turn around and move backwards, all at the same time. This classic, funny scene is well choreographed and still holds up today.

The four continue to move along the box. Finally, Slim catches a glimpse of Tubby at one end of his wall and Hyde at the other. Each runs away before he can catch them. But Slim does not give up. He raises a board he picked up and prepares to clobber the next monster that runs by. Of course, he hits Bruce, a tie-in to the scenes in the dressing rooms when Tubby hit Slim.

Tubby and Hyde both hide behind a brick wall. They slowly back up until they bump each other. They scare one another and run off in opposite directions. Slim and Bruce both yell, "There he goes!" and run into each other, reprising the sight gag that began the chase. By repeating it at the end, the director adds a sense of closure to the chase sequence.

Tubby hides behind a chimney. A sweep pops up and scares Tubby, who runs into a clothesline and knocks himself out (another repeated gag). Bobbies arrive on the roof and Slim orders them to tie up Tubby and take him away. Typical of one of Abbott's character, he is already congratulating himself. Laughing self-assuredly, he says, "Boy, will this open the Inspector's eyes." The audience knows whose eyes will really be opened.

Meanwhile, Vicky is trying to convince the police over the phone that there is only one monster loose in the city. A hairy hand covers her mouth and she faints. How Hyde escaped from a building surrounded by a mob of men and bobbies remains a mystery. But now Bruce and the police have arrived at Jekyll's house, too.

Hyde carries Vicky upstairs. Bruce hears her scream and rushes after her. Hyde opens the window and sees the bobbies waiting below. Vicky lets Bruce in the room, and he confronts Hyde. He tells Hyde there is no escape because the house is surrounded. Nevertheless, the monster tries to flee by climbing to the roof. Hyde's repeated climbing of buildings accentuates his ape-like characteristics. But he is not ape-like enough. The drainpipe breaks and Hyde falls to his death on the pavement below. A surrounding crowd watches in awe as Hyde transforms back into Jekyll. Bruce and Vicky embrace.

Originally, this ending was to have been more violent. Hyde was to attempt to jump out the window with Vicky to kill both of them. He lurches forward and almost carries her with him to the pavement. But Bruce breaks down the door and saves Vicky, who teeters on the sill. Both look down and watch Hyde transform back into Jekyll.[206]

At the police station, the Inspector looks at the map and winces. Slim and four bobbies bring in a raging, violent Tubby-Hyde. As he struggles, he bites each of the four bobbies. The Inspector points at Tubby and says it will be a pleasure to hang him. Tubby bites the Inspector's finger, accompanied by a loud crunch. A bobby clubs him and he falls unconscious.

The Inspector receives a call telling him the monster is dead. He refuses to believe it since the monster is sitting in his office. But Tubby transforms back into his normal self. When the Inspector sees Tubby, he angrily accuses Slim of purposely masquerading Tubby as the monster.

Slim is shocked to see Tubby and unties him. Instead of asking him how he got to where he is, he yells at the confused Tubby for making a fool out of him. Abbott is never concerned about Costello's welfare unless he is being directly menaced by a monster or he can make Abbott some money. Suddenly, the Inspector and the four bobbies start growling. They have all been transformed into Hydes! They chase the boys, who burst through the doors to make their escape. This may actually be the scariest scene in any Abbott and Costello film. Eerily lit, the monsters (dressed in the comforting clothes of trusted policemen) quiver and growl as they advance menacingly toward the duo. Edited to nothing more than a brief moment of screen time, the scene is a perfect capper to the film.

The ending foreshadows the finale of a multitude of horror films-to-come by concluding with a scene that leaves the audience hanging. The story is over, but story considerations are rejected in favor of a last shock. Films such as *Friday the Thirteenth* (1980) and *A Nightmare on Elm Street* (1984) would exploit this strategy until it reached the point of convention. Here, Abbott and Costello are again ahead of their time. One modern-day filmmaker, Stuart Gordon, who directed *Re-Animator* (1985) and *From Beyond* (1986), mentions in an interview (in the book *Dark Visions*) that he was affected by this film:

> I think the earliest [horror film] I can remember is *Abbott and Costello Meet Dr. Jekyll and Mr. Hyde*. I saw the movie again recently and realized that the movie ends with Abbott and Costello turning into monsters [sic]. So, it didn't have a very comfortable ending. This movie didn't end, it just kept going. I think that's what scared me.[207]

In the third grade, my best friend and I watched the Abbott and Costello movies every Sunday morning. Every Monday, we would discuss how great (or not-so-great) the movie was. At the same time, I was on my path of obsession with *The Incredible Hulk* television series. My friend, trying to be funny, told me he had seen a movie entitled *Abbott and Costello Meet the Incredible Hulk*. Today, I would be able to prove the impossibility of such a film by comparing the dates of Abbott and Costello's films with the creation of the Incredible Hulk character. But at that time, I was too young to think of such a course. Nevertheless, I did not believe my friend's claim and demanded proof of the film's existence. My friend said he only remembered one scene. Abbott and Costello were in David Banner's laboratory. They were fooling around and knocked over some chemicals. Banner kept yelling at them until he became angry and transformed into the Incredible Hulk. The Hulk then chased the comedy duo around the lab, with Costello acting scared. This was not enough for me. I demanded to see the clipping from the *TV Guide*. Days went by with my friend conveniently forgetting to bring the clipping to school. Finally, to end my badgering, he brought in a slip of paper. Written on it were a time, a channel, and *Abbott and Costello Meet the Incredible Hulk*, all in my friend's scratchy handwriting. The joke was over and we had a good laugh. But I cannot help but think that my friend's imaginary scene was inspired by scenes from *Abbott and Costello Meet Dr. Jekyll and Mr. Hyde*. The boys do infiltrate Jekyll's lab, make a mess, and incur the wrath of Dr. Jekyll, who spends much time chasing them as Mr. Hyde. As an added connection, the Incredible Hulk was based on two literary characters: the Frankenstein Monster and Mr. Hyde. Stevenson's creation inspired both Banner's transformation into the Hulk and the idea of a man possessing a dual nature, one human and the other bestial.

Stevenson's concept of the duality of man, fleshed out so well in the serious film versions, does not work here in this spoof. Karloff's Jekyll recites the theme and claims his work is based on the theory. He says every man is born with two sides to his personality—one good, the other evil. The good side keeps the evil side in check. But some are born with the inability to keep their evil side under control and so commit violent crimes. Again, this does not fit, for Jekyll's character is evil to begin with. He raises his ward from a child, shaping her the way he wants her to be, so he can marry her. When she falls for Bruce, he plots to kill him. He also kills any peer who disagrees with or mocks his work. His mistreatment of Batley and his line, "Perhaps they should never leave this house," further show his fiendish disposition. Karloff's facial expressions are perfect as they display the menace inside of him. Therefore, Hyde is just Jekyll with an ugly face and a bit more strength. Even without the head of hair, one gets the idea he would plot the deaths of all who stand in the way of his relationship with Vicky. Jekyll's potion is false, more of a werewolf elixir than anything else. This causes the entire film to ring false.

Further proof can be seen through Tubby's transformation. If Jekyll's potion did what he said, then Tubby would become a murdering fiend. Instead, Tubby scares some Londoners, barks back at some dogs, and bites some policemen on their fingers. Although he causes minor havoc, he simply wants to get away from his pursuers. The Tubby-Hyde is not a killer because Tubby is not a killer, only a childlike innocent. The Jekyll-Hyde is a killer because Jekyll is a killer; specifically, he takes the potion with the intent to kill. Instead of the dual nature of man, the film's theme should be another interpretation of appearance versus reality. One cannot judge a person by how they look, for an ugly face does not necessarily mean an ugly person. The true measure of a man is what is inside his heart, not what is on the surface.

This was the idea behind *The Incredible Hulk* on television. The Hulk was the beast inside us all, primitive and childlike, but he did not kill because David Banner did not kill. If the *Meet Dr. Jekyll* screenwriters had been brave and gone for this concept (adapting Stevenson's theme to suit their purposes) then perhaps the film would not ring so falsely. *VideoHound's Complete Guide to Cult Flicks* picks up a bit on the problems regarding the film's villain but goes in a different direction: "[Mr. Hyde] is far too serious in tone and execution, providing an off kilter counterpoint to Bud and Lou's antics. Additionally, traditional supernatural monsters, such as Dracula and the Mummy, not being the product of misguided science, hold a fonder place in our hearts than Dr. Jekyll. The archetype for A&C to play off against was simply all wrong."[208]

In many ways, *Abbott and Costello Meet Dr. Jekyll and Mr. Hyde* follows the monster spoof format used in previous films. The monster menace plays it straight. Lou encounters the monster by himself but when he tries to tell others of what he has seen, he is ridiculed and disbelieved. And Lou becomes a Hyde creature for the climax, following the tradition of having Bud or Lou become the title monster.

However, the film also attempts to deviate from previous monster spoofs. The subplot of having a beautiful girl pretend to fall for Lou is dropped, replaced by standard romantic leads and musical numbers. In fact, Bud and Lou are only secondary characters for much of the movie. Unlike previous films, their encounter with the titular monster is not accidental. They purposely set out to catch the monster so they can get back on the police force. Following that, the monster has no plans for Costello from the outset; only later in the film when he fears Lou has learned his secret does he plan to kill him. In addition, Jekyll's complex plan of action is aimed not at Abbott and Costello but at Vicky and Bruce. These changes in the formula lead to new scenes and ideas, some that work and some that do not.

The wax museum sequence, though implausible, is fun. Seeing the Monster and Dracula again, as mentioned before, is a treat. The climactic chase alone makes the film a must-see. And Mr. Hyde's makeup is quite frightening. After the Wolf Man, it is possibly the scariest makeup in a Universal horror film.

Unfortunately, Abbott and Costello's long absence from the film in the first half hour generates some static and talky scenes that mar the film. The musical numbers are out of place, and the opening battle at the suffragette demonstration is more frustrating than funny. Tubby's transformation into a mouse is too cute for a film focusing on a savage killer, and the makeup here is poor.

Still, all in all, the film is worthwhile. In fact, the final scene is the ultimate twist ending for an Abbott and Costello picture, one in which the monster side of the film gains the upper hand. As explained by Stuart Gordon, it still retains its ability to scare. It is too bad this was not the final Abbott and Costello monster spoof, for it would have been a fitting close to their "subgenre."

At the time, England considered the film to be quite frightening, awarding it an X rating because of the transformation scenes. No one under 16 was permitted to see it without being accompanied by an adult.[209] However, this reaction did not keep Bud and Lou from visiting London. After the picture was released, the comics made their second tour of Europe, stopping in London to perform at the Palladium. They enacted their haunted house/moving candle routine, along with the rubdown bit, and were well received.[210]

Abbott and Costello Meet Dr. Jekyll and Mr. Hyde had one of the best sneak previews of any Abbott and Costello film since *Meet Frankenstein*.[211] Chris Costello wrote that the movie was "not an outstanding picture from a critic's point of view but surprisingly (even to Dad and Boris Karloff) the film skyrocketed at the box office."[212] Many of the newspapers at the time, however, gave the film rave reviews. *Film Daily* called it "another big treat for Abbott and Costello fans," while *The Los Angeles Times* said it was a "real giggle-getter despite many of its ancient gags, for it has some that even Maestro Mack Sennett himself may wish he had thought of." *The Los Angeles Mirror* singled out Karloff's performance as particularly noteworthy and advised, "the spectator is best served if he forgets all about Stevenson and settles down to absorb the typical Abbott and Costello tomfoolery."[213]

Typically, current critics are not kind to the picture. Jim Mulholland states in *The Abbott and Costello Book* that the dialogue "mainly consists of a series of frightened yelps. The only funny gags are left over from their previous films."[214] James L. Neibaur maintains that this is the first film in which Abbott and Costello seem to be tired of making pictures.[215] He goes on to say that it is also the first time that Abbott looks fat and Costello looks old.²¹⁶ *VideoHound* calls the film "a lame attempt at recapturing the success of *Abbott and Costello Meet Frankenstein*,"²¹⁷ while Martin and Porter feel it is a "fun mixture of comedy and horror."²¹⁸ Maltin gives it two stars and says it is disappointing with "too few funny scenes."²¹⁹

In any case, the film deserves credit for attempting to deviate from the monster spoof formula. Of the last six movies they made for Universal, this was certainly their best (and definitely better than their final monster spoof, *Abbott and Costello Meet the Mummy*).

Craig Stevens felt pleased to be working on the film. "In those days, I was just happy to get a job anyplace. They [Abbott and Costello] were very popular and successful at the time, so it was nice to be in a film that would be seen by quite a few people, you know. That, of course, was another advantage for a young player in those days."²²⁰

In France, the picture was known as *Deux Nigauds contre le Dr. Jekyll et Mr. Hyde*, which translates as "Two Simpletons vs. Dr. Jekyll and Mr. Hyde." Titles considered for the film prior to release included the shortened *Abbott and Costello Meet Dr. Jekyll* and *Dr. Jekyll and Mrs. Hyde*.²²¹

One final note: When *Frankenstein 1970* was released in 1958, the filmmakers urged theater owners to do the usual publicity gimmicks and contests that accompanied these films. They also supplied five photographs of star Boris Karloff from five of what they called the actor's most important films. They urged theater owners to hold a contest where patrons had to guess which films the photos came from. The films included *Tower of London*, *The Old Dark House*, *The Mask of Fu Manchu* (incorrectly identified as *Mr. Wong in Chinatown* [1939]), *Son of Frankenstein*, and, believe it or not, *Abbott and Costello Meet Dr. Jekyll and Mr. Hyde*.²²²

Abbott and Costello Meet the Mummy

Released: May 23, 1955   *Running time:* 79 minutes

Directed by: Charles Lamont; *Produced by:* Howard Christie; *Screenplay:* John Grant; *Original Story:* Lee Loeb; *Director of Photography:* George Robinson, ASC; *Art Direction:* Alexander Golitzen, Bill Newberry; *Set Decorations:* Russell A. Gausman, James M. Walters; *Sound:*

Leslie I. Carey; *Film Editor:* Russell Schoengarth, ACE; *Gowns:* Rosemary Odell; *Hair Stylist:* Joan St. Oegger; *Makeup:* Bud Westmore; *Special Photography:* Clifford Stine, ASC; *Assistant Director:* Phil Bowles; *Music Supervision:* Joseph Gershenson; *Script Supervisor:* Betty Abbott; *Dialogue Director:* Milt Bronson.

Cast: Bud Abbott (Peter Patterson); Lou Costello (Freddie Franklin); Marie Windsor (Madame Rontru); Michael Ansara (Charlie); Dan Seymour (Josef); Kurt Katch (Dr. Zoomer); Richard Karlan (Hetsut); Richard Deacon (Semu); Eddie Parker (Klaris); Mazzone-Abbott Dancers (Dance Troupe); Chandra Kaly Dancers (Dance Troupe); Mel Welles (Iben); George Khoury (Habid); Veola Vonn (Dancer); Jan Arvan (Waiter); Kem Dibbs (First Policeman); Ted Hect (Anzi); Michael Vallon (Dr. Azzui); Harry Medoza (Magician); Jean Hartelle (Waiter); Mitchell Kowal (Second Policeman); Karn Tong (Chinese Busboy); Robin Morse (Waiter); Lee Sharon (Blonde Girl); Carole Costello (Cigarette Girl); Donald Kerr (Newspaper Man); John Powell (Bit); Peggy King (Singer).

Abbott and Costello's last monster spoof was also their last film for Universal. When it came time to renew their contract, the comedians demanded more money. Universal did not feel they were worth it and let them go, even though the duo had just had two streets on the studio lot named for them.[223] The boys would go on to make one more film together in 1956, *Dance with Me Henry* (not counting the Universal compilation film, *The World of Abbott and Costello*). By this time, the two were way past their prime. Abbott was nearly as fat as Costello[224] (supposedly due to his heavy drinking[225]), and his character was coming across as doddering and pushy.[226] The ravages of age and illness had affected Costello and he looked worn and ragged. In the end, *Abbott and Costello Meet the Mummy* came off as their worst monster film (and one of their poorer efforts all around).

The film was budgeted at $738,250 for a 25-day shoot, with $18,000 allotted for advertising (the lowest of any Abbott and Costello feature).[227] "[Universal] really wasn't ... behind them at that point," said Paddy Costello. "The money wasn't being spent for the script and the people that you needed to put out that kind of product."[228] Returning director Charles Lamont brought the film in one day early and $12,000 under budget.[229] The Mummy had not been onscreen in ten years, last appearing in *The Mummy's Curse* in 1944, starring Lon Chaney, Jr. The success of *Abbott and Costello Meet Dr. Jekyll and Mr. Hyde* had renewed interest in the monster spoofs,[230] so the Mummy was unwrapped, so to speak, for a return to the screen. However, his name was inexplicably changed from Kharis to Klaris.

Bud and Lou's relationship during the film was strained, according to Michael Ansara in *Lou's on First*. The two were not communicating between scenes. When the director called "Cut," Lou would go in one direction and Bud the other, with no conversation between them.[231]

Again, Bud was taking as many falls as Lou and the two were relying more on physical comedy than anything else. Most of the stunts were performed by stuntmen (although Chris Costello says Lou insisted on doing his own stunt work despite medical orders to the contrary).[232] Vic Parks again doubled for Lou and was again injured. During the finale, Parks had to run through a huge glass wall. Beyond the glass wall was a solid wall, and when Parks ran through the candy glass he hit the solid wall hard. Parks was dazed, and all he could hear was Lamont yelling, "Get out of there!"[233]

Henry Mancini, the composer who would go on to score the Pink Panther films and write the *Peter Gunn* theme, scored portions of the film, including the opening titles and the Apache dance sequence. His first work in film had been scoring portions of *Lost in Alaska* (1952).[234]

The screenplay was credited solely to John Grant, with story credit given to Lee Loeb, who had prepared a treatment for the film. The working title for the treatment was "Abbott and Costello in the Mummy," and it had an alternate ending. The character named Iben would have ordered the deaths of Abbott and Costello after Klaris and the temple had been blown up. But Costello would sneak away and reappear in drag as the Princess Ara, saving their lives.[235] Also cut from the final film was a second musical number by Peggy King called "Sing You Sinners."[236] King was a regular on *The George Gobel Show*.

Appearing in the cast was former Miss Utah Marie Windsor. Born in 1922, Windsor became famous as "nearly everybody's favorite B-feature bad girl."[237] She had appeared in thrillers such as *Narrow Margin* and *The Sniper* (both 1952), science fiction films like the turkey *Cat Women of the Moon* (1953) and *The Day Mars Invaded the Earth* (1963), and film noirs like *The Killing* (1956), but she mostly loved comedy. Lou gave her tips on timing during the film, and she later revealed he and Bud would simply improvise on the content of a scene.[238] In later years, Windsor would do mostly television shows, appearing on episodes of *The Bionic Woman* and *The Incredible Hulk*.

At the time, Michael Ansara, who played Charlie in the film, was a newcomer in Hollywood. He would go on to appear in *The Robe* and *Julius Caesar* (both 1953), and play the role of Cochise on the television show *Broken Arrow* (1956–58). He was nervous about working with Abbott and Costello because of their notorious ad-libbing.[239]

The Mummy was played by Eddie Parker, the stunt double for all the horror stars. He had doubled for Karloff in *Abbott and Costello Meet Dr. Jekyll and Mr. Hyde* and here received billing in the credits.

Also appearing in the cast was Mel Welles, a familiar face to current fans of the genre. Welles played the brilliant comic role of Mushnik in Roger Corman's *Little Shop of Horrors* (1960). He would later go on to direct his own films, including *Lady Frankenstein* (1972).

Character actor Richard Deacon, best known for his roles on such television series as *Leave It To Beaver*, *The Dick Van Dyke Show*, and *The Mothers-in-Law*, makes an early film appearance in the role of Semu, replacing H.B. Warner.[240] Deacon had numerous encounters with Lou Costello, both good and bad. Due to his claustrophobia, Deacon was nervous about the scene where he is tied up and buried. Lou overheard the prop men discussing the situation and asked Deacon if it was all right if they just sprinkled a little dirt over him. Deacon agreed and Costello had Lamont do the scene quickly so the actor did not have to spend a lot of time in the hole.[241]

Costello noticed Deacon put his hand on his hip a lot. Feeling this was effeminate, Costello asked Lamont to tell Deacon not to do it anymore. He expected actors to conform to a masculine world.[242] This was interesting and perhaps ironic because part of Costello's schtick was acting very *un*-masculine.

At one point, Bobby Barber asked Deacon to sign Costello's anti–Communism pledge which he was having everyone on the set sign. Deacon refused, even though he knew this was just Costello's way of showing his patriotism. Barber was angry when Deacon did not sign. He told the actor that if Lou found out, Deacon would never again work at Universal. But the matter was never mentioned again.[243]

Abbott and Costello Meet the Mummy is not the duo's worst film, but it does, at times, display much sloppiness. For example, Bud and Lou call them themselves Abbott and Costello throughout the film but are listed in the credits as Peter Patterson and Freddie Franklin.

The film opens with some appropriately Egyptian sounding music that still retains the tone of *Abbott and Costello Meet Frankenstein*'s theme. Little cartoon figures of Abbott and Costello appear onscreen with the credits, but there is no attempt at animation, another sign of how the studio no longer cared about their once–number one comedy team.

For a change of pace, the film's story opens with spoken narration:

> "It has been said that a man's best friend is his mummy. In Egypt today, this theory is to be in great dispute — for two bold adventurers are about to discover another kind of mummy."

This unfunny narration adds nothing to the film.

At a nightclub, a man and three women fight in an acrobatic dance number. At the time, this was a popular but violent dance form known as "apache dancing."[244] Bud and Lou enter the club and are seated at a table. We never learn just what they are doing in Egypt or how they got stuck there. A woman falls off the stage and knocks Lou over. Already it is evident the boys will be relying mostly on slapstick for laughs. In fact, Bud takes a pratfall right after helping Lou up. Bud takes so much abuse in this film that the straight man/comic roles almost seem reversed.

The waiter offers Bud a flaming shish kebab. Lou yells, "The meat's on fire!" and splashes the meat (and Bud) with water. Bud asks, "How stupid can you get?" Costello replies, "How stupid do you want me to be?" He could very well be asking this of Lamont. Most of the jokes in the film are recycled, and the numerous pratfalls are painfully unfunny. In this scene, even the pacing is off. Too much time is spent on the static image of the nightclub show. Universal had returned to their old formula of adding musical numbers to Abbott and Costello comedies. These numbers have since dated their films.

Bud dries off and returns as the act concludes. The waiter brings another shish kebab and Lou again douses Bud. The joke is no funnier the second time.

At a nearby table, Dr. Gustav Zoomer is interviewed by the press. He says he has discovered the mummy of Klaris, Prince of Egypt, and inside Klaris' sarcophagus is a clue that will lead to the location of the tomb of Princess Ara. No one knows why Universal changed the Mummy's name from Kharis to Klaris. Apparently, the Mummy in this film is not the same as in the earlier series, though the studio could have easily tied the spoof to the series by making the Mummy Kharis. Dettman and Bedford state: "It isn't surprising that [the Mummy] was renamed Klaris in this film, for consider the similarities between him and Klarabell in the then-popular *Howdy Doody Show*—both were clowns and both about equally terrifying."[245]

Overhearing the conversation are two threatening Egyptians who order a third man to send a message to Semu. He is to tell Semu that Klaris has been located and will be returned to his people. They add that Dr. Zoomer will not go unpunished.

Bud walks by Zoomer's table and hears the professor say he is looking for two trustworthy men to accompany him on his trip to the States. Bud finds out who Zoomer is and hatches a plan to return to America.

When another man asks for Rontru, a beautiful woman emerges. Upon hearing the news of Zoomer's discovery, she orders her two henchmen, Charlie and Josef, to steal Klaris. They ask her if she is afraid of the curse, but she says there is "no curse that a gun or knife can't cure." She tells them to follow the doctor home. Anything that might happen to him will be blamed on the curse.

At Dr. Zoomer's house, the doctor speaks into a tape recorder, telling where he found the tomb. The followers of Semu, Hetsut and Iben, shoot a poison dart into his neck and the doctor dies. They hide the body.

Bud and Lou arrive at Zoomer's house. Bud explains how they will accompany the Mummy to America. Naturally, Lou thinks Bud is talking about Zoomer's mother and is confused when Bud says the Mummy is a he. This is just the type of wordplay we expect from Abbott and Costello. The film needs more of it.

Hetsut and Iben open the sarcophagus and tell Klaris he will be returned to his people. The Mummy is still alive!

His appearance is very shabby; the bandages are obviously a suit. One critic mentioned that the Mummy's body looks much like the Creature from the Black Lagoon. Strangely, no explanation is offered as to how or why the ancient Mummy is still alive, though we do find out later how he is *kept* alive. The writers obviously felt such background was not important to this film.

The two men are about to carry out the sarcophagus when they hear the doorbell. They hide as Bud and Lou let themselves in the house. Bud is suspicious so he sends Lou to look in the room with the artifacts. As Lou looks around the room, one follower tries to choke him and the other tries to stab him with a knife. Lou narrowly averts each disaster without ever knowing the danger he is in. This is reminiscent of scenes in *Abbott and Costello Meet Frankenstein* and *Abbott and Costello Meet Dr. Jekyll and Mr. Hyde* in which Costello narrowly escapes death from a menace he is unaware exists.

Costello sees the wooden statue of a woman which he at first mistakes for Mrs. Zoomer. He almost slaps it on the behind but catches himself. He then opens Klaris' coffin. Klaris sits up and scares him. Lou runs out of the room yelling one of his trademark cries of "Hey, Abbott!!"

Naturally, Bud does not believe the 4,000-year-old Mummy is still alive. But he does want to take a picture of it. When he and Lou return to the room, they find the Mummy and his casket gone. Hetsut and Iben have taken the sarcophagus downstairs. But they cannot find the sacred medallion which has the clue to the tomb of Princess Ara. They search the doctor's body but decide to give up because Klaris has gone too long without sustenance.

The scenes that follow are all made up of bits and pieces of standard Abbott and Costello gags, beginning with an oft-repeated exchange from Bud and Lou. Bud says, "There's someone in this house who doesn't belong here." Lou agrees: "I know who it is — me."

Bud gives Lou a camera, has him hide, and orders him to take a picture of anyone who enters the room. After Bud leaves, Lou opens a closet and finds the body of Dr. Zoomer. Lou has opened closets and found dead bodies in *Hold That Ghost*, *Who Done It?*, and *Abbott and Costello Meet the Killer, Boris Karloff*. Watch the open-eyed corpse of Dr. Zoomer very closely in this scene. When Costello hits him on the head, his eyes close as he falls to the floor.

When Lou realizes the doctor is dead, he runs out to get Bud. Hetsut and Iben continually move the body and hide it different places around the room. Every time Lou brings Bud back, the body is gone. When Bud leaves, Lou finds the body in a different spot. This is a variation of the "Changing Room" routine from *Hold That Ghost* that was also used in *Abbott and Costello Meet the Killer, Boris Karloff*. Throughout the scene, Bud thinks Lou is mentally ill, just as he has in the previous monster spoofs.

Eventually, Lou sees someone hiding behind the shower curtain in the bathroom. He hits the stranger with his camera. Bud falls out — just like in *Abbott and Costello Meet Dr. Jekyll and Mr. Hyde*.

Lou returns to Zoomer's office where Hetsut and Iben have placed the doctor's body at his desk. The tape recorder plays Zoomer's voice and Lou thinks the dead man is talking to him. This scene echoes the transcription scene in *Who Done It?*

Lou hears the doctor's murder on the tape and screams. This brings in Bud, who crashes into the door. He listens to the tape and realizes the doctor has been murdered. He wants to go to the police but is afraid the body will disappear. He has Lou take a picture for proof. But Lou takes a picture while Bud is placing the body in the chair. Meanwhile, Hetsut and Iben give up their search for the sacred medallion. They take Klaris back to Semu even though they know they will have to face Semu's wrath.

Bud and Lou must have an early Polaroid camera because the picture is ready immediately. Bud has Lou write "This is Dr. Zoomer" on the back of one of the photos and seal it in an envelope. They leave the house, not knowing they are being watched by Madame Rontru's men, Charlie and Josef. Lou tells Bud he shot Zoomer's body three times and his head twice. Lou is, of course, referring to taking pictures, but Rontru's men think the two are cold-blooded murderers. Similar confusion occurred in *Hit the Ice*.

Bud has a boy deliver the envelope containing the photograph to the police.

In the hidden tomb of Klaris, Hetsut and Iben report to high priest Semu. The followers of Semu celebrate the return of Klaris to his people with a dance number. This slows down the pace of the film.

Semu prepares a potion to provide sustenance for Klaris. What is in the potion is not revealed. In the earlier Mummy films, tanna leaves were used to revive Kharis.

Semu notices that the sacred medallion is missing. Hetsut and Iben explain that the doctor hid it. Semu orders them back to the house to find the medallion. If they fail, they will die.

In an outdoor cafe, Bud and Lou ponder the situation. Lou approaches a French woman who accuses him of trying to make a date. As she berates him, she tells him her address and phone number. This is the first great bit in the film. Bud finally intercedes. The woman tells him things in French to which Bud repeatedly answers, "No, lady, I don't think I can." Lou hears all this and finally says, "Hey, Abbott! What's she saying? Maybe I can!"

Bud buys a newspaper and cannot understand why the newsboy is afraid of him. When he reads the article about Zoomer's death, he sees the picture of himself with Zoomer's body. The police think Bud is the murderer! The newsboy tips off the cops, who investigate.

Bud and Lou escape disguised as peddlers begging for alms. The cops follow them into the street. This street scene is somewhat reminiscent of the street scenes in *Raiders of the Lost Ark* (1981) when Indiana Jones is chased by Nazis while his girlfriend Marion hides in a basket.

Bud orders Lou to play the flute so they will not look suspicious. As Lou plays, a cobra emerges from a basket, attracted to the music. Lou sees it and loses his breath. Bud tells him to keep playing but Lou cannot, so they switch places. This time the snake comes out of a different basket, frightening Lou, who runs off. This is the start of the film's running gag, a variation of the "oyster in the soup" routine. Although funny, it makes a common error. Snakes are attracted to the rhythm and movement of the instrument's player, not the music.

The police pursue Bud and Lou and corner them on a street. Bud tells Lou to play the flute while he performs the Indian rope trick. Bud climbs the rope and is suspended in the air while Lou plays. The cops leave and Lou stops playing, causing Bud to fall into a fruit cart. Lou knocks him out and wheels him away. In earlier films, situations like this would happen solely to Lou, but this late in their careers Bud became the focus of abuse just as much as Lou.

At Zoomer's home, Rontru, Charlie, and Josef arrive to search for the sacred medallion. They keep an eye out for Lou, who they think is a "baby-faced killer," emphasizing Lou's child persona.

Bud and Lou also return to the house in search of the real murderer "who always returns to the scene of the crime." They turn on the recorder so when the murderer hears Zoomer's voice he will investigate. Then they can grab him. Lou is scared. Bud tells him to be brave and be a man. "Be tough like me," he says, like an older brother.

Lou imitates Bud, repeating over and over, "Nothing scares me." But his inner child emerges and he starts to cry. He decides to record his tough voice to be strong. Accompanied by music fit for Superman, he records himself talking to an imaginary prisoner. He says he has a gun and orders his quarry to put up his hands. When he plays it back, Bud overhears and thinks someone has cornered him. When he finds out it is Costello, he slaps him. This gag is similar to the transcription scene in *Who Done It?*

Bud and Lou decide to search the trophy room, so Rontru and her men hide, with Rontru taking the place of the female statue. Bud orders Lou to look for a secret passage by knocking on walls and objects. Lou sees the "statue" and knocks on Rontru's ass with his hat. She kicks him and he flies into the wall. Lou ends up holding a vase, which he wants to use as a piggy bank. When he shakes it, he finds the sacred medallion. Rontru breaks from her pose and orders her men to get the medallion. Bud and Lou make a run for it. Lou's attitude here perfectly captures his child character. He yells, "Finders keepers!" when the villains want the medallion.

In a gag borrowed from *Abbott and Costello Meet Frankenstein*, Bud and Lou run into a room and barricade the door with a dresser, but the henchmen open the door and push the dresser into the next room. The cops arrive on the scene, so Bud and Lou race back to the trophy room. Now they are trapped, with men at each door trying to burst in. They formulate a good plan (finally showing some smarts) by opening both doors at the same time and letting the two parties crash into each other.

Unfortunately, one of the cops collars Lou, and Rontru and her men identify him as the murderer. Lou starts the tape recorder and everyone mistakenly assumes they are being held at gunpoint. Bud and Lou escape and the police follow. Semu's men arrive in time to overhear Rontru say she knows Lou has the medallion. They return to Semu with the news and he decides to accompany them when they go to retrieve it.

In a marketplace, Bud wonders why the medallion is so important. They try to hock it but the sight of it only frightens the shopkeeper. Upon leaving the shop, the boys run into Rontru, who comes on to Lou and offers to buy the medallion for $100. Again a beautiful woman flirts with Lou while ignoring Bud in order to manipulate the boys.

Bud smells something fishy and asks for $5,000. Rontru angrily agrees but she does not have the money on her. She says she will make the payoff at the Cafe Baghdad. She leaves behind a smitten Lou. Bud calculates how he will spend the money, naturally giving himself the larger share. Lou picks up a flute and begins to play. A snake emerges from a basket but Lou does not see it. He covers the basket with his hat while he fixes his flute. When he plays the flute again, the hat rises in the air. Grabbing the hat, Lou sees the snake and runs. The running gag progresses nicely.

Lou runs right into the shopkeeper, who now apologizes and offers to buy the medallion. But Bud will not sell. Semu's men emerge as Lou explains he is meeting Rontru at the cafe. They chase after Bud and Lou with knives but the boys escape. Semu stops his men from following, telling them to wait until dark.

At the Cafe Baghdad, Peggy King sings a song. Like the musical interludes in early Abbott and Costello films, this song is intrusive and slows the picture's pace.

Bud and Lou arrive. Lou sees a flaming shish kebab and gets a devilish glint in his eye. Bud warns, "No, you don't," an amusing reference to the gag in the opening scene.

With no sign of Madame Rontru, the boys take a table and order two coffees and two hamburgers. (Apparently, hamburgers are an integral part of Egyptian cuisine.) Nevertheless, the burgers are brought to the table along with catsup.

Bud still thinks the medallion may be fake, so he calls a waiter over to the table to look at it. The waiter is frightened. He says the medallion "means death to whoever holds it." Bud immediately slips it to Lou.

Bud and Lou pass the medallion back and forth, placing it in each other's pockets. This is one of their oldest routines. Lou even tries to slip it under some flowers a young girl is selling. But because they are wilted, she gives the flowers to Lou for free, unknowingly returning the medallion. The flower girl is played by Lou's daughter Carole, who had previously appeared in *Abbott and Costello Meet the Keystone Kops* (1954). Originally, she was to have dropped a tray of food and a pitcher of water on Lou.[246]

Lou puts the medallion in Bud's hamburger but Bud switches the plates. They enact another old routine in which each knows the other is trying to slip him a mickey. So they continually distract the other's attention and switch the plates. Eventually, one gets wise and only pretends to make the switch. The other, hearing the sound, switches the plates and gives himself the mickey. It is a very funny routine, previously used in *Pardon My Sarong* and *The Naughty Nineties*.

Lou tricks Bud into giving himself the burger with the medallion. The looks on their faces are priceless as Bud realizes he has received the medallion and Lou revels in his superiority over Bud. But Bud wins out. He puts the medallion in the catsup. Of course, Lou ends up putting the medallion on his burger. Naturally, Lou uses catsup because it is well known, thanks to the "mustard" bit, that he does not like mustard.

Lou eats the burger and unknowingly eats the medallion. As he chews, loud crunches of metal are heard on the soundtrack. Though Lou's expressions of surprise are funny, this scene pushes credibility and suspension of disbelief to the limit. Scenes like this one make it clear the boys were playing strictly to a kiddie audience.

Rontru finally arrives and takes Lou to a private dining room, leaving a frustrated Bud at the table. There, she asks to see the medallion but Lou refuses. She has him hang up his hat and coat while she puts on some soft music. A hand reaches out from different holes in the wall to search through Lou's coat for the medallion. Lou sees the hand and bats at it with his hat, blaming termites. For once Lou is not frightened by what is going on. He is actually angry because his coat is being searched.

A hand emerges from a lion's head on the wall and pulls the coat into the mouth to be searched. It is a good visual gag because, to Lou, it looks like the lion is eating the coat. Lou gets his coat back after making a wisecrack and places it on an Egyptian statue. The statue begins picking the pockets. This is the end for Lou, and he attempts to leave. But Rontru makes him stay by giving him the money. Lou breaks the fourth wall and looks at the camera, letting us know he has no intention of putting the money in his coat. He puts it in his pants pocket.

Rontru and Lou sit down and have a drink. A hand comes out of the floor and picks Lou's pocket, taking all the money but one dollar. In what seems to be an improvised bit of business, Lou knocks on the table and the hand returns. Lou gives him the dollar he missed and then tries to run out. Rontru's men grab Lou and bring in Bud. They demand the medallion and Lou admits he ate it.

Meanwhile, Semu's men tell him Hetsut was arrested by the police for Zoomer's murder. This is an all-too-convenient way of dropping the false murder charge plot and is never properly explained. Apparently, an autopsy uncovered the truth. "Let him hang," says Semu. Realizing Rontru has taken Bud and Lou to the house of Dr. Azzui, he decides to pay a visit there.

At the doctor's house, Madame Rontru forces Lou behind a fluoroscope at gunpoint. She x-rays Lou's stomach and sees a marble, a safety pin, and some buttons. Bud has a funny line when he says, "I lost a tie clasp two years ago, see if it's in there."

In a scene reminiscent of *Here Come the Co-Eds*, Charlie shakes up Lou in order to get a better view of the medallion. Letters from the medallion's chain spell "HELP" under the fluoroscope. This time Charlie forces Bud to help shake Lou. They swing him around and he flies into the ceiling. If you watch Michael Ansara in this scene, you will see he is trying hard not to laugh.

Vic Parks recalled how he was shot in the air 15 feet by compressed air to film this scene. Two guys on the ceiling were supposed to catch him. Then he would dangle his legs through the hole. Parks demanded mattresses be placed below in case the guys missed him. After some debate, Lamont agreed. Sure enough, the guys missed Parks and he fell back to the ground — onto the mattresses. They shot the scene again and this time they caught him.[247]

Bud climbs a table to pull Lou down, but Lou lands on the other end and sends Bud into the ceiling. This time Rontru is able to see the hieroglyphics on the medallion but she is unable to understand them. Just then Semu arrives to offer his services as a translator, saying he is a student of archeology. Josef does not trust Semu and warns Rontru against working with him. But Rontru plans to kill Semu after he translates the hieroglyphics.

Rontru explains that the medallion is in Lou's stomach. As Semu, Richard Deacon delivers a witty line here when he says, "What an extraordinary place to keep it." He translates the medallion, which reveals the way to Princess Ara's tomb. He offers to guide the expedition and Rontru agrees. She also decides to take along Bud and Lou in case the x-ray is damaged and they need to get to the medallion. As plans for the expedition are put together, Rontru orders Charlie and Josef to follow close behind.

Semu, Rontru, Bud, and Lou travel into the desert. They arrive at the temple ruins where Semu's followers wait in hiding. While they make camp, they discuss the curse of Klaris. Rontru says she fears no man, but Semu explains that Klaris guards the temple of Ara. It's a good thing the scriptwriters inserted this dialogue, for by this point most viewers have forgotten the Mummy is even in the film! Klaris is absent from the screen much too long, which detracts from the value of the picture. After all, the title is *Abbott and Costello Meet the* Mummy!

Semu sneaks into the temple through a secret entrance in a rock while Bud and Lou pitch the tent. He tells his followers he has brought the one with the medallion, and the followers pray to Klaris.

Meanwhile, Rontru secretly meets with Charlie and Josef and tells them she plans to melt down the treasure in the tomb and recut the jewels. One of Semu's men listens in as Rontru mentions that everyone else is expendable. Semu is informed of Rontru's betrayal, and he declares all will die after the feast of Klaris. They prepare for the celebration.

Lou follows instructions to "pitch the tent" by throwing it at Bud. Bud throws it back and Lou falls through the secret entrance into the hidden temple. This scene (and subsequent sequences in the tomb) seem to be forerunners of similar scenes in Steven Spielberg's *Raiders of the Lost Ark*. Maybe Spielberg was inspired by this film as a child — or maybe not.

Just as he was in *Abbott and Costello Meet Frankenstein*, Lou is chased by a vampire bat. He finds a decaying mummy, runs into a giant lizard (possibly influenced by the giant monster movies so prevalent in the fifties), and finally ends up with a skeleton on his shoulders. This is the stuff the audience have been waiting for. The delight of the monster spoofs is seeing Lou do his scared routine. At last, he has a chance to be menaced by more monsters.

After running into the lizard a second time, Lou discovers the temple. He sits by the sarcophagus, not realizing the Mummy is emerging from it. He turns around but misses seeing Klaris. He looks in the casket and sees nothing. Klaris creeps up behind him. Finally, Lou runs into the Mummy, who tries to strangle him. Lou escapes. In this scene, one can see how truly pathetic the Mummy costume looks. Obviously, it is a zipped-up suit. In addition, the Mummy emits growls that sound like "RAHH!"— the type of noise kids make when they are scaring each other. As a movie monster, the shambling Mummy was never all that terrifying — but he was never this ludicrous.

Lou overhears Semu say he will kill everyone after the celebration. After again being frightened by a bat, Lou leans against the wall and ends up back with Bud. He tells Bud he has found the Mummy.

Bud wants the Mummy for himself so he can make a fortune off of it. In a blatant error, Lou tells Bud they should inform Rontru and Semu about the discovery. Why would Lou want to go to Semu when he just overheard Semu plan to kill him?

The boys rediscover the secret entrance to the temple. Echoing a running gag from *Abbott and Costello Meet Dr. Jekyll and Mr. Hyde*, Bud says, "Follow me," then pushes Lou through the secret entrance.

Rontru orders her men to stay out of sight. They argue over the best time to kill Semu. Meanwhile, Lou takes Bud to the crypt, but Klaris is gone. Bud orders Lou to sit by the sarcophagus. Then, when the Mummy returns to attack Lou, Bud will whistle. Lou can then grab the Mummy. Lou would go along with the plan except for one small detail — Bud cannot whistle. So they exchange places. Naturally, the Mummy arrives and attacks Lou. Bud tries to whistle in order to warn him but cannot. This scene is hilarious.

Bud runs out. Klaris follows behind Lou. Lou bends down and sees an extra pair of feet. This propels him into his scared routine. The "feet routine" was used again in the famous Colgate Comedy Hour clip when Lou met the Frankenstein Monster and the Creature from the Black Lagoon.

Klaris squeezes Lou and he spits out the medallion (in effect, Klaris gives Lou the Heimlich Maneuver!). He hands the Mummy the medallion and runs out. Bud and Lou leave the temple and tell Rontru that Semu and his men plan to kill them. Rontru passes the information on to Charlie and Josef, who emerge from hiding. She orders her men to set up a trap for Semu. She also orders Bud and Lou to dig a large hole.

About to dig the hole, Bud and Lou launch into a rare verbal routine (rare for one of the later monster spoofs anyway). It is refreshing to see them return to the comedy they do so well. Here, Lou is confused when Bud tells him to take his pick of a pick and a shovel. With classic wordplay, Lou cannot understand that the pick is Bud's "pick." This scene was added during the film's production.[248]

Lou digs while Bud plans. Lou discovers an artifact. Bud takes it and pushes Lou, who falls down the secret entrance to the temple. Bud sits down to rest and also falls into the temple.

Semu is captured by Rontru and her men, who decide to hold him as a bargaining chip.

In the tomb, Bud and Lou search for a way out. Bud boosts Lou up to a shelf where he sees another mummy. Lou falls down on top of Bud.

They look for another exit and hear music. The dance is going on as planned. Semu's men decide to search for their missing leader. Bud, in the meantime, opens a coffin and finds a secret passage with a decayed mummy hanging on the door. Lou follows Bud through the passage.

Josef finishes digging the hole while Charlie dresses up like Klaris. No explanation is given for this course of action. Apparently, the crooks plan to trick Klaris' followers. They decide to dump Klaris in the hole and substitute Charlie in his place. They keep Semu tied and gagged under some canvas.

Bud wants to find Semu and exchange their lives for the medallion. But Lou explains he gave the medallion to the Mummy. Bud says they must find Klaris.

Charlie and Josef open Klaris' casket. When Klaris sits up, Charlie knocks him out cold. (As if the Mummy could be knocked out!) Josef gets rid of Klaris, and Charlie takes his place.

Bud and Lou return to the tomb with plans to hide Klaris from the crooks. Then Bud will dress up like Klaris and take his place. But when they open the sarcophagus, Charlie pops out and grabs Lou. Bud knocks out Charlie and together the boys lift him from the coffin and take him out.

Josef buries Klaris in the hole. Semu still refuses to disclose the secret of Ara's treasure. Rontru and Josef take a metal detector and explosives and begin searching.

Bud and Lou bury Charlie in the same hole housing Klaris. Bud finds the leftover bandages and dresses up like the Mummy. Not only is this another example of one of the comedians becoming the monster, it also sets up the common mistaken identity plot so prevalent in comedies.

Rontru and Josef search for the treasure but are forced to hide when Semu's followers begin looking for their missing leader.

While Bud dresses as the Mummy, Lou completes the burial of Charlie. Klaris revives and begins to rise but Lou knocks him out again with his shovel. Charlie then begins to emerge from the other end of the hole but Lou knocks him out, too. Confused, he tries to tell Bud what has happened, but Semu's groans interrupt him. Finding Semu, they prop him up next to the secret entrance and he falls into the temple.

Lou leads Bud into the temple so they can save the treasure. Bud, dressed as the Mummy, looks like he lost twenty pounds. Obviously, he was replaced by a stuntman when "under wraps."

Klaris and Charlie awaken at the same time. Klaris frightens Charlie, who runs into the temple. The Mummy also heads into the temple.

Rontru and Josef discover the empty tomb. Rontru sets the explosives. Bud and Lou sneak through the corridors and spot Semu's followers. Bud runs away and Lou unknowingly takes the real Klaris by the hand. Together they hide until the followers have all gone. Then Klaris frightens Lou away. Bud then returns and drags Klaris off, thinking he has Costello. Klaris frightens him away, too. In a scene reminiscent of *Abbott and Costello Meet Dr. Jekyll and Mr. Hyde*, the three mummies back into each other. Klaris then scares away the two fakes. This scene might actually have been funny had it not been a direct and contrived steal from the previous spoof.

Rontru orders Josef to set the explosives. Meanwhile, Bud searches for Lou, followed by Charlie and Klaris. Where Lou has disappeared to is anybody's guess. The three mummies again meet up in the tomb. Rontru and Josef are confused — they do not know who is who. Josef is so taken aback by the sight that he faints.

Madame Rontru orders Charlie to raise his hand but all three mummies do as she asks. She solves the problem by shooting at their feet. Charlie and Bud run off but Klaris advances on Rontru. She shoots at him but bullets have no effect. In a classic (and stupid) cliché, Rontru realizes bullets won't stop him and so throws the gun at the Mummy. Why did characters always do this in the old monster movies? If bullets have no effect, a thrown gun would certainly have none either! Crooks on the *Superman* television series always tried the same strategy and obtained the same results.

Rontru beats at Klaris with a torch but Klaris grabs it and throws it aside. The torch lights the fuse connected to the explosives. This brings up another plot hole. Why would Rontru, who spent the whole movie looking for the hidden treasure of Princess Ara (which would make her fabulously wealthy) suddenly decide to blow up the place? Did she think the explosion would uncover the treasure? Did she ever stop to think the explosion might forever bury the tomb — and her with it? Blatant plot holes like this (big enough to drive a jeep through — or at least a camel) help make this one of the worst Abbott and Costello films.

Semu is freed by his followers. He tells them they must save the treasure. Meanwhile, Klaris struggles with Madame Rontru and throws her down. She picks up the dynamite, tosses it at the Mummy, and runs to the door. There she is met by Charlie, Bud, Semu, and the followers. Klaris raises the dynamite in his hands. Semu tries to talk Klaris out of destroying them. As the Mummy advances, they all back up.

Oh, yeah — Lou is running around somewhere. He casually walks into frame as if he became bored waiting in his trailer and wanted to see what was going on. By this time, we had forgotten he was even in the tomb. Klaris throws the dynamite to Lou. Bud tells him to throw it back to Klaris, which he does. The dynamite blows up, destroying Klaris and his tomb. It also destroys Josef, who had fainted and was lying behind the tomb. (The writers probably forgot about him.) The explosion also clears the entrance to the tunnel, unearthing Princess Ara's tomb and treasure.

A sad Semu whines about how a legend is all that remains now that Ara's secret has been unearthed. Bud tells him the whole world should know of the legend and says he has a way to make the legend of Klaris last forever.

In the most ridiculous solution imaginable, Bud and Lou build a nightclub called Kafe Klaris on the site of the tomb. Inside, Semu and his followers serve as waiters and the musicians dress as mummies. A packed house dances and drinks on opening night. This is a crazy and totally unsatisfying climax. Why would Semu and his followers ever agree to such a sacrilegious notion (especially one that reduces them to nothing more than hired help)? And what about the murders Semu and his followers committed or were a party to? And what has happened to Madame Rontru and Charlie? There are too many unanswered questions; obviously, if one makes it this far into the film, one should not be bothered about logic.

Lou shows up and performs a bit with a zip-up tuxedo. He grabs a nearby horn and Bud shows him how to play it. As Bud plays, two sensuous arms rise up out of a nearby urn. A beautiful girl emerges and passionately kisses Bud. Lou is amazed. He takes the horn from Bud and tries another urn. In a perfect capper to the running gag, Lou plays the horn and a huge, ugly snake rises out of the urn. Lou takes no notice, certain that a beautiful girl is waiting for him. When he leans in to kiss her, the snake flicks its tongue at him. Lou does a double take and crashes through a huge glass mirror. This final bit was later repeated in the compilation film *The World of Abbott and Costello*.

Upon completion of the picture, Abbott and Costello rode the number one float in the 1954 Macy's Thanksgiving Day parade.[249] They were still popular with their fans. In fact, some of the critics at the time gave the film positive reviews. *Variety* called it "one of their best comedies in some time."[250] *The Hollywood Reporter* said the film was "a considerable improvement over the last Abbott and Costello comedy ... both comics sound some echo of their great days, but their material is pedestrianly hokey.... With a sound story both [Lou] and Bud could probably be great again."[251]

Modern critics are universal (no pun intended) in panning the film. *Creature Features Movie Guide Strikes Again* calls it "the least of the Abbott and Costello film spoofs"[252] (the only real criticism among a paragraph of bad puns). Jim Mulholland writes, "the plot is ridiculous even by Abbott and Costello standards."[253] He also says the makeup for the Mummy is ludicrously bad.[254] James L. Neibaur claims it is their "best picture in quite some time," yet "painful to watch."[255] Brunas, Brunas, and Weaver comment, in passing, about the film. They write that the Mummy "upstages a sadly aging and painfully unfunny comedy team."[256] They add, "Eddie Parker ... stalks about some interesting Egyptian sets looking more like a bandaged Creature from the Black

Lagoon."[257] *VideoHound* calls the film an "okay comedy"[258]; Maltin says it is an "amusing adventure"[259]; and Martin and Porter feel the movie has some amusing moments but drags out the "same tired vaudeville routines."[260]

Oddly, however, the film is still referenced today in a positive light. An episode of the NBC sitcom *Men Behaving Badly* had the two main characters arguing over why, if they are so smart, they are still entertained by lowbrow comics like Abbott and Costello. One character says, "It works on so many levels. Like when Bud rescues Lou from Mr. Bacciagalupe, we recognize it as man saving himself from the tyranny of absolute power. When Lou gets stuck on that exercise belt ... well, it symbolizes man becoming ensnared in the fruitless pursuit of perfection." To this the other character replies, "Watch out for the stairs, Bud!" The film they are watching is none other than *Abbott and Costello Meet the Mummy*—referred to by name.[261]

Abbott and Costello Meet the Mummy contains most of the elements that make up the Abbott and Costello monster spoof formula. The title monster, the Mummy, is basically played straight. Although he never kills anyone in the course of the film, Klaris still intends to murder those who cross his path, evident in his attempts to choke Lou and destroy the tomb with dynamite. Lou is the first to "meet" the monster when he comes across him in Zoomer's house, and Abbott, of course, refuses to believe him. And, again, Bud and Lou stumble into the plot by accident rather than initiating any of the horror action that follows.

Left out of the previous monster romp but restored here is the subplot that has a beautiful woman pretend to be smitten with Costello in order to manipulate him. Madame Rontru plays that part, romancing Lou in order to obtain the medallion.

A wild chase typically caps the film, but not before Bud has "become" the title monster. In this case, he is joined by Charlie when they both masquerade as Klaris. Unfortunately, the reasoning behind both masquerades is never adequately explained, detracting from the enjoyment of the movie.

Strangely, in this film, the actual characters of Abbott and Costello have started to become interchangeable. Bud is still the older, parental figure, but he has lost a lot of his con man edge. In fact, Lou beats him in the "slipping a mickey" routine.

Lou still retains his childlike characteristics but seems wiser and even a bit world-weary. Things that would normally happen to Costello (being wanted for murder, climbing the rope and falling, masquerading as the Mummy) now happen to Abbott. This would have been unthinkable in their earlier films.

The reliance on more slapstick and physical humor (enacted equally by both men) and the change in characters are just two of the reasons the later Abbott and Costello films are so bad. The scripts got weaker and the boys got tired — so tired that they did not care about making distinct who was Abbott and who was Costello. Ironically, when they started their career on radio (on Kate Smith's show), listeners complained they could not distinguish between the two comedians because their voices were so alike. This prompted Costello to adopt a higher pitched, nasal voice that he used from then on. History repeated itself, only now Abbott had put on so much weight he started to *physically resemble Costello!*

No one ever cares to delve into the higher meanings and themes of *Abbott and Costello Meet the Mummy*, due, most likely, to the fact that there does not seem to be anything there to explore. The plot possesses more holes than a piece of Swiss cheese; the monster is barely in the film long enough to make a mark; the film has obviously been targeted for the kiddie market; and the dialogue is weak and often painfully unfunny. One of the few mentions of the picture in the context of a critical study occurs in John Denne's essay on the monster film in relation to society. He classifies three types of monster films: 1) the atmospheric monster movie, where the environment in which the struggle takes place is the monster's own or the society is distorted and changed by the monster and his forces; 2) the bipartite or bipolar monster movie, where the struggle occurs between and among two distinct environments; and 3) the social monster movie where society's environment remains very much intact and dominant and the monster operates within it, not in his own.[262] He cites *Abbott and Costello Meet the Mummy* as an example of the social monster movie but does not give any reasons for its inclusion.[263]

One wonders if he ever saw the film. The social monster movie deals with the problem of deviance within society and the ill effects of nonconformity. In other words, it vindicates the status quo.[264] While it may be true that in the earlier Mummy films (*The Mummy's Tomb, The Mummy's Ghost, The Mummy's Curse*) the classic Mummy characterization is a deviant in a world he never made, here the story is set in the Mummy's homeland of Egypt. Klaris is at home among the temples, tombs, and deserts of the film — which invalidates Denne's claim. It is Abbott and Costello who are the foreigners, the intruders, sticking their noses into affairs not of their culture, society, or business. They do not dress like Egyptians (unless in disguise), do not act like Egyptians (Lou extinguishes the shish kebab, thinking the meat is on fire), and are constantly at odds with Egyptians (the crooks, the cultists, and even the police).

Consequently, the film could be classified as an atmospheric monster movie since the environment is the monster's own and the heroes are the outsiders. The Mummy and his forces (the followers of Semu) are working to retain their own status quo at the expense of the outsiders. More aptly, the film is an example of a bipolar monster movie. The world of Abbott and Costello is at odds with the world of the Mummy. The struggle is symbolic of the whole idea behind the monster spoof — the horror genre at odds with or combating the comedy genre. In effect, each one of the "Abbott and Costello Meet the Monsters" films could be classified as bipolar, for each details a struggle between a world of horror and a world of comedy. Although Abbott and Costello survive each movie, their victory is always questionable. At the close of *Abbott and Costello Meet Frankenstein*, they find themselves still fighting monsters when the Invisible Man surprises them in the boat. In *Abbott and Costello Meet the Invisible Man*, Lou first becomes an Invisible Man himself, then a deformed freak. In *Abbott and Costello Meet Dr. Jekyll and Mr. Hyde*, the movie refuses to end until the boys find themselves confronted with a roomful of monsters. These films were ahead of their time because the endings fused the world of comedy (represented by a final gag to elicit a laugh) and the world of horror (the dark, frightening undertone of the gag), leaving the viewers subtly confused as to which reaction they should have. The filmmakers were venturing into black comedy!

Unfortunately, *Abbott and Costello Meet the Mummy* concludes on a comic note (the capping of a running gag) with no hint of black comedy. This signaled the end. The Universal horror film became the Universal science fiction film and Abbott and Costello soon retired from the screen. Along with sci-fi, the studio continued doing the formula pictures in which they always specialized, with further entries for *Francis the Talking Mule* and *Ma and Pa Kettle*. They also produced numerous westerns with Jeff Chandler and Audie Murphy, and the romantic melodramas of Douglas Sirk.[265]

The era of fun horror spoofs was over — but not forgotten. Roman Polanski's *The Fearless Vampire Killers* (1967) took lessons from these films by having the vampires play it straight (in fact, the picture is quite scary). Roger Corman poked fun at the genre with *A Bucket of Blood* (1959) and *The Little Shop of Horrors* (1960). And, in the seventies and eighties, the "splaffter" film emerged, combining gruesome gore with black comedy to produce some of the funniest yet scariest films ever made — including *An American Werewolf in London* (1981), *The Howling* (1981), *The Evil Dead* (1982), *Re-Animator* (1985), *The Return of the Living Dead* (1985), *Tremors* (1988), and *Dead Alive* (1993). These movies owe a lot to Abbott and Costello and the Universal monsters.

As do we all. For me, the monster spoofs have been a constant source of pleasure since childhood. Almost everyone I know has seen at least one of them and has found the experience enjoyable. Their video sales are consistently high (in fact, I recently overheard a clerk at a video store tell a patron interested in sampling the comedy team that he could not go wrong with one of their monster movies), and they still show up now and again on television. Like the monsters Abbott and Costello fearlessly faced and fought, these films can never die.

Part Three

The Other Horror-Comedies

Hold That Ghost

Released: August 6, 1941   *Running time:* 85 minutes
Reissued: August 19, 1948, and December, 1949 (with *Hit the Ice*)

Directed by: Arthur Lubin; *Screenplay by:* Robert Lees, Frederic I. Rinaldo, and John Grant; *Original Story:* Robert Lees, Frederic I. Rinaldo; *Associate Producers:* Burt Kelly, Glenn Tryon; *Director of Photography:* Elwood Bredell, ASC; *Art Director:* Jack Otterson; *Associate:* Harold M. MacArthur; *Film Editor:* Philip Cahn; *Musical Director:* H.J. Salter; *Musical Numbers Staged by:* Nick Castle; *Dialogue Director:* Joan Hathaway; *Sound Supervisor:* Bernard M. Brown; *Technician:* William Fox; *Gowns:* Vera West; *Set Decoration:* R.A. Gausman.

Cast: Bud Abbott (Chuck Murray); Lou Costello (Ferdinand "Ferdy" Jones); Richard Carlson (Doctor Jackson); Joan Davis (Camille Brewster); Mischa Auer (Gregory); Evelyn Ankers (Norma Lind); Marc Lawrence (Charlie Smith); Shemp Howard (Soda Jerk); Russell Hicks (Bannister); William Davidson (Moose Matson); Milton Parsons (Harry Hoskins); Frank Penny (Snake-Eyes); Edgar Dearing (Irondome); Don Terry (Strangler); Edward Pawley (High Collar); Nestor Paiva (Glum); Paul Fix (Lefty); Howard Hickman (Judge); Harry Hayden (Mr. Jenkins); William Forrest (State Trooper); Paul Newlan (Big Fink); Joe LaCava (Little Fink); Bobby Barber (Bit Waiter, not in final cut); Ted Lewis and His Orchestra (Themselves); The Andrews Sisters (Themselves).

The four films previously discussed form a pattern, a small group of horror spoofs following a formula. But Abbott and Costello made other horror-comedies besides those four. These pictures do not quite fit into the previously mentioned formula; hence they are being discussed separately. *Hold That Ghost* is one of the team's best films but stands alone as an example of the old dark house spoof or haunted house comedy (a genre most comedy teams have ventured into at one time or another). *The Time of Their Lives* is a borderline horror-comedy in that it focuses primarily on comic fantasy along the lines of *Topper* (1937), *Blithe Spirit* (1945), and *The Cock-Eyed Miracle* (1946). *Abbott and Costello Meet the Killer, Boris Karloff* actually does follow the "meet the monsters" formula to a point, but does not have a monster as a menace, instead combining the formula with the murder mystery. In fact, it is actually a part of the "horror whodunit" subgenre of which Universal was so fond (but more on that later).

Hold That Ghost was the team's fourth picture released by Universal but was actually the third filmed. After their successful debut in *One Night in the Tropics*, the boys were signed to do *Buck Privates*— but this time they were supposed to be the stars. It seems, however, Universal did not fully trust them to carry the picture on their own so they included the Andrews Sisters and a healthy helping of musical numbers. As *Buck Privates* was being readied for release, the boys set about filming the script that would become *Hold That Ghost*. (Supposedly, many of the ghost routines seen in the movie had been among those used when Abbott and Costello first auditioned for Matty Fox at Universal.[266])

The young up-and-coming comedian Bob Hope had made a big splash with two horror-comedies in which he co-starred with the beautiful Paulette Goddard. Both films were based on two successful plays from the now defunct old dark house genre, *The Cat and the Canary* (1939) and *The Ghost Breakers* (1940). Both stories had been filmed before, but years earlier when the genre was in full swing (just as silents were giving way to talkies) and never with such an emphasis on comedy. At a time when horror was only just beginning to come back, and when the old dark house comedy was long dead, studio heads were surprised at how well the two films did and wanted to cash in on the success. Universal was particularly interested (after all, horror had always been their domain), so they set in motion two horror-comedies that would incorporate all the elements of the genre: secret panels, masked killers, clutching hands, and supernatural occurrences that could be explained away at the end. One of those productions became *The Black Cat* (1941), an enjoyable romp starring Broderick Crawford, Hugh "Woo-Woo" Herbert, Basil Rathbone, and Bela Lugosi. The other script, titled *Don't Look Now* had its moniker changed to *Oh, Charlie* and was tailored for the new comedy team of Abbott and Costello. (The title was later changed to the more salable *Hold That Ghost*.[267])

During filming of *Oh, Charlie*, the grosses from *Buck Privates* came in and they were phenomenal. (In fact, the film single-handedly saved Universal from bankruptcy.) The studio had a big winner on its hands and new stars in Bud and Lou. Production on the horror-comedy was halted in order to rush the boys into another service comedy that would cash in on the success of *Buck Privates*. The boys were again teamed with the Andrews Sisters and this time crooner Dick Powell came along for the ride. The resulting film, *In The Navy*, also did well, and *Hold That Ghost* became the team's fourth film to be released.

Hold That Ghost was a step forward for Bud and Lou in that the story centered around them, not the romantic leads. Unfortunately, production on the picture did not go as smoothly as planned. The shooting schedule during the first half of the film was delayed when Lou fell ill. He left the studio early three days in a row, then missed a full day and a half of work under doctor's orders. The second half of production was delayed due to bad weather and a search for a gas station location. Eventually, the studio just built the gas station set at a cost of $2,500. It was used again in *Pardon My Sarong*.[268]

The supporting cast assembled for the film was one of the team's best. Comedienne Joan Davis, on loan from Fox,[269] had made her debut in Mack Sennett two-reelers and had appeared in quite a few films. She is best known for playing in both the radio and television series *I Married Joan*. She is truly funny in *Hold That Ghost*, so much so that Lou became a bit jealous of her talents. Purportedly, he complained whenever she was given a close-up or good line. When asked about the rumors regarding Lou's jealousy of fellow performers, Paddy Costello replied:

> I don't know anything about that. Again, it's not being on the set eight or 12 hours a day and watching them work, being a part of it that way. I wouldn't see things like that. And it's like he wouldn't come to me, a small kid, and say, "Hey, Paddy, I'm really jealous of that guy 'cause he's so damn funny...." It's like his [IRS problem], is he going to come discuss that with me? Hell, no. My knowledge of that is not an intimate knowledge. It's not what he would have discussed with me. I

never, ever heard him say anything bad about any performer ... everybody that he worked with, he had nothing but, I think, good things to say about. Because they all — a lot of these people — all came up the same way. It was a lot of hard work, you know, working on the burlesque circuit and travelling and really trying hard to hone your craft. And he had a lot of people work for him — buddies that had been on the stage with him. He was good that way — very, very good to people he knew before he became famous. Very, very good, very good. I don't know where something like [stories of his jealousy] would come from. If it's actually true, I don't know.[270]

Two future horror and sci-fi stars appeared in the film. Evelyn Ankers was on the verge of becoming the scream queen of the forties by appearing in a glut of Universal horror films, including *Man Made Monster* (1941), *The Wolf Man* (1941), *The Ghost of Frankenstein* (1942), and *Captive Wild Woman* (1943). Richard Carlson had appeared in the previously mentioned *The Ghost Breakers* and would go on to a prolific career in the 1950s as the star of such science fiction classics as *It Came from Outer Space* (1953), *Creature from the Black Lagoon* (1954) and the strange horror film *The Maze* (1953).

Perennial gangster Marc Lawrence was cast as the "Charlie" of the film's shooting title, while Shemp Howard, one of the original Three Stooges and brother to Moe and Curly, played a bit part as a soda jerk. Howard was another actor who people say provoked Lou's jealousy and supposedly Howard's best stuff from the Abbott and Costello films ended up on the cutting room floor.

During the film's preview, the audience missed the presence of the Andrews Sisters (they had appeared in both *Buck Privates* and *In the Navy*.)[271] This backed up the studio brass, who wanted the film to be more along the lines of *Navy*'s structure and include musical numbers.[272] So, the film's original ending was dropped and a new prologue and epilogue added. Since Joan Davis had returned to Fox and was involved in a new production, she was not able to be in the new footage and her part in the re-takes was written out.[273] The new footage contained musical numbers by the Andrews Sisters, Ted Lewis and His Orchestra, and an appearance by character actor Mischa Auer, whose only previous genre appearance was in *The Monster Walks* (1932). Along with the original ending, the boys' "herd of cows" routine was dropped from the script (but later used in *Ride 'Em Cowboy*).[274] Unfortunately, these new sequences cause most of the plot holes and mistakes in the finished film.

Hired to direct was Arthur Lubin, a no-frills craftsman with a long list of B movies to his credit.[275] He had directed *Buck Privates* and was immediately given *Hold That Ghost* afterwards. In later interviews, Lubin told stories about working with the comedy duo. He said Bud was actually the brighter of the two and was easily able to get Lou back to the script when his ad-libbing went too far. He also said Lou hated to memorize his lines but took direction well. He mentioned the boys enjoyed showing nude pictures of their wives to cast and crew because they were so proud of their women, who had formerly been strippers in burlesque.[276] Budgeted at $190,000 with a 20-day shooting schedule,[277] Lubin went seven days over schedule and more than $10,000 over budget.

The Breen Office was concerned by the gangsters in the script and demanded the character of Moose Matson take only two or three shots at the police (while the police officers could shoot as many times as they liked). This didn't seem to bother the writers, who were more worried about the film not being funny enough. When they saw the finished product, they wanted their names taken off of it (having visualized the movie as being much funnier). When they saw it with a howling audience, however, they realized how funny it truly was.[278]

Like the earlier *Abbott and Costello Meet Frankenstein*, the film opens with an animated title credits sequence. The same sequence (of a ghost chasing the comedians) was used for Olson and Johnson's *Ghost Catchers* (1944).

The first scene takes place at the Chez Glamous nightclub. A shot of a neon outline of Ted Lewis dissolves to the real thing in the first of many directorial flourishes. Lewis sings a song for the crowd and asks his trademark, "Is everybody happy?" A black man in a tuxedo joins Lewis on stage for the next number and Lewis says, "Charlie, my boy!"

Maître d' Gregory is told by a young busboy that the relief waiters have arrived. Grouchy Gregory yells at the nervous young man. "What are you staring at? Ice water!" Already, this character is set up as an antagonist for Abbott and Costello, but his part is so minor he does not live up to the audience's expectations. It is not actor Mischa Auer's fault, though, it's just due to the fact that these scenes were tacked on after the film was completed.

Gregory heads for the kitchen and we overhear Lou's voice coming from inside. It sounds as though Lou is robbing the place. Gregory bursts in and finds the two comedians shooting dice with the help, a definite reminder of the famous dice scene in *Buck Privates*.

Bud and Lou go by the names of Chuck Murray and Ferdy Jones in this film. Chuck explains that the employment agency sent them to the restaurant and Ferdy adds that they used to work at a gas station. Gregory is already angry with them and he orders Ferdy to pull down his coat. When Ferdy does, his vest pops up with an added sound effect, setting up a gag for later in the film.

Gregory tells Ferdy, "One mistake out of you and I'll throw you out!"

"Yes, you will," says Ferdy.

"Yes, I will!" repeats Gregory.

"I said you will," says Ferdy.

Costello used this joke time and time again. One can only wonder why, since it is not all that funny. It is just an example of using the tone of voice to trick someone who is not paying attention to what is actually being said. Bugs Bunny used the same trick repeatedly on Elmer Fudd and Daffy Duck.

Lou gets hit with the door on his way out of the kitchen so he has to catch up to Chuck and Gregory on the club floor. When he arrives he is all excited because he has just seen the Andrews Sisters. Gregory, who has given Bud all the orders, tells him to make a waiter out of Ferdy. He leaves and Ferdy comments, "A snooty sort of a fellow," with a great line reading from Costello.

Chuck instructs Ferdy on pushing a chair in and out for a customer, an obvious set-up for a payoff to come. He also tells Ferdy about showing the checker his slip, which worries Ferdy because he, as he tells Chuck, is not wearing one, another mix-up based on Lou's habit of taking everything literally and recognizing only one definition of a word.

Ted Lewis sings "Me and My Shadow," as an unidentified black man mimics his every movement. Such blatantly racial humor would today be considered politically incorrect, but audiences (and performers) at the time thought nothing of it.

Chuck continues teaching Ferdy how to be a waiter by telling him there are three questions he must be ready to answer. The first is how much is dinner, and the answer is three dollars. If someone says that is too much, then Ferdy should tell the person to talk to the manager. If the person says he will not eat at the restaurant, then Ferdy should tell him that if he doesn't, someone else will. Naturally, when Ferdy waits on his first table, he screws up. He causes a man to fall on the floor by pulling out the chair at the wrong time. The man berates Ferdy:

"Why'd you pull that chair out?" demands the irate patron.
"Three dollars," answers Ferdy.
"I'll report you for this," says the man.
"Go tell the manager."
"Why I oughta punch you in the nose!"
"If you don't, someone else will."

This is followed by Lou's trademark whistle. It is a good set-up, but the joke falls flat and is not all that funny.

Ted Lewis introduces the Andrews Sisters (Maxene, Patty, and Laverne) and they sing a number. All they do is stand in place, sway back and forth, and sing. Their type of entertainment is dated and their appeal has diminished over the years. Many modern video viewers fast-forward through this scene when watching the film (though there are some who watch these pictures because of the memories of such numbers). The comedy team movies were patterned after radio and vaudeville shows in which comedy and music coexisted. Audiences at the time expected the musical numbers. Today, this structure is passé, as is the musical itself.

A wealthy customer, Alderman Birch, arrives and Gregory asks about the man's wife. In a rare bit of risqué humor, Gregory realizes Birch has brought along his mistress, a bubbly young lady who calls him "Daddy." They are given one of Ferdy's tables.

In a stupid bit that drags on without hitting one funny note, Ferdy argues with Birch about serving them some soup. Ferdy wants to bring them the soup but Birch refuses it. When Birch finally agrees to some soup, Ferdy informs them they are all out. The scene does finally become funny when Ferdy tells the young lady to listen to her father. Birch is indignant and tells Ferdy he is not the girl's father. Ferdy is delighted and begins to flirt with the girl. Chuck calls Ferdy away from the table.

Lawyer Bannister (an appropriate name considering how closely it resembles "barrister") arrives and asks where Moose Matson (a notorious gangster) is sitting. Bannister is distracted by Charlie Smith, an oily sort who followed the lawyer to the club. Smith is angry because Moose beat him to a payroll job. Now he wants a cut or he will go to the police. This scene, tacked on after the film was completed, completely contradicts later action and is, therefore, useless. First of all, Smith's dialogue is just meaningless and unnecessary. Secondly, Bannister and Smith are painted as enemies, yet a few minutes later they are working together. Finally, Moose's money (presumably from the payroll job) ends up going to Bud and Lou at the end of the film, meaning they now possess stolen money! Why wouldn't the authorities take it away from them?

Bannister sits down with Moose and tells him the will he drew up for him will hold up in court. He also tells him Smith wants a cut from the payroll job. Moose says Smith must *find* the money before he can get any of it. Bannister asks Moose to tell him where it is, but Moose only says he keeps the money in his head.

Ted Lewis tells everyone to be happy and dance. Birch's girl wants to dance, but Birch will not and they have a fight. Both storm off just as Chuck and Ferdy bring their food. "Eat it yourself!" snarls Birch, so the two take him at his word. They begin to feast on the duck (leading to the obligatory moment when Chuck says "duck" and Ferdy does just that).

"Is everybody happy?" asks Ted, and Ferdy says, "Everybody — me, too!" Instead of carving the duck, he spanks it with his knife. Gregory catches them and ends up with the duck in his face. The dubbing of the next few lines is clumsy: Gregory tells them they are fired and Ferdy says, "Back to our old jobs at the gas station."

Until recently, the print usually shown on television began here, with the boys at the gas station lamenting about being thrown out of the nightclub. According to their uniforms, which say "Chuck and Ferdy's Station," they own the gas station. Why would the boys want to be waiters when they own their own business?

Ferdy apologizes to Chuck and sings like Ted Lewis, using an oil pump as a microphone. Chuck says "Give me that!" so Ferdy takes him literally and squirts him in the face with oil. Chuck slaps him, getting oil on Ferdy's face. In another bout of politically incorrect humor, Ferdy comments on how they both look like "shadows."

Ferdy assures Chuck he will not be a gas station attendant all his life. Chuck scoffs when Ferdy says someday Ted Lewis and the Andrews Sisters will work for him. In a nonsensical line (that is still funny) Ferdy says, "Don't look now but your eye is dripping."

Chuck writes the station prices on a chalkboard — eight gallons for $1.00, not including ethyl. The two do a bit where Ferdy believes "Ethel" to be a real person. In an early draft of the script, Ferdy was to ask Chuck why ethyl was more expensive and Chuck was to reply, "You can go further with ethyl." The Breen Office demanded this line be cut.[279]

A man asks Chuck and Ferdy to park his car for a few hours and Ferdy wildly backs the car into a tight space. It is an amusing effect done by reversing and speeding up footage of someone pulling out of a spot. The angry man says Ferdy should have his license taken away and Chuck replies, "I'll see that he does as soon as he gets one"—a rare throwaway joke for Abbott.

Moose Matson pulls up and asks for some gas. For some reason, the boys try to sell him everything *but* gas. When he finally threatens them, Chuck pumps the gas. Ferdy actually climbs inside Moose's car and begins cleaning the back of it.

In a macabre moment of black comedy, Ferdy finds a cache of pistols and takes one out. He points it at his head and pulls the trigger, but nothing happens. (Obviously, the childlike Ferdy thinks the guns are toys, but the idea is too serious to be funny—similar to the scene in *Pardon My Sarong* in which Abbott tries to talk Costello into committing suicide.) When Ferdy points the gun out the window and pulls the trigger, it goes off, surprising him. It also attracts the attention of the police, who recognize Moose, a wanted criminal. Moose takes off just as Chuck is climbing into the car to retrieve Ferdy, and a car chase ensues.

The police shoot at the car and one of the bullets unties Ferdy's bow tie. A bit of dialogue shows Ferdy to be nothing more than big kid:

"I want to get out of here!" whines Ferdy. "I want to go back to the gas station!"

Moose points the gun at him and demands, "What is it you want?"

"I want my Mama!"

Moose makes Ferdy drive so he can shoot at the cops. Frightened, Ferdy drives like a maniac. Moose is hit by one of the bullets and orders Ferdy to pull over. Dying, Moose asks for Lefty, but Chuck says Lefty is not there. Moose hands the boys a copy of his will. We never learn who Lefty was supposed to be.

As originally scripted, the next scene shows a judge in the probate court ruling Moose's will to be legal. The film, however, cuts to Bannister's office where the lawyer reads the will to the boys. Moose decreed that whoever is with him when the "coppers dim his lights" will be the inheritors of his worldly possessions. But, Bannister tells the boys, there is no evidence of any fortune. Moose always said he kept his money in his head. There is only an old tavern known as the Forrester's Club on what used to be Highway 29. At this point, another bit of business was cut in which Bannister shows the boys an architect's rendering of the club.[280] Chuck is delighted with their new holdings, and Bannister introduces them to his associate, Charlie Smith, who will take them to the property and hand over the keys. Amazingly, these two enemies are now working together.

Bannister shoots Charlie a serious look and introduces the boys. Smith tells them they will take a private bus chartered from Harry Hoskins to the tavern. Ferdy asks if it is not too much trouble and Smith assures him it will be a pleasure to take them for a ride. It is a great line reading from Marc Lawrence, foreshadowing Bela Lugosi's cool remarks to Wilbur in *Abbott and Costello Meet Frankenstein*.

They make plans to meet the next morning, but Ferdy is worried. Outside, he tells Chuck he wants to go back to the gas station. Chuck berates him for not wanting to better himself. Suddenly, gangsters (led by Smith) shoot at the boys, hitting only Ferdy's hat. Ferdy faints.

The next morning, the boys arrive with luggage and groceries to meet Harry Hoskins. Chuck orders Ferdy to help Harry load the bags. Ferdy takes Chuck's suitcase and hurls it over the car onto a passing bus while Chuck, fast talker that he is, tries to impress Harry with the story of their inheritance. Ferdy tells Chuck, "Don't you wish you were goin' south ... that's the way your bag went!"

Chuck and Ferdy learn Harry is expecting other fares. As if on cue, the beautiful Norma Lind shows up. She heads inside a nearby drugstore for some breakfast. Lou seems smitten with the blond. "Sure, we'll wait for you — anything for you," he says.

Chuck asks Ferdy if he is trying to be a cavalier. Where he comes from, Chuck explains, a cavalier is a guy who takes a girl out, wines and dines her, and takes her home without even asking for a kiss. Where Ferdy comes from, his partner answers, a guy like that is called a sucker.

The next to arrive is Camille Brewster, a radio actress, who plows right into Ferdy. (Her name was originally to have been Daisy Brewster.[281]) "Why don't you look where you're going?" growls Ferdy. "You blind or something?" "Blind nothing," replies Camille, "I hit you, didn't I?" It is the first of many effective wisecracks she gets throughout the film. Joan Davis is perfect for the part, and she makes a worthy foil for Costello. It is a shame they did not work together again.

Camille explains who she is and demonstrates her famous scream which opens the "Tales of Terror" radio program. She says she is quitting radio to return to the movies — as an usherette.

Inside the drugstore, the doctor berates soda jerk Shemp Howard for not having freshly squeezed orange juice. The doctor is never given a last name, though some sources refer to him as Dr. Jackson.[282] He explains to the soda jerk that people need vitamin C. People like Norma who, he points out, has a slight pituitary deficiency. He explains that he is doing research into glands and vitamin consumption, but Norma thinks he is feeding her a line. As he fumbles for his credentials, the soda jerk tries to pass off the old orange juice as freshly squeezed. The doc pours it away, so the jerk calls his manager, Mr. Jenkins (a brief cameo by Harry Hayden, who would turn up as Mr. Crandall in *Abbott and Costello Meet the Killer, Boris Karloff*). Before a confrontation can occur, the doctor realizes he is late and rushes to catch the bus — Hoskins' bus. Norma follows.

Charlie Smith finally arrives and privately yells at Harry for picking up extra fares. Smith gets in the vehicle, rudely pushing in front of Camille. Chuck is about to do the same thing when Ferdy stops him. Chuck realizes his mistake, but Ferdy stopped him because he wanted to get in first. Ferdy bumps his head on the car and Chuck says, "Go ahead — ruin the man's car!"

A scene was cut from the script in which the crew stops at a roadside diner for lunch. Ferdy would have asked what was on the menu, to which the cook would have said, "I got a duck in the icebox." Ferdy would then have replied, "Go ahead. We'll wait till you come back."[283]

On the road, Norma attempts conversation with the doctor, who is preoccupied with a book. Ferdy flirts with a nervous Camille. She asks if he is married, then asks Chuck, "He's old enough, ain't he?" Ferdy says he is old enough because he plays games — he plays post office. Camille says that is a kid's game but Ferdy says, "Not the way I play it." Costello used this joke time and again throughout his career.

Night falls, along with a thunderstorm, and the car arrives at the tavern, a wonderfully spooky setting. Seemingly falling apart at the seams, the joint is a perfect haunted house. In fact, Camille thinks it looks like the setting for one of her radio dramas, "The Death of the Howling Corpse." In a great moment easily overlooked, Chuck shushes her and points to Ferdy as if to say, "Not in front of him!"

Harry says the roads might be bad and suggests spending the night at the tavern. Everyone (except Camille) agrees this would be for the best. They exit the car one by one and Ferdy comments, "It's a good thing we have all these groceries." A shot of Harry finds his eyes suddenly flashing with menace, making for a creepy moment.

On the porch, Chuck finds that his key does not work. Ferdy decides to batter down the door and takes a running start. Of course, the door opens and Ferdy goes flying through the room and into the wall. Cobwebs cover him like a wedding veil.

With everyone preoccupied, Harry is able to drive away with their luggage. Charlie explains it is the old wildcat bus racket — collect the fares then strand the passengers and make off with their luggage. Lou yells after the crook and Camille laments the loss of her nightgown and her new pair of "mules." Lou takes her literally and asks why the board of health does not say anything about Camille keeping a pair of mules under her bed. Before the confusion can continue, a flash of lightning scares the two inside the tavern to join the rest.

The doctor starts a fire while Charlie goes down in the cellar to "rustle up some real heat." The lights go out. Chuck searches for a switch and says, "I feel a damp opening." He actually has his hand in Ferdy's mouth. Meanwhile, downstairs, Charlie searches for Moose's money.

Norma admires the doctor's fire — and his smile. But the doctor, stereotypically naive, is unable to catch the romantic drift of the conversation, which frustrates Norma.

Camille and Chuck look in the cupboards, both hitting Ferdy with the cupboard doors. Ferdy tries the sink but the faucet just makes a loud noise. Ferdy plays with the faucet and does a bad imitation of a choo-choo train, like a little child would do. Chuck slaps him. He gives him a bucket and tells him to go outside and get water from the pump. Bud and Lou do a variation of the "I'll search in here — you search out there" routine before Ferdy admits he is afraid to go outside by himself. Chuck tells him to talk to himself if he is afraid to be alone. Ferdy says he gets too many stupid answers.

Outside, Lou starts in on his scared schtick, which he will continue with the remainder of the film. Finding the pump, he pumps the handle furiously but no water comes out. Predictably, when he looks in the nozzle the water comes splashing out into his face.

Charlie continues to search the cellar. Chuck opens the door and tells him to come up for supper. Hands creep out from the furnace and grab Charlie around the neck. Choking him furiously, the hands drag Charlie back into the furnace. This is the scariest moment in the whole film (and one lifted from any old dark house thriller).

At dinner, Ferdy rudely reaches for some soup only to be slapped by Chuck. "Don't reach!" admonishes Chuck. "You want something, ask for it. You've got a tongue, haven't you?"

"I can reach further with my hands," replies Ferdy. This joke was another of those used numerous times throughout Abbott and Costello's careers.

Camille notices Charlie is missing (she calls him "tall, dark, and gruesome"), so Chuck orders Ferdy to go to the cellar and call him. Frightened, Ferdy painstakingly makes his way downstairs, calling "Oh, Charlie" (hence the film's original title). He sees Smith's flashlight on the floor and runs back to the table.

Ferdy tells everyone what he saw and, amazingly, they all decide to keep eating! Apparently no one really cares about poor Charlie Smith, since instead of searching for him they opt to sample the soup. There follows some amusing reaction shots as everyone makes a "yuck" face after tasting the soup. Camille has the best reaction: she pushes the soup away and calmly says, "Just like mother used to make. It stinks."

The doctor thinks the water could be bad. Chuck says, "I'll find out; taste it, Ferdy," a precursor to his bit in *Abbott and Costello Meet Dr. Jekyll and Mr. Hyde* when he tells Lou to "Follow me," then pushes him ahead. Ferdy is about to try a glass of water when Chuck adds, "It might be poison." Ferdy is now scared, but Chuck says, "What are you worrying about?" Costello's reaction sells the scene. Through a subtle gesture he seems to be saying, "Yeah, he's right." The bit that follows is good, too. Shaking uncontrollably, Ferdy is unable to bring the glass to his lips. So he holds the glass at the end of his tie with one hand, and with the other pulls on the tie so that the glass is brought to his mouth. Genius!

The water is bad, which intrigues the doctor. Before the new prologue and epilogue were added, the water subplot was to play an important role in the story. But as the film is now, that subplot never pans out.

Norma wishes a band was present so they could dance between courses, foreshadowing the film's conclusion. Chuck sees an old record player and cranks it up, playing a waltz. Norma asks the doctor if he would like to dance. Richard Carlson actually delivers a good gag line when he says, "I'd love to. I must learn sometime."

Ferdy asks Camille to dance and she graciously accepts. In the comic highpoint of the film, she and Costello perform a hilarious duet. During their routine, Ferdy drops Camille, steps in a bucket of water (not once but twice), slips and slides, and destroys a piano. He and Camille get in a splashing battle, dousing each other with water until both are soaked. Camille gets her derriere stuck in the bucket, and the dance concludes with Ferdy beating on the bucket like a bongo while Camille wiggles her tail feathers. The scene is hilarious, enhanced by the cutaways to Bud who reacts appropriately to Costello's destructiveness. Amazingly, the scene was filmed with Richard Carlson and Evelyn Ankers seen clearly watching in the background. How they kept a straight face is anyone's guess. Nevertheless, the scene works beautifully, thanks to the flawless timing of the two seasoned comics. In fact, the comic ballet was one of Davis' specialties,[284] and Lou supposedly thought she was stealing the scene from him (which she was).

The two dry off and Ferdy says, "I'm like a little flower after a heavy rain — I'm droopin'," one of his nonsensical but funny lines. Now that they have all finished eating, the party suddenly remember that Charlie Smith is still missing and decide to search for him. Ferdy pulls a lamp off of the fireplace and a secret passage opens to a hidden room. The room was a speakeasy, used by the club during prohibition. Camille says it reminds her of the secret door in "The Case of the Mummy's Claw." (The writers should have given her titles that were actual Universal horror films or mysteries. It would have been funnier had she said, "This reminds me of the secret door in *The House of Fear*," or "This is just like the *Secret of the Blue Room*.")

In the dialogue that follows, Chuck and Ferdy reveal they whooped it up during prohibition times. Camille says she was too young to be out drinking in those days (most likely a lie), then panics when she sees Smith's carnation on the floor. Instead of screaming, Camille, a professional screamer, is only able to gasp in horror.

There follows an abrupt cut to someone going down into the basement. The short shot is unnecessary and was obviously used to make a transition between scenes. The film cuts back to the men deciding to finally search for Smith. The girls are told to stay there, and Ferdy joins them. When Chuck tells him "You're not a girl," Ferdy says he played with dolls when he was young. This bit, and the accompanying dialogue, hints at a homosexual side of Lou that was exploited more fully in *Abbott and Costello Meet Frankenstein*.

The men search the cellar and Lou looks inside the furnace. He sees the outline of a man and two glowing eyes. The man blows out Lou's candle. Lou's facial expressions in this scene are priceless — he in no way wants to open the door and look in the furnace, yet he has to. He panics after seeing the man and tells the others someone has blown out his candle. Chuck tells him it was the wind and Ferdy says, "Since when does the wind eat garlic?" anticipating the joke in *Abbott and Costello Meet*

Frankenstein when Bud tells him the noise he heard was the wind. "It should get oiled," says Lou.

Meanwhile, Norma and Camille reluctantly decide they should help by searching upstairs. Heading up the staircase, Camille is reminded of a scene she played in "The Case of the Haunted House." Norma remarks on how funny it is that Camille can scream on cue in her radio plays, but when she is *really* scared, nothing comes out. Camille starts to gasp again and Norma chuckles. But Camille is truly frightened, this time by two eyes glowing in the darkness. Norma sees them and lets out one of the screams Evelyn Ankers became famous for. This payoff for Camille's screaming bit comes too soon and is not funny enough.

The men come up to investigate. In a hilarious moment, Camille tells them they saw a fiend with fangs and makes an ugly face to imitate it. Ferdy yells "Ooh! Ooh!" When Camille makes the face, Ferdy makes for the door. The mere suggestion of the fiend is enough to make him panic! Of course, the fiend is revealed to be nothing more than an owl, an old gag that would be repeated in *Abbott and Costello Meet the Killer*. (Costello even answers the owl when it says "Who, Who" in both films.)

The group now decides to go upstairs together, but Ferdy breaks down and refuses—he is too scared. Chuck argues, then relents, and Ferdy is left at the bottom of the staircase. The others start down a long hallway and look into the bedrooms. This hallway is another wonderfully atmospheric set, reminiscent of a similar one in Paul Leni's *The Cat and the Canary* (1927).

Meanwhile, Ferdy notices a creepy statue of a woman and speaks to it. "How do you do? Are you the hatcheck girl?" A hairy arm reaches out and snatches Ferdy's hat. This sends Ferdy upstairs in a flash. This is an amusing gag, setting up an even funnier payoff later on.

Upstairs, Ferdy tries to tell Chuck what happened but Chuck will not listen. If you watch Costello closely, he pantomimes what happened to Evelyn Ankers, who coolly ignores him. This is easily missed but worth a chuckle.

The gang checks out one of the rooms and starts making it up for bedtime. Ferdy helps Camille and Chuck make one of the beds. They do a bit where Camille keeps telling Ferdy to slip the sheet under the mattress. Ferdy takes her literally and puts the entire sheet under the mattress instead of just tucking it in. Chuck and Camille get angry at Ferdy. Ferdy gets frustrated and jumps on the bed. It collapses. All in all, the bit is not paced very well and seems to drag on too long. Costello's reaction shots are poorly placed in the scene and do not match up well. But the payoff is good — Camille says, "Well, looks like we're gonna sleep together," and Lou replies with his trademark whistle through the teeth. It is impossible not to pick up on the thoughts going through his head.

Chuck, Ferdy, and the doctor decide to look for other rooms and say good night to the girls. Chuck tells Ferdy to put one of the lamps on the highboy. Ferdy asks him what he said and when Chuck replies "highboy," Ferdy says, "Hi ya Chuck." The reference is dated, and today the joke does not work.

Chuck and Ferdy find another room, and the initials "MM" on the bed tell them it's Moose's room. Ferdy asks what happens when one pulls the cord hanging by the bed. Chuck explains that you pull it to get your breakfast. Ferdy pulls it and says "Ham and eggs." A curtain opens, revealing a door. Chuck tells Ferdy to open the door but Ferdy says he knows what happens in those mystery movies — every time you open a door, a dead body falls out. Chuck proves he is wrong by opening the door, revealing nothing but an empty closet. Ferdy is ashamed: "I'm gettin' to be a real big sissy." He slams the door and Charlie Smith's body, bound and gagged, falls out from behind the curtain. Ferdy faints. Chuck brings him around but Ferdy faints again.

Chuck drags Ferdy out of the room and yells for the doctor. Everyone comes running and Chuck says, "It's murder!" Camille thinks Ferdy has been killed and she faints. Ferdy come to and thinks Camille is dead and faints again. This is one of the film's best bits, with the music perfectly matching the actions.

The doctor examines Smith's body and tells the others Smith was strangled. Ferdy asks if that is serious. "The man is dead!" yells Chuck. Ferdy says, "Oh, that's serious." They used this blackly comic joke often, specifically in *Abbott and Costello Meet Frankenstein*.

There is a pounding at the front door, so the group heads downstairs to answer the door. Two men come in saying they are police officers. Chuck tells them he and Ferdy own the place, having inherited it from Moose Matson. Ferdy adds, "We were very close to him at the time of his surmise." The doctor tells them a dead man is upstairs and Ferdy explains there was something stuffed in his mouth.

"He had a gag in his mouth!" says Chuck.

"If he did, he didn't have a chance to tell it." replies Ferdy.

Chuck and the Doctor then lead the cops upstairs, but the cops eye Ferdy suspiciously, backing him up to the statue. After everyone goes up, Ferdy asks the statue if it knows what happened to his hat. Plop! The hairy arm replaces the hat, sending Lou screaming up the stairs. It is a good capper to the earlier joke.

Upstairs, Smith's body has disappeared. The cops decide to look around the tavern and advise everyone to leave. Ferdy wants to follow the advice because he is afraid to sleep in Moose's bedroom. Chuck decides to find him a new room. The doctor heads downstairs to have some warm milk before retiring.

The cops find the secret passageway in the speakeasy. A scene was deleted here in which the two cops were revealed to be gangsters named Irondome and Strangler, who were there to meet with Rosy, Snak-Eyes, Glum, and High Collar. They would decide to scare away the intruders and quickly find the money because Lefty and his boys had escaped from jail and were on their way to the tavern.[285] This scene should have been retained. It would have made the story a lot clearer by explaining who the gangsters are at the climax, and what was meant by Moose's cryptic mention of Lefty when he died.

Chuck finds Ferdy a new room with a private bath. Ferdy says, "I won't take a bath. No one's going to catch me with my ... coat off." Chuck leaves Ferdy to sleep in his own room and Ferdy gets undressed. Just as in the later *The Noose Hangs High*, Ferdy's nightclothes are revealed to be under his regular clothes. After neatly folding his pants, he sloppily tosses them on a coatrack, then leaves the room. He has no idea he has tripped a switch, and when he is gone, wall panels slide open and tables flip over to transform the bedroom into a casino—complete with slots, a roulette wheel, and even a bed that becomes a dice table.

After washing up, Ferdy returns and lies down on the dice table. What follows is the famous changing room routine, a variation of the moving candle bit where Lou experiences weird occurrences that disappear when Bud enters the room. It takes Ferdy a few moments to realize his room has changed. (Actually, this scene is somewhat spooky due to its use of music and lighting.) Ferdy screams and runs out, taking his pants with him—which causes the room to return to normal.

At first, Ferdy thinks he is dreaming as he tries to explain what happened to Chuck. Returning to the room, they find it normal and Chuck tells Ferdy he is imagining things. "Chuck," says Ferdy, "I can't imagine things like that, I'm not that clever." Chuck tries to placate Ferdy by pretending to see all the gambling devices, but he succeeds in calming Ferdy only by switching rooms with him.

In Chuck's room, Ferdy again puts his pants on the clothes hook, triggering a lever that now causes Chuck's room to turn into a casino. Ferdy checks to make sure his old room has not changed and retrieves the rest of his clothes. Upon returning, he is shocked to see that the new room has changed. When he rushes to get Chuck, he grabs his pants and the room changes back to normal. Chuck tells him to stop working himself up into one of his frenzies. Ferdy says he has not made any "frenzies" since he's been in the place.

Chuck drags him back to the room with a chokehold and forces Ferdy to go to bed. He puts Ferdy's clothes on the rack and the room changes with Ferdy in it. Ferdy runs out and grabs Chuck but, of course, the room changes back. Exasperated, Ferdy cries out, "Did you ever?" then decides to find his own bedroom.

Norma goes downstairs to visit the doctor, who is busy testing the tavern's water. Norma attempts to flirt but the doctor absentmindedly answers "Huh?" to every question. Norma takes off the doctor's glasses to admire his eyes and he almost kisses her, only to remember his experiment. Furious, Norma stomps upstairs without hearing the doctor compliment her on her beauty. This is a nice, romantic scene, not nearly as intrusive as the romantic subplots of the other contemporary Abbott and Costello movies.

In a new bedroom, Ferdy tries to sleep but is too frightened. In a scene right out of *The Cat and the Canary*, hands creep out of the wall and try to choke him but they just miss. A knock at the door distracts Ferdy and when he answers it, he finds no one is there. The door closes behind him and Ferdy finds he is locked out. He rushes to get Chuck, rousing his partner out of bed. A great throwaway gag has Chuck leaving to check Ferdy's room and Ferdy climbing into Chuck's bed. Chuck angrily grabs him and they return to Ferdy's room.

The door is now unlocked, but the room inside has been ransacked. Chuck is angry because he thinks Ferdy did it. After slapping Ferdy, he turns away and Ferdy points his finger in Chuck's back to protest. Chuck thinks Ferdy pulled a knife on him and slaps him. This scene does not work. Chuck is too quick to assume Ferdy is behind the mess when there is no provocation for such an assumption. And he should know Ferdy would never pull a knife on him.

A hand opens the door to the girls' room where we find them still awake. Camille decides she wants some warm milk and asks if the doctor is still downstairs. Norma says, "His body is," which frightens Camille until Norma adds that the doctor's mind is a million miles away.

On the stairs, a ghost appears behind Camille. Although the ghost is obviously a man in a sheet, it is still effective due to the way he comes up behind Camille on the steps. Camille hears the ghost's footsteps echoing behind her as she descends, so she tries a trick. When she reaches the bottom of the staircase, she does a little "shave-and-a-haircut" two-step and the ghost taps a reply. Camille turns, screams, and faints. The panicked ghost runs upstairs. This scene is similar to one with Costello and John Dierkes in the later *Abbott and Costello Meet Dr. Jekyll and Mr. Hyde*.

The ghost runs into Ferdy's room and hides in bed with him. Camille's scream brings everyone running and Camille tells them she saw a ghost — with fangs (just like in the owl scene). The doctor is appropriately disbelieving when he says, "What — again?"

Meanwhile, Ferdy thinks Chuck has crawled in bed with him to apologize (what kind of apology is he expecting?). When he sees it is a ghost, he runs to the top of the staircase. "Hey, hey!" he yells. "He's in my room! — in my bed! — pulling the covers over his head! Come on!" Costello's delivery makes this a funny moment.

A gag from Camille keeps everyone downstairs just long enough so they miss seeing the ghost: "I'm afraid to have you go up there ... without me." When they reach Ferdy's room, all that is left of the ghost is a white sheet. "There's your ghost," says the doctor. Norma thinks it is all a joke and Chuck wonders why everything always happens to Ferdy. Ferdy realizes he is undressed and sheepishly slips away.

Discussing the matter, the group decides someone is trying to scare them away. They also realize the detectives have disappeared. The men decide to search for the detectives while the women get ready to leave.

Downstairs, the doctor expresses his regret at being unable to finish his water experiment, since he was on the verge of an answer. Later, he will tell the boys that he has solved the water mystery, so somewhere along the line he must have finished the experiment. Anyway, the whole water subplot becomes moot thanks to the changes made in the film prior to release.

The doctor and Chuck split up to look for the detectives. Chuck sets the frightened Ferdy down at a table with a map and tells him to find the best way back to town. Ferdy is worried about the ghost coming back, but Chuck says the ghost is just a rumor. Ferdy answers, "I don't care if he's the landlord!"

Chuck tells Ferdy to call him if he needs him by hollering "Oh,

Chuck!" Ferdy tries it before Chuck has even left the room, then asks, "What kept you?" When Chuck leaves, Ferdy realizes he is alone and says, "Oh, Chuck," increasing the volume until he is screaming. Chuck runs in and the frightened Ferdy tells him not to wait for him to yell "Oh, Chuck" anymore, but to come back on the "Oh."

Camille comes in, so Chuck has her sit with Ferdy and look at the map. What follows is the moving candle scene. The premise is the same as in the changing room scene, only this time Camille participates. Ferdy continually sees a candle move back and forth and up and down but Camille is always distracted. Frightened beyond belief, Ferdy cannot get her to look at the candle, he can only sputter and mumble. Finally, Ferdy calls for Chuck; but when Chuck comes in, the phenomenon has stopped and Camille is unable to back up Ferdy's story because she has not seen anything. Much of the humor comes from Lou's scared routine — he seems to know exactly how long to drag out his gestures and his pantomime. He also delivers some good lines. When Bud tells him not to be so scared and that he is not alone, Lou replies, "No, not much."

A ghost (again a gangster in a sheet) enters, unseen by Ferdy and Camille. He stands behind the two comics and slaps Ferdy. Ferdy tells Camille not to slap him, but she says she did not do it. The ghost then slaps Camille, whacking her pretty hard. She gets angry at Ferdy and warns him not to slap her again. "And you're supposed to be a boy scout..." she says tearfully. When Ferdy says he did not do it, they realize a third person is in the room. The ghost covers Ferdy with the sheet as he puts out the candles. In the dark, Ferdy grabs what he thinks is the ghost and says he will lift up the sheet and see who it really is. The lights come on, showing an embarrassed Camille walloping Ferdy. The gag is quite risqué for the time.

Chuck and the doctor come in and Ferdy explains what happened. The doctor decides to check on Norma. Chuck thinks the crooks in the house are after Moose's bankroll and explains to Camille that Moose kept the money "in his head." Ferdy points to a moose head on the wall and says, "You mean in that thing?" Now Chuck has to explain to Ferdy that this was just a figure of speech.

Usually, Bud and Lou's verbal routines hedge on the fact that Lou takes everything literally and confuses the meanings of words. The roles seem to switch here when they launch into a routine about figures of speech. Ferdy says he knows what a figure of speech is; it is like "water went under the bridge." Chuck says, "What bridge?" He scrutinizes every example Ferdy subsequently provides, and Camille even gets in on the act. When Ferdy offers, "gone with the wind," she asks, "What wind?" The bit is drawn out way too long and does not quite work simply because the role reversal does not fit into character. Plus, it is dumb — Chuck explains what a figure of speech is then turns around and ignores his own words by quizzing Ferdy on his examples.

The bit is interrupted by the film shifting to the doctor checking on a pouting Norma. She is angry with the doctor for ignoring her advances, and they argue. A cutaway shows a hand opening the door to the room. When they cut back to the doctor and Norma, he has lost his glasses — an error in continuity. Norma is in the process of telling the doctor she does not need his protection when the picture frame behind them moves and a hand with a knife emerges. The doctor wrestles with the hand and it disappears. What follows is the worst dialogue exchange in the film:

> DOCTOR: Darling, are you hurt?
> NORMA: No, dear.
> DOCTOR: Darling, you called me dear.
> NORMA: Dear, you called me darling.

After this disgusting display, they kiss. It is so passionate the two do not notice the knives being thrown at them. (They do not hit them, of course, just the wall behind them.)

Downstairs, Ferdy is still arguing with Chuck and Camille over figures of speech. He mentions, "never the twain shall meet." Camille asks, "What twain?" and Ferdy replies, "The twain on twack thwee." He has reached the end of his rope and he asks what started this argument. Camille reminds him that he thought money was hidden in the moose head. Ferdy decides to prove there is no money inside and, standing on a chair, puts his hand inside the moose head.

Costello has some good lines here as he talks to the moose head. Referring to his hand, he says, "This one's going in; this is the one I eat with," an ad-lib. When his hand gets stuck, he cries out, "I'll never join your lodge," also an ad-lib.[286]

Naturally, Ferdy has found Moose's money, but he pulls it out without even realizing what he is doing (he thinks the tongue is peeling). Chuck and Camille become ecstatic at the sight of all the cash. When Ferdy is finished, he is ready to argue but Chuck says, "No more arguments!

Ferdy, I love you!" Ferdy blushes and says, "He loves me," displaying the homosexual side of his character once more.

Ferdy finally realizes they are rich and goes nuts. Norma and the doctor rejoin the group and Chuck fills them in on what has happened. Suddenly, a crook holding a gun enters and demands the cash. "I've been hunting that dough for weeks!" says the crook, a flunky who worked for Moose and does not want to see someone else "get the gravy." Chuck, Ferdy, and the doctor grab the crook and knock him out. Ferdy is left to drag out the body.

Chuck declares that they are now "sitting on top of the world." In an apt reference to their earlier routine, Ferdy says, "That's a figure of speech," to which a new voice adds, "Just like 'reach for the sky.'" A gang of crooks has entered the scene, presumably the ones who have been trying to scare them. According to the deleted scenes, they could be Lefty and his gang, but one can't be sure. Bannister never shows up again; we do not know which were the fake detectives; the mystery is never solved; motives are never made clear. Thanks to all the cutting, the loose ends are never tied up. But no one seems to mind and, in truth, most viewers won't care when watching the film. It is too fast-paced and funny; there is no time to stop and think about what is going on.

The gangsters order Ferdy to hand over the money and insultingly call him fatty. Chuck needlessly informs Ferdy they are referring to him. Ferdy says, "Fatty? I lost 43 pounds since I've been in the place." In a rare moment of courage, Ferdy knocks the gun from a gangster's hand, grabs the bag of money, and races upstairs. Chuck and the doctor attempt to stop the other crooks.

Ferdy runs up the stairs in fast motion. The gangsters follow and shoot at him in the hall. Ferdy hides in Moose's bedroom. The gangsters follow. They open the closet but Ferdy is not inside. Thinking he is behind the curtain, they shoot at it, causing the body of Charlie Smith to fall out. Ferdy comes out of hiding and says, "He come back again." The gangsters seem shocked by the appearance of Smith's body, which shows that they did not kill him. He was apparently killed by the first crook, the one knocked out by our heroes.

Ferdy runs out. The two gangsters order the third to look after the body while they chase Ferdy. They run downstairs. Ferdy emerges from beneath a sheet in the hall and starts to sneak away. The gangsters return upstairs, causing Ferdy to run into one of the rooms. Presumably, it is the same room, but the gangster left behind to take care of the body is gone—as is the body. (We never see them leave.) Ferdy hides in the closet, which now holds the body of Harry Hoskins—a body not there a few moments earlier when the gangsters were looking for Ferdy. These errors are just plain sloppy and show that there was not a lot of thought going into the shooting of these climactic scenes.

Ferdy emerges from the closet dazed. He shambles into the hall, where the gangsters shoot at him. They chase him through one of the bedrooms where, in the process, the hat rack is knocked over. The room changes into a casino which distracts the gangsters—one of them even gets stuck in the bed as it becomes a dice board.

Ferdy slides down the banister and flies into the wall, a stunt performed by Lou's brother, Pat Costello. He starts back up the stairs only to meet the gangsters halfway. Ferdy then single-handedly beats up all the gangsters. It seems out of character to have Lou be so good in a fight, but again the fast pace keeps one from noticing.

Chuck has Ferdy throw him the money. Soon, he and the doctor are brawling with the crooks. Ferdy disappears out of the room and imitates a police siren. The crooks think the siren is real and take off. Ferdy enters through the front door with a big grin and Camille exclaims, "My hero!" Originally, the gangsters were to tie everyone up only to have crooks named Big Fink and Little Fink show up. The two gangs were then going to fight until the police arrived. Another deleted scene had the cast keeping the crooks at bay by throwing phonograph records at them.[287]

With all the crooks gone and morning upon them, the tavern is much less scary. Chuck and Ferdy count their money, with Ferdy doing the old "one for you, one for me, two for you, one two for me" trick, a routine that seems more appropriate for Bugs Bunny.

Somehow the doctor finished his experiment, because he tells the boys the tavern's water has great therapeutic value. He advises them to open a health resort. "The water here will make sick people feel like dancing." Chuck and Ferdy decide not only to do that but to also make it a nightclub; then they can hire Ted Lewis and the Andrews Sisters.

In the original conclusion, the money turned out to be counterfeit, so the water subplot would have been more important. The hotel would have been turned into a posh resort with the doctor, Norma, and Camille on staff—with Camille acting as staff dietician.[288] The ending had Chuck and Ferdy telling an elderly guest named Mrs. Giltedge to pull the bell cord if she needs anything. Ferdy would demonstrate, revealing that old closet out of which would pop the body of Charlie Smith. The movie would finish on a close-up of Camille screaming.[289]

The film actually ends at Chuck and Ferdy's nightclub on opening night. Ted Lewis is there asking, "Is everybody happy?" The house is packed and Chuck and Ferdy, clad in tuxedos, survey the crowd. Chuck tells Ferdy to make sure every dollar goes in the cash register; he does not want to check up and find Ferdy short. Naturally, Ferdy throws in a gag and says, "Wait a minute — what's my size got to do with it?"

The doctor and Norma show up, postponing their honeymoon so they can attend the grand opening. Both will be working for the boys at the resort. Norma asks what happened to Camille and Ferdy says they had a runaway marriage: "She bought the license and I run away." This is right in line with a Costello characterization. His characters love women and love to play the field but shy away from commitment. On their radio shows, Costello would often make jokes such as, "Marriage is like a cafeteria — you take what you want, then pay for it later," or "Marriage is a three ring circus — the engagement ring, the wedding ring, the suffer-ring."

Ferdy opens the cash register and realizes there is a bell, foiling his money-laundering scheme. Chuck catches him and angrily warns him to keep his hands out of the till. Waiters come up and bring the bills, and Ferdy tucks the money inside his tux. A bit with Bobby Barber as a waiter that would have appeared here was dropped. Stills of Costello signing Barber's bald head still turn up occasionally.[290] This was the film where Abbott and Costello first met Bobby Barber and he quickly became their off-set stooge.

Gregory, the maître d' from the opening, shows up as one of the waiters. He was sent from the same employment agency that sent Chuck and Ferdy to his club. Ferdy takes the opportunity to humiliate Gregory, including getting Gregory's vest to pop up in his face. Strangely, Gregory still gets the upper hand over Ferdy in this scene. Ferdy barks orders at him until finally Gregory barks back, making Ferdy back down.

Ted Lewis introduces the Andrews Sisters and they sing the song "Aurora." The Breen Office, on reading the script, objected to a line from this song that said, "I'll give you this and give you that," citing sexual suggestiveness. Another line, "Is it me or just my money," proved offensive to Latin Americans, according to the office's South American expert. But since the song was already a hit in South America, no changes were made.[291]

Chuck checks up on Ferdy later in the night and wants to look in the register to see how well they are doing. Ferdy tries to distract him by pointing out some pretty girls but Chuck stands firm. When he opens the drawer, Chuck finds it empty. Ferdy tries to run away but Chuck chases after him and drags him back into frame. There is a strange cut here and a voice saying, "Ohhh." It sounds like Ted Lewis but it could be either Abbott or Costello. I like to think it is actually a real ghost haunting the tavern.

In a final nod to the running gag, Chuck slaps Ferdy for taking the money, causing his vest to again pop open — this time revealing all the money. Ferdy looks down and says, "Now who put that there?" Fade out.

Hold That Ghost, the first film to truly showcase Lou Costello's flair for pantomime,[292] was a success. In fact, audiences found Costello's scared reactions so funny that Universal inserted a spook-house scene into the team's next picture, a service comedy called *Keep 'Em Flying*. The scene, in which Lou gets lost in a funhouse and meets up with a gorilla, had nothing to do with the rest of the picture but satisfied fans who wanted to see a frightened Costello.

In a sense, *Hold That Ghost* is a one-joke picture based on the old "scare 'em" principle where villains attempt to scare the comedians out of the old house.[293] But this is the set-up for most of the old dark house spoofs. The old dark house genre usually had a group of people trapped in an old house or mansion looking for some kind of treasure. A masked killer (one of their own number) tries to scare away the others or kills them off one by one through the use of secret passageways and scare tactics (such as fake ghosts). Oftentimes, the house already has a reputation for being haunted (upon which the killer capitalizes), but, in the end, all supernatural manifestations are explained away. This kind of picture was popular during the silent era and at the rise of the talkie. Films like *Dracula* and *Frankenstein* in 1931 bravely forced the audience to accept the supernatural events as real from the outset and did not explain them away as hoaxes. By this time, the old dark house genre had begun to spoof itself, making the main character a funnyman whose frightened antics created an amount of comedy equaling the amount of horror in the film.

Naturally, this type of movie lends itself well to comedians looking for new vehicles. Bob Hope, the Bowery Boys, the Ritz Brothers, Laurel and Hardy, the Three Stooges, Hugh Herbert, and many other comics all did old dark house comedies of one type or another at some point in their careers. Many did quite a few. It is only natural Universal would place Abbott and Costello in such a setting for their first foray into horror-comedy.

Strangely enough, the film in some ways fits into the pattern the boys established in their "Meet the Monsters" series. Naturally, no one but Costello sees the supernatural goings-on, and he is disbelieved by Abbott (although Camille, also playing a comic part, sees some ghosts herself). The villains engage in a complicated plot and try to do away with Abbott and Costello in order to get what they want. (Complicated might be an understatement — a multitude of loose ends and mistakes never explained constitute the film's major flaw.) Although there is no femme fatale out to use Lou, he does attract the attentions of Camille. With Norma interested in the doctor and Camille flirting with Lou ("He's old enough, ain't he?"), Bud is again left with no one. Unlike in future films, he does not seem to mind. He is content to remain asexual, interested only in making a better life for he and Ferdy. (Even at the film's end, Chuck is more interested in seeing how much money they have made than he is in looking at all the pretty girls.) The film's climax has the comic world (Abbott and Costello) defeating the horror world (the gangsters), but the original ending would have seen the horror world triumphant. *Meet Frankenstein* possessed the twist of having the Invisible Man show up; *Meet the Invisible Man* saw Costello end up with his feet on backwards after turning invisible; and *Meet Dr. Jekyll* featured the creepy scene in which nearly all of Scotland Yard turns into monsters. *Hold That Ghost* would have had a similarly dark conclusion in which Costello opens a closet to find the body of Charlie Smith popping up again — a far superior ending to what was actually used.

Part of the aforementioned pattern has either Abbott or Costello becoming the monster at some point in the film. *Hold That Ghost* arguably contains a moment like this. The gangsters spend the film trying to scare everyone out of the tavern using ghosts. (The thing Ferdy seems to fear the most.) In the end, Costello scares the gangsters away by imitating a police siren (the thing the thugs fear the most). By turning the tables, he goes from scare-ee to scare-er, and hence becomes the title goon.

Hold That Ghost has no deep meanings or themes; it is, as were most of the old dark house comedies, just plain fun. There are not as many quotable lines for buffs as in some of their other films, but the high energy and fast pace of the picture make up for it. Much of the humor in the picture comes from the anticipation of the gags to come,²⁹⁴ especially with the moving candle and changing room bits.

The film also shows off to best advantage the main idea behind the team's verbal gags: Lou Costello has so many arguments with Bud Abbott (and others) because he takes everything that is said literally. A word cannot have two meanings in Costello's universe. So, he misinterprets such common phrases as "He has a gag in his mouth," "Slip it under the mattress," and "Show him your slip." This leads to an underlying feeling that there is no difference between reality and fantasy, or at least the unreal world created through words. In our daily speech we use similes and metaphors to compare and contrast things but in the Abbott and Costello world, similes and metaphors do not exist. Something cannot be like another thing or stand for another thing, it has to be only the thing it is. This is reflected throughout the entire film. It is why when Moose Matson says he keeps his money in his head, the money is kept in a moose head. It is why Chuck and Camille argue with Ferdy over figures of speech demanding he give proof for each figure of speech he mentions. It is why Costello becomes so confused and thinks he is dreaming when his room changes suddenly into a casino.

Reviews at the time were mostly favorable. *The Motion Picture Herald* said, "It is doubted if any two comedians ever got so many laughs in one picture any time, any where." *Motion Picture Daily* felt the film was "by far the corniest comedy the Abbott and Costello duo has committed ... 'corniest' is, in this case, a synonym for best." The *New York Times* felt the boys were "immensely funny" but also felt the film was too long and was slowed down by the musical numbers. And the *New York Morning Telegraph* said "*Hold That Ghost* is good, rowdy, risible slapstick. But it should have been better Abbott and Costello."²⁹⁵

Modern reviews are also favorable. Jim Mulholland admires the film's "fine, eerie atmosphere,"²⁹⁶ and says it is the "team's best film next to *Buck Privates*."²⁹⁷ The *Creature Features Movie Guide* says, "There are a few funny moments amidst the total nonsense."²⁹⁸ Ted Okuda wrote: "In the field of scare comedy, no one surpassed Bud Abbott and Lou Costello, Universal's top box office attraction of the 1940s." He adds: "*Hold That Ghost* ranks as one of the team's best, although it suffers from the same segmentized structure that mars most of their early pictures (there's several entertaining but unnecessary musical interludes). But the comedy routines are first rate, relying heavily on Costello's hilarious scared reactions."²⁹⁹ Leonard Maltin calls the film "prime" with a "fine cast" and picks the moving candle scene as the movie's highlight.[300] The *Video Movie Guide* rates the film as a "super comedy" and adds, "You may have to watch this one a few times to catch all the gags."[301] *VideoHound's Complete Guide to Cult Flicks* praises the screenplay: "Screenwriters Robert Lees and Fred Rinaldo crafted a solid comedy script for the team (with the usual special material by regular writer John Grant)."[302] *Universal Horrors* devotes an entire chapter to the film and is the strongest in its praise, saying:

> As trite and hackneyed as the old dark house gags were at the time of *Hold That Ghost*'s release, it didn't make a bit of difference to audiences back then or today, almost a half-century later. *Hold That Ghost* has so much comic vitality and spirit, any attempt to criticize its considerable excesses pales in light of the picture's uninhibited joys. Bluntly put, it's one of the best horror farces ever made and, arguably, A&C's funniest film. Though *Abbott and Costello Meet Frankenstein* surpasses the film in terms of novelty, star names and production values, *Hold That Ghost* has the edge in several respects: the boys were younger and more agile in 1941 and their old burlesque routines (which were constantly revitalized by chief writer John Grant, an ex-vaudevillian himself) hadn't yet grown stale from overuse.[303]

The boys re-created *Hold That Ghost* for radio audiences on Louella Parsons' *Hollywood Premiere* on August 1, 1941.[304] But the influence of the film continued on. Olson and Johnson's bizarre spoof *Ghost Catchers* (1944) had a funny scene in which the duo's clothes are ripped off of them by a ghost — while at the same time they verbally agree that there are no ghosts because they had seen *Hold That Ghost*. "Remember Abbott and Costello in *Hold That Ghost*?" asks Olson. "The whole thing turned out to be gangsters." They casually talk about the film, noting how preposterous it was. They even mention the moving candle bit! Brunas, Brunas, and Weaver comment how that "unusual in-joke sticks in the mind after everything else about *Ghost Catchers* has faded from memory."[305]

Later, the Universal compilation *The World of Abbott and Costello* would use clips from the car chase in the film, ignoring all of the other, better scenes (including the comic ballet, which one would think should have been first choice).

Today, the film remains one of the team's most popular. An example from an eighties television show displays how the content of the picture might be forgotten but the title itself lives on. In an episode titled "The Resurrection of Carlini" on the television show *The Greatest American Hero*, reluctant superhero Ralph Hinkley (William Katt), FBI Agent Bill Maxwell (Robert Culp), and Ralph's girlfriend Pam Davidson (Connie Selleca) search a villain's hideout for clues to a killer's location. Bill and Pam are split off from Ralph as he tries to pick up psychic vibes off items in one of the rooms. Exploring a closet, Bill and Pam are startled when some boxes fall. Ralph catches up to them to find out what happened, and Pam comments that it is nothing — just Leo Gorcey and Huntz Hall doing *Hold That Ghost*.[306] She got the names wrong (those are the Bowery Boys), but the mention of the Abbott and Costello film brings a smile just the same.

The Time of Their Lives

Released: August 16, 1946   *Running time:* 82 minutes
Reissued: May 1, 1951 (with *Little Giant*)

Directed by: Charles T. Barton; *Produced by:* Val Burton; *Executive Producer:* Joe Gershenson; *Screenplay by:* Val Burton, Walter DeLeon, Bradford Ropes; *Additional Dialogue by:* John Grant; *Director of Photography:* Charles Van Enger; *Film Editor:* Philip Cahn; *Musical Score and Direction:* Milton Rosen; *Art Direction:* Jack Otterson, Richard H. Riedel; *Director of Sound:* Bernard B. Brown; *Technician:* Jack A. Bolger, Jr.; *Set Decoration:* Morgan Farley; *Gowns:* Rosemary Odell; *Hair Stylist:* Carmen Dirigo; *Director of Makeup:* Jack P. Pierce; *Assistant Director:* Seward Webb; *Special Photography:* D.S. Horsley, ASC, and Jerome Ash, ASC.

Cast: Bud Abbott (Cuthbert Greenway and Dr. Ralph Greenway); Lou Costello (Horatio Prim); Marjorie Reynolds (Melody Allen); Binnie Barnes (Mrs. Prescott); John Shelton (Sheldon Gage); Jess Barker (Tom Danbury); Gale Sondergaard (Emily); Robert Barrat (Major Putnam); Donald MacBride (Lieutenant Mason); Anne Gillis (Nora); Lynn Baggett (June Prescott); William Hall (Connors); Rex Lease (Sergeant Makepeace); Harry Woolman (Motorcycle Rider); Harry Brown (Second Sergeant); Walter Baldwin (Bates); Selmer Jackson (Curator); George Carleton (First Guard); Vernon Downing (Leigh); Boyd Irwin (Cranwell); Marjorie Eaton (Bessie); Wheaton Chambers (Second

Guard); Kirk Alyn, John Crawford, Myron Healey, Scott Thomson (Dandies).

Ticket sales on Abbott and Costello films declined in the mid-forties as audiences tired of seeing the same old routines over and over again. In response, Universal put the boys in two pictures in which they did not work as a team. At the time, this experiment was a failure, but in retrospect, it produced two of the more interesting Abbott and Costello features.

Little Giant (1946) featured Lou as a would-be vacuum cleaner salesman who goes to the big city, with Bud as his boss. (Bud actually plays two roles in this film, as he would in *The Time of Their Lives*.) Unlike in the latter movie, the two performed one routine together: "$7 \times 13 = 28$."

For the next picture, the boys were put in a film that, for the first half, was a period piece. The rest of the movie turned out to be a light ghost fantasy, inspired by the likes of *Topper* (1937) and *Blithe Spirit* (1945).

Late in 1944, Val Burton had written an original treatment for a film called *The Ghost Steps Out*, which was developed as a vehicle for Abbott and Costello. The treatment was similar to the finished A&C film, except the ghosts were Guinette De Rome and Cedric Brown, a dandy and his black valet.

In April of 1947 (nearly a year after the picture's completion), lawyers for John Cecil Holm pointed out the alleged similarities between the script and Holm's Broadway play *The Gramercy Ghost*. Both sets of lawyers reviewed the studio's assignment file and realized the treatment was written in 1944. Neither party seemed to have the need to take action against the other, so the matter was dropped.[307]

One of the team's better supporting casts was assembled for this picture. Marjorie Reynolds was a great choice to play Melody Allen in the picture. Born in 1921, Reynolds had toiled for Monogram as the intrepid reporter in the Mr. Wong series before Paramount picked her up. She starred in *Holiday Inn* (1942) and *Ministry of Fear* (1944; with Ray Milland) before being loaned to Universal to appear in the Abbott and Costello film. After *The Time of Their Lives*, she acted in *Heaven Only Knows* (1947) and played Babs on the TV series *The Life of Riley* (1953–1958).[308] She later appeared on an episode of Abbott and Costello's TV show called "Peace and Quiet" in 1953.

Also in *The Time of Their Lives* was popular comic actress Binnie

Barnes. Born in London in 1905, the sophisticated actress began her career in two-reel comedies before making British features.[309] She had appeared in *The Private Life of Henry VIII* (1933) and *It's in the Bag* (1945) and would make a few more films before retiring in 1955. She returned to the screen in 1966 for *The Trouble with Angels* and its sequel.

Some well-known names from the fantasy genre made appearances with the boys in this film. Gale Sondergaard had won a Best Supporting Oscar for her work in *Anthony Adverse* (1936) before becoming Universal's premiere villainess. Some of her horror work included her famous role in the Sherlock Holmes entry, *The Spider Woman* (1944), as well as its 1947 follow-up, *The Spider Woman Strikes Back* (not a sequel to the Holmes film). She also appeared in *The Cat and the Canary* (1939), *The Black Cat* (1941), and *The Invisible Man's Revenge* (1944). According to a *Time of Their Lives* preview handout, Sondergaard was an accomplished linguist who had to learn a seventh language for this film — medieval Latin — so she could read her lines in the séance scene. Supposedly, these lines were from an original incantation discovered in a work on ancient witchcraft. Of course, this information was most likely made up for studio publicity purposes.[310]

John Shelton had appeared in a handful of previous horror-comedies, including *The Ghost Comes Home* (1940), *Whispering Ghosts* (1942) with Milton Berle, and *A-Haunting We Will Go* (1942) with Laurel and Hardy.

Former child actress Anne Gillis had previously appeared in *In Society* (1944) with Abbott and Costello before being seen here. Bud's nephew Norman, fresh from serving a stint in the navy, was used as his uncle's stand-in.[311] Two fantasy notables also appeared in bit parts as dandies — Kirk Alyn, the Superman of the serials, and Myron Healy, an actor who would specialize in B sci-fi pictures in the fifties.

The Time of Their Lives was the most expensive Abbott and Costello picture to date. It was originally scheduled for 48 days but ran two weeks over. It came in at $830,625, out of which Bud and Lou received $111,000. Much of the budget went to special effects, particularly the opticals used to create the ghost effects. These were achieved by first photographing the set with nobody on it, then covering everything with black velvet and photographing the scene with the actors. These two pieces of film were then overlapped so that it looked as if you could see right through the actors.[312]

Cinematographer Charles Van Enger worked closely with director

Charles Barton to achieve the realistic effects. Barton took home $15,500, with a provisional bonus of $5,000 upon completion of the picture. This was his first Abbott and Costello film and he would direct the next seven, including all-time favorite *Abbott and Costello Meet Frankenstein*. Barton knew how to work with the often-difficult Abbott and Costello and initiated the three-camera technique with them, using three cameras at the same time so as not to lose any part of Bud and Lou's antics.[313]

Abbott and Costello were not the easiest actors to work with during the making of this film. The team was at its lowest ebb. Lou wanted to branch out and try roles with a Chaplinesque pathos which left Abbott as nothing more than a supporting character in the team's movies.[314] Bud did not like the new direction the team was going, thinking it was going to lead to a breakup of the two.[315] What it did lead to was a lot of fighting between them. Barton commented in Chris Costello's book: "When I started working with them and directing their films in 1946, I could sense an animosity between them. In one film they wouldn't even speak to one another. In another they'd have a riff one day and the next day it would be completely forgotten. Lou went through spells when he wanted to reverse the billing of their names. I don't think it was ever Lou's idea as much as the henchmen that were around him. (Bud had his cronies around too.)"[316] Lou even pulled a stunt where he wanted to switch roles with Abbott. Three weeks into shooting, Costello called Barton and said unless he and Abbott switched roles, he would walk off the picture. He felt Bud had the better part. With half of the film already shot, Barton refused to give in. Costello sat it out for two weeks while the crew shot around him as much as possible. Finally, Lou returned to the set with no explanation and completed the film.[317] Regarding the team's fighting, Paddy Costello said:

> There's another thing going on here, too. They were together for something like 26 years and that's a hell of a long time for two people to be together. A lot of marriages never last that long…. I think maybe you outgrow certain things. I always think they achieved what they set out to do and they did it well. They were on the stage, movies, radio, television; they had it all — it's like, so what do you do now?[318]

Lou was also up to his old trick of stealing props from the set before shooting was finished. Often, costly re-takes had to be shot because of the disappearing items. One prop he took was a beautiful grandfather's clock, sending a truck to pick it up during a lunch break.[319] Lou had to be promised he could keep the clock after shooting was completed before he would agree to bring it back. (This story has also been told in regard to *Abbott and Costello Meet Frankenstein*.)

The production did start on a happy note, however. The first day of shooting was Lou's fortieth birthday and his family came down to the studio to surprise him with a cake.[320]

Universal publicity had a field day with the film. According to a preview handout, the cast and crew were prevented from smoking cigarettes during filming. Barton provided them with a number of small sticks with a knob at one end — like little tympanum drumsticks — to act as a substitute for nervous cigarette lighting.[321]

The film opens with a candlelit book on a period table. The credits are printed on the pages of the book.

The first shot shows Danbury Manor, a beautiful mansion in King's Point, New York. A title card tells us the location and the setting: "1780, the war of the revolution was in its fifth year...." A fancy dress ball is going on inside the manor.

Inside, four guests admire the portrait of Tom Danbury's fiancée, Melody Allen (who is seen dancing). They agree that Tom is a lucky man because Melody is adored by all.

Butler Cuthbert Greenway is called in. Cuthbert is the first of Bud's two roles in the film. He is asked by one of the guests if he recommends a particular vintage and Cuthbert relies, "Yes, sir, (hic) it's delicious ... or so the other guests tell me." It is a great introduction for Bud and just the first example of the good use made of his talents in the film. Bud has a chance to really act and he takes full advantage of it. He also gets a lot of laughs, breaking his straight man role to play a character. Lou's jealousies might not have been as misplaced as some thought. Unfortunately, the line is a bit tragic when recalling Bud's problems with alcohol. He was supposedly an alcoholic in real life and would start drinking at 4 P.M. — like clockwork — every day.[322]

In the kitchen, Cuthbert helps himself to more drink but is caught by maid Nora, who chides him. Cuthbert says he will give up drinking if Nora marries him (he has even saved up enough money to pay her bond to Danbury). But Nora refuses; she would rather stay in bondage. "So," says Cuthbert. "You're still in love with that little, fat, stupid tinker!" Of course, he is referring to Lou, who plays Horatio the tinker. There is a foreshadowing of the "Meet the Monsters" formula here in that Bud can never understand why a beautiful girl would be more interested in Lou than in himself.

Another maid informs Nora that Horatio is on his way to the house. Cuthbert calls him a "lazy, fat tub" but Nora defends her beau, insisting he is not lazy. The scene immediately cuts to Horatio on his horse, fast asleep. It is another good introduction and it deserves the laugh it gets.

Horatio puts his horse in the barn. Nora calls to him and he bumps his head on the barn door. While dismounting, he pulls hay all over himself and sneezes uncontrollably. It is still the same old Lou Costello, even in this period setting.

Nora brings Horatio a snack and asks where he has been. Horatio explains using double-talk and tongue twisters. He tells Nora how much he loves her. They kiss and fall in the hay—a literal "roll in the hay," the first of many sexual connotations in the film.

Horatio cries out in pain and Nora thinks it is because of her kiss. But Horatio is sitting on a pitchfork. She pulls it out, accompanied by a "SPROING" sound effect one would normally find in a Three Stooges short.

Finally sitting down to eat, Horatio tells Nora to take the first bite because then it will be sweeter (a very romantic line). Nora complains about the pestering Cuthbert, angering Horatio, who threatens to give the butler the dirtiest look he has ever seen. (Horatio's nonviolent nature makes his sudden death a few minutes later much more shocking). Nora is happy the two will be leaving the next day but Horatio sadly reveals he no longer has the money to pay her bond. His customers could not pay their bills and many were starving, so he bought them food. Horatio's speech here is cheesy but it pays off—at the conclusion, he reveals he lost the rest of the money in a card game. This is funny because Abbott and Costello were known for the poker games they played in between shooting. They would lose thousands of dollars a day playing cards with the cast and crew. Ironically, on the set of *The Time of Their Lives*, the boys were fighting so much they gave up their card-playing habit.[323]

Nora is disappointed but Horatio assures her his business will soon be booming. He has received a personal recommendation from General George Washington, which he reads aloud to Nora, not knowing Cuthbert is eavesdropping. Nora wants to show it to Melody Allen, thinking Melody will help them to elope. Nora takes the note and leaves the excited Horatio with his dinner.

Cuthbert steals Horatio's dinner before making his presence known to the wary tinker (there is a hint the two have had previous confrontations). Cuthbert says he just wants to congratulate Horatio, tricking him by saying Nora has told him of the marriage plans. Horatio says "'Od's Bodkins!" for the first time, the exclamatory phrase he uses throughout the rest of the film.

Cuthbert says Tom Danbury will not be happy about Nora breaking her bond, but there is something Horatio can do to get in good with the master. There is a large trunk Tom wanted to take on his honeymoon but he has lost the key. Cuthbert tells Horatio, "If you could open that trunk, I could put you in very good."

Horatio opens the trunk and Cuthbert tricks the tinker into stepping inside it. A variation of the previous joke is used (in a bit of overkill), but Cuthbert eventually locks Horatio inside the trunk and leaves him in the barn.

Meanwhile, in the garden, Tom and Melody kiss. Tom says they will soon have titles — Sir Thomas and Lady Danbury. Melody reminds him that after the war there will be no titles, but Tom hints the Colonies may not win the war. A carriage drives by and a suddenly nervous Tom rushes Melody inside the manor, promising to explain later.

Tom meets with co-conspirators Bramwell and Lee and they decide to talk in private. Bessie the maid tries to keep the evil Cuthbert from telling Tom what Nora and Horatio are planning. Cuthbert orders her into the kitchen and looks for Tom. Nora sees Cuthbert coming and hides in a closet in Danbury's study. Tom and his cohorts enter and Tom orders Cuthbert away. The three then discuss their plans. It turns out they are traitors to the revolution! The two men tell Tom his plan is working fine — Benedict Arnold has agreed to surrender West Point, which will end the war. But Arnold will only surrender to Tom, and the two men urge him to go to West Point. Meanwhile, Melody listens outside the window and learns the truth about her fiancée.

Tom finds Nora in the closet and takes from her Horatio's letter from Washington. They decide to deal with the patriotic tinker later, prompting Nora to call her master a traitor. Tom orders the men to "take care of her," meaning kill her, and Melody watches in horror as the men take Nora away. Tom hides Horatio's letter in the secret drawer of a clock on the mantle.

Melody changes into riding clothes in the barn and hears Horatio screaming from the trunk. By this time, Horatio has his head and feet pushed through each end of the trunk. (Comedians stuck or hiding in trunks seems to be a common occurrence, as evidenced by the Marx Brothers in *A Night at the Opera* [1935], Bob Hope in *The Ghost Breakers* [1940], and Dean Martin in *Scared Stiff* [1953].) Melody pulls a gun on Horatio, who tells her who he is. She helps him out of the trunk and informs him that the Colonies and General Washington are in danger and that they have to warn the revolutionaries of Tom's plan. Horatio knows the location of the nearest army base, so they saddle up two horses.

In the meantime, rebel soldiers are on their way to the manor. Major Andre has been captured and the papers in his boot exposed the plot. They are on their way to arrest Tom.

In the stable, Melody gives Horatio a horse pistol ("What do *I* shoot with?") and says they must leave. Horatio wants to tell Nora where he is going. Melody almost slips and tells him of Nora's fate (a sad moment) but catches herself and says there is no time. They take off (with Horatio riding his horse backwards).

Seeing the troops, Melody and Horatio mistake them for Tom's friends and ride off in the opposite direction. The soldiers mistake the two for traitors and chase them. Bullets fly and Melody and Horatio are shot and killed. This scene is unexpected and, as a result, shocking in its brutality. No one ever expected to see Costello get killed in one of his own films.

The soldiers decide the only burial the "traitors" deserve is to be thrown down the well. They then put a curse on the souls of the traitors — accompanied by a weird shot of the bodies lying at the bottom of the well. "Hear me, ye faithless souls," says Major Putnam. "May you lie there in everlasting torment with but one name to identify your rotting bones—'traitors.' And unless some evidence proves us wrong, I curse your miserable spirits to be bonded to Danbury Manor till crack of doom!" The Major nails a sign to the well that reads, "Here were buried two traitors, Sep. 23, 1780."

The spirit of Horatio Prim materializes in a cloud of smoke. Melody's spirit also appears, frightening Horatio. They realize they are ghosts when Horatio's hand passes through Melody's body (a good effect). The scene then takes a turn for the worst by employing the oldest gag in the universe. Horatio drinks from the well and the water pours out of the bullet holes in his body. To add insult to injury, Lou performs it twice!

Horatio and Melody do not realize what has happened to them until they read the sign and see their own bodies in the well. They hear noises and see the soldiers looting and burning the mansion. Horatio says his letter from George Washington will prove their innocence, but he does not know where it is. Melody realizes it was the letter Tom took from Nora and admits to Horatio that Nora was kidnapped. Angered, Horatio runs off to save his sweetheart.

Horatio sees Cuthbert leaving on Horatio's horse, Lancelot. He tries to give chase but when he reaches the gate he is repelled by an invisible barrier. Costello shows off his pantomime skills as he is repeatedly pushed back by the force field. Melody remembers the curse and slowly it dawns on the two ghosts that they are trapped forever on the mansion grounds. "Why didn't you get Paul Revere to help you?" asks Horatio as the two return to the well.

Time passes, shown by markings on trees and a weather montage. (Supposedly, the fog seen in the montage was made of titanium chloride, a smoke-screen chemical developed by the army during the war.[324]) By the year 1946, Melody and Horatio have been sitting in their tree near the well for 165 years.

In a strange scene, Melody starts coming on to Horatio, unable to hold back her sexual desires. Horatio is embarrassed but seeks Melody's permission to ask a favor. An excited Melody urges Horatio to ask his favor but is disappointed when he simply wants her to scratch his back. She throws him out of the tree. Apparently, sex is an option for these ghosts (who are obviously attracted to each other), contrary to the title of the atrocious Bo Derek film *Ghosts Can't Do It* (1990). Again, this is an example of the emphasis on sex. Obviously horny, Horatio and Melody remain faithful to their lost loves, yet hope to be reunited with them for the promise of sex.

Danbury Manor has been rebuilt and restored. A car pulls up with new owner Sheldon Gage, his fiancée, June Prescott, and her aunt, Mildred (Milly) Prescott. They meet the housekeeper, a sinister looking woman named Emily, who was sent by an employment agency. As they enter, Mildred asks Emily, "Pardon me, but didn't I see you in *Rebecca*?" a reference to the famous Alfred Hitchcock film. Inside, Emily tells the group the history of the house as they admire its beauty.

Dr. Ralph Greenway, Sheldon's psychiatrist (and one of the best in New York), arrives. Milly does not like Ralph, and June asks her not to give him a hard time. Sheldon is recovering from a breakdown and June does not want Mildred to upset him. But Mildred does not have any faith in Ralph. (Even in a respectable position as a doctor, Abbott is still seen as a con man and a quack.)

Downstairs, Ralph takes credit for the restoration and tells Tom his great-great-grandfather was the Danbury's butler. Emily enters with a plaque for the well. She mentions to the group that no one has ever found out the identities of the two traitors in the well. She goes on to explain that the ghosts of the traitors always throw the sign over the fence. Everyone scoffs at the idea of ghosts, but Emily is a firm believer. Nevertheless, she puts up the new plaque.

Horatio wants to throw away the new plaque, but Melody says it will not do any good. Horatio says he overheard Sheldon say he will open the place up to tourists every Saturday between the hours of two and four. Unable to stand the thought of all those people believing him to be a traitor, Horatio makes a momentous decision — he will haunt the house. Melody tells him to wait, explaining that no self-respecting ghost does any haunting before midnight.

Melody floats gracefully from the tree to the ground, something not in the original script.[325] Horatio forgets he too can do this and clumsily jumps to the ground. Throughout the film, his ghostly "powers" fade in and out of control.

At midnight, everyone is asleep. Ralph has taken sleeping pills and Emily reads in bed. Horatio looks in the window. Melody comes up behind him and scares him. Even as a ghost, Costello is still afraid. "Don't do that," he says. "You almost scared the life out of me."

Melody wants to go inside with him but the window is locked. She turns invisible by doing a little shimmy (which The Breen Office cautioned must not be too suggestive[326]) and passes through the wall. Horatio tries the same thing but gets stuck in the wall. Melody has to pull him all the way inside. Paddy Costello recalled being on the set for those effects:

> That was a fun one to be on, too — to watch them work there. And when they would get somebody to disappear like in that movie, they had them shake, do this little shake. Well, they'd be shooting and they would have them shake and then you would see them. The director would tell them to leave or whatever, or to cut — and they would just walk off. So they would stop and walk off.... When I watch the movie, I can still see them doing that. I can still hear the director saying, "that's it." And then, *you* watch them disappear on screen, but I'm in my mind seeing them just stop, turn around, and walk off.[327]

The ghosts are amazed at how much the restored mansion resembles the original. Lou tries to light a candle but it is electric and he has no idea what electricity is. When he accidentally turns on one of the lights, he is scared and tries to blow it out. Melody hits the switch by accident and the light goes out. They figure out how to turn the lights on and off and what powers them. Melody has a cute line when she says, "What an astonishing idea! Probably got it from Ben Franklin — he's always inventing things!"

The flickering of the lights awakens Ralph, who, as it turns out, is a very nervous man himself. Ralph says to himself, "Be calm! Be reasonable!" the start of a running gag.

Downstairs, Melody is amused by the "haunting" but Horatio is frightened. Melody finds Tom's memoirs (Horatio thinks she said "grandmas") while Horatio knocks over a table, again awakening Ralph.

Melody reads the dedication. Tom's memoirs are dedicated to his country and to Melody, whose love he betrayed "for vainglorious ambition." They admire the portrait on the wall, but Melody says it belongs in the library.

Ralph, in the meantime, looks at himself in a mirror. Bud shows off his acting talents as he tells himself to pull together and practice what he preaches.

Horatio picks up the phone and the operator says, "Number, please." Horatio yells out, "Spooks!" Ralph comes downstairs, so the two ghosts "unmanifest" themselves by turning invisible — but Horatio is unable to fade away. Ralph enters and Horatio mistakes him for Cuthbert. Ralph looks around and Horatio realizes Ralph cannot see him. He tests his theory by waving in Ralph's face like a little kid. He also whistles but Ralph still does not know he is there. Horatio is then ready to kick Ralph but the doctor sits down.

Horatio mocks Ralph while he looks for a match to light his cigarette. Ralph finally bends over, allowing Horatio to kick him and send him flying over the chair. Emily then enters the room, providing Costello with one of the best lines in the film: "Zounds! What well did she come out of?"

Ralph accuses Emily of kicking him, but the housekeeper is in some sort of trance. Ralph snaps her out of it. She reports that the ghosts are present and they are offended. Ralph is skeptical, but Emily explains she is psychic — she can even hear Horatio laughing. Emily also tells Ralph that she did not kick him, the ghosts did. He becomes nervous when she tells him the ghosts are after him. He tells her not to tell the others, lest they think she is crazy. She goes back to bed.

Ralph admires the harpsichord and plays a few notes. As Ralph is leaving, Horatio plays on it, sending Ralph out of the room in a flash. (According to studio publicity, the rare, old harpsichord was filled with electrical controls because the original mechanism did not provide enough tone volume for the music expected of it.[328]) Horatio is happy; he is finally getting his revenge on Cuthbert, and he has so much more planned. Viewed now, it is almost as if Costello is delighting in finally turning the tables on Abbott!

Melody discovers that the portrait is actually the original painting and, when she finds that the same harpsichord key sticks, she realizes everything in the house is original. Now they can look for the letter and prove they are not traitors! They decide to start searching the library, and Melody disappears through the door. Horatio is about to follow but he takes a moment to yell out the window, "Nora! It won't be long now!" There is a hint of sexual longing in these words, eclipsed by a great gag: it looks like Horatio will fade through the door like Melody, but at the last minute he opens the door and walks out.

Horatio goes through the books (with the help of fast motion photography) but cannot find anything. Melody is still staring at the painting and offers a suggestion to look in the clock. But Horatio tells her no one has ever put a secret drawer in a clock.

The two continue searching and make a mess. They find a radio and Horatio turns it on. A crime drama about the "Phantom" is playing and the two believe the program to be real. When the radio voice tells a character to "start singing," Horatio sings. When it says, "Everybody blow!" the two start blowing. When gunshots are broadcast, Melody makes herself disappear while Horatio panics. This scene is reminiscent of the transcription room scene in *Who Done It?* (It would have been even funnier had the program playing on the air been an Abbott and Costello radio show.)

The radio awakens everyone in the house, and Ralph hides under his bed. June hears the commotion and says, "Sounds like the radio." "It can't be the Revolutionary War!" replies Milly. Everyone starts heading downstairs.

Meanwhile, the ghosts have turned invisible and Horatio heads for the door while carrying a candlestick. Sheldon enters the room just as Horatio is exiting, and he is beaned by the candlestick. When the girls find Sheldon they think he is cracking up again. Ralph is called down and Emily also appears, turning off the radio. They gather in the library to figure out what is going on.

Ralph says they need a stimulant and asks where the brandy is kept. (Although this is a funny line, it shows Ralph may not be a very good doctor because he does not know alcohol is a depressant.) Horatio sees "Cuthbert" is coming and again disappears. His shadow, however, stays behind until Horatio whistles and says, "Come on!" Horatio then trips Ralph, and his little kid persona emerges when he says, "I tripped you! I tripped you!"

Upset, Ralph fetches a bottle from the cabinet but Horatio puts it back. Ralph gets it out again and pours himself a drink. Horatio samples the drink and spits it out — on Ralph. "No, no, this can't happen to me," says Ralph as he drinks his drink. "Be calm. Be cool." He puts a cigarette in his mouth and searches for a light. Horatio lights it for him and Ralph says, "Thank you." Ralph realizes what has happened and Abbott performs a great double take. This is a funny sequence utilizing convincing special effects reminiscent of the Invisible Man series.

Ralph listens to his heartbeat with a stethoscope: Horatio toots into it, sending Ralph into the next room where he collapses.

Horatio laughs until he sees a drink being poured by itself. Of course, Melody is doing it, turning the tables on Horatio. "You're a bad boy," she says, using a variation of Costello's famous catchphrase. She reminds him that they have to find the letter. Melody decides to search upstairs and Horatio will search the cellar. Melody again wiggles suggestively and turns invisible.

Upstairs, Melody goes through one of the closets and finds a beautiful gown. Downstairs, Horatio finds a file cabinet and searches one of the drawers. When he slams the door shut, another pops open and hits him. He flies into some bottles and ends up with his head inside one. This gag was not in the original script.[329]

Melody, dressed in the gown, puts on some perfume. "If Tom could only see me now," she says wistfully. Melody obviously still desires Tom.

Downstairs, Ralph revives and tells the others the ghosts have a grudge against him. He explains what he has seen and Shelly backs him up. But June believes Sheldon has simply communicated his hysteria to the doctor.

Milly makes fun of Ralph and Sheldon and decides to go to bed. On the staircase, she passes Melody, who is invisible except for the gown.

Milly says hello, does a double take, screams, and collapses. The gown falls off Melody, who runs back upstairs. This is a bit risqué because Melody is now nude (though still invisible).

The others rush to Milly's aid as she regains consciousness. Ralph shows her the discarded gown and she faints again. Bud has a good moment when June arrives with some liquor. "I'll take that," he says and grabs it away from her. June still does not believe there are ghosts, even though the other three swear they have seen them. Still, she is unable to come up with a reasonable explanation for the phenomena. Suddenly, the lights go out, causing Milly to become hysterical. The scene cuts to the cellar where we see the reason for the blackout. Horatio is caught in the generator and is being electrocuted. This gag drags on way too long, and Costello even compounds the problem by sitting on the generator a moment later and doing the whole bit over again.

Melody appears. She is frightened and wants to go back to the tree. Horatio throws things at the offending generator until he knocks out the power for good. He picks up a light bulb and it lights up in his hand (shades of Uncle Fester). Horatio uses it like a baton and conducts an imaginary orchestra. Finally, he and Melody decide to leave and they head out, light bulb in hand. This scene is also too long and not very funny.

Outside, a dog chases after the "floating" light bulb. Horatio trips over a tree branch and drops it. He turns visible, which frightens the dog. Its eyes roll (a gag stolen from Petey in the Our Gang shorts) and it runs off. Although the gag has gone on too long, this scene does boast some impressive lighting.

June now believes something supernatural is going on. Emily declares that the ghosts have been frightened off. June wants to go back to town, but Sheldon wants to figure out who the ghosts are and what they were doing. This leads to the scariest scene (perhaps the only scary scene) in the film. They decide to conduct a séance, with Emily in the driver's seat.

June is reluctant to take part in the seance but she is convinced otherwise. Sheldon reads from Major Putnam's record of the two traitors and they learn about the curse. Sheldon says they must get to the bottom of the ghostly manifestations. Ralph agrees, which surprises Milly, who reminds him that he wrote many articles exposing séances as fakes. (Bud has always had a streak of hypocrisy in his characters.) Sheldon agrees that if the séance does not work, they will return to the city in the morning.

The participants put their hands on the table and make their minds blank. Emily says some mystic words. In the tree, the ghosts feel themselves being pulled toward the house. A strong wind blows them inside and Emily feels their presence. Horatio whines that he will never haunt them again if they just leave him alone, but the guests cannot hear or see the ghosts. Sheldon explains aloud that they want to help them. He says they should rap on the table in reply to his questions — one for no, two for yes. Melody urges Horatio to cooperate and he climbs under the table. Horatio raps yes, he can hear them. He taps yes, they will help them. Ralph asks if they are the spirits of the two traitors. This angers Horatio and he pounds Ralph's foot, a funny moment. Ralph flies back in his chair. "Why do they always pick on me?" he asks.

The others realize the question has offended the ghosts. They ask the ghosts if they are not actually traitors and Horatio raps yes. Horatio tries to identify himself to them but they are unable to hear him. Melody suddenly has an idea and she leaves the room. Emily, sensing the ghosts' departure, tries to call them back.

Melody and Horatio return, with Horatio carrying the portrait of Melody from the other room. June identifies one of the spirits as Melody Allen and Horatio confirms it by rapping twice. They try to guess the identity of Horatio by guessing his profession. He is not a soldier or a gentleman so they use the old rhyme — he is not a rich man, but he is a poor man; he is not a beggar man, but he is a tinker. Sheldon remembers reading about a tinker in Danbury's diary. The diary says that Nora had later written to Tom asking about information on Horatio Prim's whereabouts, but both the tinker and Melody had disappeared the night of the fire. Hearing this makes Horatio sad. The acting in this scene is tremendous. One's heart goes out to Horatio when he hears about his long lost Nora (who apparently was not killed by Danbury's men).

In the diary, Tom confesses that he stole Prim's letter and hid it in a secret drawer. Ralph says that if Horatio had a letter from George Washington then he could not have been a traitor. Horatio quickly raps twice to confirm this. June realizes the ghosts have been looking for the letter so they can remove the curse. The ghosts get excited and dance happily.

Sheldon asks the ghosts if they know where the secret drawer is, but they do not. Suddenly, many raps come from beneath the table and it starts to rise. Horatio and Melody become scared because they are not behind the phenomenon. It is a creepy scene, made more so by having

Emily speak in a man's voice and call out, "Melody! Melody!" Many feel this is the picture's most memorable scene.

Melody realizes Tom is speaking through Emily. "I've come to help you," says the ghostly voice. "It must be Danbury speaking through Emily," observes Sheldon. "Oh, fine," says Milly, "a ghost-to-ghost broadcast." (This surely was not the first time that old chestnut was used in a movie.) It seems like Binnie Barnes is given all the lines Costello would normally have.

Melody wonders why she cannot see Tom. "You can't, you poor kid," says Horatio. "He's got his wings, but we're still grounded."

Ralph tells Tom they want to help, too. Tom recites a poem: "Start at twelve, turn twice to three, At ten past one, t'will open be." Emily then collapses as the spirit leaves her body. Bud has a great line when he asks, "Would you mind repeating that last part?"

Emily recalls nothing of what has happened and abruptly goes to bed. Sheldon figures out that Tom was talking about a clock, so they decide to search each one in the house. Melody tells Horatio that it has to be the library clock because Tom only had the letter in there. Horatio is excited and wants to yell to Nora. He makes a dash for the window as Melody is making her own dash to the door and they run right through each other. In the process, they find they have switched clothes. This is another gag not in the original script.[330] It is a good addition, adding a little of what today would be known as gender confusion but was then an innocent laugh-getter.

The ghosts return to their rightful costumes while everyone else searches for the clock. The ghosts try to direct their attention to the clock in the library. Horatio causes confusion by tapping Ralph (he thinks it is Milly) and Sheldon (he thinks it is June)—a gag reminiscent of the slapping scene between Costello and Joan Davis in *Hold That Ghost*. Finally, Melody directs their attention by opening the door to the library.

Sheldon realizes the clock in the library is the one they want but tells the group that this clock is a reproduction. The original is in a New York museum. Sheldon had approached the museum's board of directors but they would not even talk to him and barred him from the museum. (There seems to be some back-story missing here.)

The group feels bad because they've come this far but seem unable to help the ghosts further. Ralph decides to go to New York and get the clock in order to atone for the sins of his ancestor Cuthbert. Melody tells this to Horatio, who is so excited he kisses Ralph. Ralph thinks it was Milly who kissed him and plants a huge one on her in return. Naturally, he is slapped.

At the museum the next day, director Prof. Dibbs tells Ralph he can neither take the clock nor examine it. So Ralph steals the clock by hiding it under his coat and masquerading as an obese man. When the clock chimes while he is stalled by a suspicious guard, Ralph says, "four o'clock — how time does fly. And so must I!" He runs out leaving the guard behind. When Prof. Dibbs finds out about the theft, he calls the police.

At the mansion, Shelly is concerned for Ralph, and Emily says even the ghosts are worried. Milly, still the cynic, makes a big production over sitting down by asking, "Pardon me, is this chair taken?" The chair is promptly pushed in for her by ghostly hands, causing her a new bout of anxiety.

The doorbell rings and the group rushes to see who is there. Horatio gets so excited he forgets to completely phase through the door and gets stuck.

Lieutenant Mason of the state police greets the group. He is waiting for Ralph to show up with the clock. Another police officer hides their car so Ralph will not see it when he arrives.

Shelly tries to explain to Mason why they need the clock. In the meantime, Melody tells Horatio they must keep Ralph away from the house so the police do not take the clock before it can be searched.

Mason, of course, does not believe Shelly's crazy story. Shelly offers proof. He and June call for Melody and Horatio, hoping they will make their presence known. But the ghosts are heading for the gate. Outside, Horatio calls back to them, "Oh, we'll be back in a minute!" Ironically, Lou's line reading makes him sound like Joe Besser's character, "Stinky," from the Abbott and Costello television show of the fifties. (It is a funny moment and a good capper to the scene.)

Ralph pulls up in his car. The ghosts try to warn him but Ralph drives through them. Horatio tries to throw a cannonball on a chain in order to stop him. But as he swings the chain, it winds around him and the cannonball conks him on the noggin — a great sight gag.

Ralph is about to sneak inside but Emily catches him and warns him. She tells him to hide in the stable. Melody thanks Emily for her help. But the cop has seen the car and he calls for Mason.

In the stable, Ralph recalls the rhyme and tries to open the clock's secret drawer. Before he can do so, he hears the cop and goes to the door to see what is happening. Melody urges Horatio to finish opening the clock, but Mason and the cop enter with guns drawn. Mason takes the clock out of Horatio's hands (without seeing Horatio, of course) and leads Ralph outside. Like the little kid he is, Horatio pouts and cries.

Ralph tries to explain to Mason at the car, but he is handcuffed and put in the vehicle. Milly tells Ralph to plead insanity because he is an expert at it. Mason joins Ralph in the back seat of the car. Horatio continually yanks Mason's hat down around his ears, infuriating the officer, who blames it on Ralph. Ralph maintains his innocence but Mason is so mad he pulls Ralph's hat down.

When the car tries to pass through the gates, it stops because Horatio is sitting in the car. The cops are dumbfounded. This twist is implausible, however; the car should continue on its way, leaving Horatio behind. Nevertheless, they are unable to leave. The cop gets out to check the car and Melody tells Horatio to try to work the automobile. They plan to hide Ralph and the clock in the well until the police leave.

Mason decides he wants to drive and gets out of the car. Horatio pulls his cap down again, and this time Mason blames his partner. The whole cap-pulling business was never in the original script and was added during production.[331]

The car suddenly backs up and drives off through the yard. Horatio is behind the wheel but no one can see him. The cops watch in awe, with Mason screaming at Ralph to stop. But the frightened Ralph has no idea what is going on. According to studio publicity, the ghost car effect was achieved by fitting the vehicle with dual controls and a second steering wheel under the cushions of the rear seat where the driver hid, peering through a gauze screen in order to drive.[332]

According to Furmanek and Palumbo, Bud Abbott had to learn how to drive a car for this film. He had never driven an automobile before, so the studio built an electric car with which he could practice. He would drive it down Ventura Boulevard to his restaurant, and the cops would let him go without bothering him.[333] (Bud later said he almost hit Lou while driving in this scene![334]) This story actually disproves an anecdote related in the television special *Abbott and Costello Meet Jerry Seinfeld*. Seinfeld states Bud was once pulled over by a cop because he had a cigarette dangling from his mouth. It was fire season in California and there was a smoking ban in effect near the hills. Bud asked the cop what made him think he was smoking. The cop indicated the cigarette in his mouth. Bud replied, "I have shoes on but I'm not walking." The cop could not dispute this, so he let Bud go.[335] The fact Bud never drove disproves this tale, but the same story has been told about Lou. Either the incident actually happened to Costello or the story is just another example of entertainment apocrypha. After all, the duo have used the joke over and over again in their routines and public appearances.

Horatio chases the cops with the car until they close the gate. The car heads for the gate, then turns around at the last second. The car hits the well head-on, sending Ralph and the clock flying out of the car and into the bushes.

The steering wheel floats around, then comes to rest on the debris. It is an unconvincing effect due to a plainly visible wire attached to the wheel. Horatio becomes visible — he is upside down on top of the steering wheel. Melody also turns visible as everyone else arrives on the scene.

Ralph revives and tries to tell the cops he is not to blame. Suddenly, the clock chimes. The drawer has popped open and the letter is found. Melody and Horatio hug.

Emily explains that the curse has been lifted and the spirits are no longer bound to the land. Together, the ghosts run to the gate. But before leaving, Horatio hands the steering wheel to Mason. He says thanks, then does a great double take.

At the gate, the ghosts are nervous about finally leaving. Horatio offers, "Ladies first," and Melody passes through the gate. Horatio tries to cross the barrier but finds himself held back. He cries, but Melody realizes his coat is stuck on the gate and frees him. They leave together.

A glittering ray of light shines down. Melody hears Tom calling for her. She says good-bye to Horatio and they admit they will miss each other. Horatio offers to have Tom and Melody over for dinner. Surprisingly, Horatio and Melody walk off in opposite directions. (Perhaps this is a hint that Tom is someplace different from where Nora resides, possibly paying for his treachery.)

Horatio is all alone, but soon he hears Nora calling to him. He walks up to the pearly gates where Nora waits on the other side. They kiss.

"Now that I'm here," says Horatio, "nothing can keep us apart. Let me in." But Nora cannot. She points to a sign on Heaven's gate — "CLOSED FOR WASHINGTON'S BIRTHDAY" (a wonderful closing gag). Horatio is dumbfounded. "'Od's Bodkins!" he says.

The ending in the script was quite different from the one actually filmed. After Melody and Horatio said good-bye, Horatio would go on and spot Cuthbert dressed as an angel and running off clutching a harp. He is pursued by two similarly dressed men holding tridents who yell, "Stop thief! Bring back that harp!" Horatio shakes his head and says, "Same old Cuthbert." When he finally meets up with Nora he asks her what it is like in heaven. She says she does not know because she has not been inside yet. The powers that be gave her special permission to wait for Horatio. "It wouldn't be heaven without you," she says, and as they embrace, Lancelot (with wings like Pegasus) emerges from the mist and carries off the reunited lovers.[336]

Some consider this to be the first Abbott and Costello film in which the humor is derived from characterizations and situations rather than the boys' stock routines.[337] That could very well be true; even *Little Giant* contained one of their patented sketches. True also is the fact that virtually no elements of the future monster spoof formula can be found here.

Instead, the film fits neatly into the ghost fantasy subgenre. Just bordering the realm of horror-comedy, the ghost comedy contains virtually no scares and is better seen as a situational comedy in which one or more characters just happen to be ghosts. Characters in the film might react to the ghosts with fright but there are no fright scenes for the audience, just laughs.

These fantasies usually feature likable lead characters with a zest for life who are tragically cut down in their prime. They return as ghosts or spirits and haunt another likable character, one who does not have as much zest for life and needs to be taught the value of it. The spirits have to fulfill a task or complete an errand before they can happily retire to the afterlife. The human character risks his life, his career, and his sanity to help the ghosts, who become the best friends he ever had. Although seen as crazy by his friends and family, the human character helps the ghost solve their problem and complete their task while at the same time learning a valuable lesson about life from the spirit. An intriguing premise with multiple variations, the ghost fantasy formula still pops up today in comedies like *The Sixth Man* (1997) and even in more serious films such as *Ghost* (1990).

The Time of Their Lives follows this formula to a tee. Horatio and Melody have everything to live for and are about to be married when they are mistakenly shot down. They cannot get into heaven until their innocence is proven, and so they engage the help of the mansion's new residents. The humans help the ghosts get into heaven, while at the same time the ghosts help the human characters open up to new ideas (June and Milly), regain their nerves (Sheldon), and make up for sins of the past (Dr. Greenway).

These types of films are usually light and fluffy and, although they skirt darker issues, never become too serious. *The Time of Their Lives* actually goes a bit deeper in that the problem the ghosts must solve is on two levels. On the basic level, the ghosts must prove their innocence. Seen as traitors, they must reveal the truth to the world. In this world, how others perceive you is all important—if you are seen as a traitor, then you *are* a traitor (which may be why Major Putnam's curse actually works). The ghosts cannot rest until their character is restored, until history is made right. It is not necessarily a fair world, but truth makes up the backbone of justice and integrity. The ghosts have to prove their innocence even though their consciences are clear. The thought that someone might perceive them as traitors is enough to bind them to the earth.

The second level, and the underlying problem that must be solved, deals with sexual fulfillment. The ghosts yearn to be cleared of the charges against them because they have unfinished business—they never consummated their love with their intendeds. Sex is the true driving force behind their actions. Hints of this come out again and again. Both Horatio and Melody are romantic, sensual beings. Melody is first seen dancing with Tom while being admired by all the men in the room. Later, when they talk, both seem anxious to be married and to be lovers. Later, as a ghost, Melody uses a provocative shimmy to turn herself invisible, another device marking her as a sexually charged being.

Horatio is also seen in a similar way. He is overjoyed to see Nora, and they excitedly talk about freeing her from bondage so they can be married. Horatio is an old school romantic—he tells Nora to take a bite out of an apple first so that when he bites it, it will taste sweeter. He even attempts to imitate Melody's shimmy (though Costello's character necessitates this becoming a comedic device).

As ghosts, no sexual drive or longing is lost for Horatio and Melody. Melody hints to Horatio that they should briefly forget their fiancées and enjoy each other's company. For Horatio, this means having his back scratched, but Melody is suggesting they go a lot further. Melody is also attracted to Sheldon, evident when she wonders who the nice, young man is. (Melody seems to have more of a sexual drive than Horatio, though Horatio continually expresses longing for his lost Nora.)

Melody and Horatio are killed before they can sleep with their future spouses (this is, after all, the time of the Revolutionary War). As ghosts, they want to leave the earth so they can be reunited with these people. Melody speaks of her lost Tom with sad eyes and a longing to see him when his voice calls to her during a séance. Horatio takes every opportunity to call out the window, "Nora! It won't be long now!" Heaven for them is the orgasm; it is sexual fulfillment and satisfaction — quite a bold statement for the time.

Apparently, the film was too bold and too different for the public. Fans were not interested in seeing Bud and Lou on separate sides and would accept them only as a team. Unsurprisingly, Bud liked his role(s) in this film, the best in his career. He wrote a short piece for *The Saturday Evening Post* in 1949 in which he stated Greenway was his favorite role because the parts were reversed and he finally got to take the punishment from Lou. "I enjoyed the reversal of the usual Abbott-Costello film formula because it was a novelty and because I thought it would help us at the box office. The picture was fast-moving, with lots of laughs and some fine trick photography."[338]

Critics at the time were not impressed with the effort, shrugging it off as another in the long series of comedy-fantasies Hollywood was grinding out.[339] Some did praise the film, however. *Variety* said, "Direction is well-aimed at the belly laugh level and the trick photography is handled with flawless technique ... film sags only in the script where Abbott and Costello could use some fresh, bright material instead of the easy and tired way out." *The Hollywood Reporter* stated, "Something new is being offered by Abbott and Costello, something gay and riotously brand new ... the best Abbott and Costello show to date."[340]

Contemporary critics all agree that the film is one of the team's finest works. Leonard Maltin says the picture is one of the team's best, calling it "imaginative, funny, and well-done."[341] The *VideoHound* also feels it is one of the best A&C comedies.[342] Martin and Porter sum it up as "one of Abbott and Costello's most unusual features" and compare it favorably to *I Married a Witch* (1942) and *The Canterville Ghost* (1944).[343] Stanley labels it "a classic example of the team at its best."[344] Jim Mulholland states, "Lou ... gives the performance of his career. Bud ... showed that he was capable of being a fine character actor."[345] Furmanek and Palumbo take an unusual step back from their material and give personal comments, calling Lou's performance the most endearing of his career and remarking that the duo did not need their old routines to charm us.[346] Brunas, Brunas, and Weaver also recall the film fondly, but with their usual reservations. After labeling it one of Abbott and Costello's best outings they go on to say, "The story is solid, the look and tone of the film is right, and much of the time it's funny when it wants to be."[347] They did feel the last third of the picture seems to belong to a different movie because the car chase is "second-drawer slapstick" and Bud's antics with the clock are nothing more than "typical movie nonsense."[348] However, they make an interesting point when they call *The Time of Their Lives* "an Abbott and Costello movie for people who don't like Abbott and Costello."[349]

At the time, the film was not heavily pushed as a ghost fantasy, which is surprising considering how popular this type of picture was. Publicity material gave no indication that the film was a fantasy. It also did not advertise the fact that Lou played a period character. The film's poster, ads, and many of the publicity stills (not to mention the cover of its video box) featured Abbott and Costello in contemporary business suits rather than their period costumes.[350]

The movie's trailer did emphasize the fact that Lou was a ghost and played up the comedy antics arising from such a situation.[351] It portrayed the picture as a light fantasy and, although Bud's role was not emphasized, called it "Something new from Bud and Lou."

Unfortunately for the film, it came at a bad time. As mentioned before, the public was not interested and the result was a poor box office return. This was the last film the duo did before Universal's restructuring, and, because the returns were bad, the new management came in with an intense dislike for Abbott and Costello.[352] It would take *Abbott and Costello Meet Frankenstein* for the team to have another box office winner and for the studio management to again accept the comedy duo as one of their top draws.

World War II temporarily interrupted the flow of the team's pictures to Europe. When the conflict ceased, France and Spain quickly snatched up all the old Abbott and Costello films. During the summer of 1947, *The Time of Their Lives* was the only American film making money in Madrid.[353] They must have known then that the film was one of the team's best pictures. It is a shame it took the rest of the world so long to find out.

Abbott and Costello Meet the Killer, Boris Karloff

Released: August 22, 1949 *Running time:* 82 minutes
Reissued: March 23, 1956 (with *Abbott and Costello Meet Frankenstein*)

Directed by: Charles T. Barton; *Produced by:* Robert Arthur; *Screenplay by:* Hugh Wedlock, Jr., Howard Snyder, and John Grant; *Original Story by:* Hugh Wedlock, Jr., and Howard Snyder; *Director of Photography:* Charles Van Enger; *Art Direction:* Bernard Herzbrun and Richard H. Riedel; *Set Decorations:* Russell A. Gausman and Oliver Emert; *Music:* Milton Schwarzwald; *Film Editor:* Edward Curtiss; *Sound:* Leslie I. Carey and Robert Pritchard; *Costumes:* Rosemary Odell; *Hair Stylist:* Joan St. Oeger; *Makeup:* Bud Westmore; *Special Photography:* David S. Horsley, ASC.

Cast: Bud Abbott (Casey Edwards); Lou Costello (Freddy Phillips); Boris Karloff (Swami Talpur); Lenore Aubert (Angela Gordon); Gar Moore (Jeff Wilson); Donna Martell (Betty Crandall); Alan Mowbray (Melton); James Flavin (Inspector Wellman); Roland Winters (T. Hanley Brooks); Nicholas Joy (Amos Strickland); Mikel Conrad (Sergeant Stone); Morgan Farley (Gregory Milford); Victoria Horne (Mrs. Hargreave); Percy Helton (Abernathy); Claire DuBrey (Mrs. Grimsby); Harry Hayden (Lawrence Crandall); Vincent Renno (Mike Relia); Marjorie Bennett, Gail Bonney, Henrietta Taylor (Maids); Harry Brown (Medical Examiner); Frankie Van (Bozzo); Billy Gray (Boy with Arrow).

Although Jim Mulholland (in his *Abbott and Costello Book*) considers *Abbott and Costello Meet the Killer, Boris Karloff* to be part of their horror cycle,[354] the truth of the matter is that the film is more a spoof of murder mysteries than it is horror movies. In fact, like earlier Universal films such as *The House of Fear* (1939) and *The Strange Case of Dr. RX* (1942), the picture is a horror whodunit, a hybrid genre mixing comedy, horror, and mystery in a blender to create a bizarre concoction of thrills and chills.

The film is included in this study because it does follow the horror spoof formula closely. It was Universal's official follow-up to the success of *Abbott and Costello Meet Frankenstein* (though *Mexican Hayride* appeared in between) and attempted to emulate the previous film's style. It even featured the same producer and director!

Storywise, no monsters or supernatural beings are present, which is why the picture is not grouped with the first four discussed in this book. Instead, the film is closer in concept to *Who Done It?* which was also a murder mystery. In fact, the two films are quite similar. In each, Abbott and Costello are stuck in the middle of a murder mystery case. They attempt to solve the case, only to find the killer is after them because Costello is holding on to a crucial piece of evidence (in *Who Done It?* it is a rubber glove; in *Killer* it is a handkerchief — although we will see that this is not really the case). The duo find themselves pursued by the police, who believe they are in league with the killer. In the end, Abbott and Costello win the respect and admiration of the police by helping them solve the crime and, more importantly, catch the killer before he can get away.

On closer examination, the two films turn out to be quite different. The settings are naturally distinct, but so is the tone. In the first one, Abbott and Costello rely strongly on their old routines (including a variation of "Who's on First?" involving watts and volts and the "Alexander 2222" bit) and on physical gags involving props (such as water fountains, elevators, and limburger cheese). The actual murder mystery is just a device for Lou to exhibit his scared schtick, and when the murderer is revealed, it seems as though the people on the set had randomly picked one of the contract players to do the deed. *Killer* actually takes the time to set up a complicated mystery plot and uses less of the Abbott and Costello stock routines. The same amount of belly laughs are there, but this time it is actually possible for mystery buffs to attempt to solve the case, since the killer is given a probable motive.

The original treatment for what became *Abbott and Costello Meet the Killer, Boris Karloff* was submitted by Hugh Wedlock, Jr., and Howard Snyder as a vehicle for Bob Hope and was entitled "Easy Does It." It follows the plot of *Meet the Killer* closely, except the main character is a radio star named "Easy Davis." At the point of a nervous breakdown, Easy plans a getaway to the Arrowhead Springs resort and spa. But the lawyer for the show's sponsor (Amos Strickland) insists he continue his broadcasts. He arranges to do the show from the resort, but when he arrives, he discovers Strickland's dead body in his room. Easy finds he is the number one suspect in the murder investigation and must solve the mystery in order to clear himself. Universal bought the story but reworked it as a project for Abbott and Costello under the title *Abbott and Costello Meet the Killers*. Oscar Brodney contributed to the script without taking any screen credit.[355]

Swami Talpur, the part Boris Karloff would play, was originally a female character named Madame Switzer. Karloff signed to appear on February 5, 1949, necessitating the change. He would be a "name" guest star for the film, and it was hoped his name would make a connection with *Frankenstein* in the minds of the public.[356] Most likely, the producers hoped the Karloff name would give the project a general connection with the horror genre. This was just the type of role many critics accused Karloff of walking through, saying he did not give his all to such parts because he felt they (or the project) were beneath him. Sara Karloff does not agree with these assessments:

> I think my father gave 150 percent every time he walked on the set. I think he was well known for being a consummate professional, always ready with his lines and always gracious and appreciative of his co-workers. And to say he walked through his part I think would be categorically something he would never do. I mean, he was delighted to be a working actor and he respected the profession, and he was *immensely* gratified by the opportunity to continue working.[357]

A year earlier, Karloff had turned his nose up at the idea of even seeing *Abbott and Costello Meet Frankenstein*, yet here he was appearing in a similarly veined spoof. Maybe he was willing because he did not have much to do in the film yet earned billing in the picture's title. He would have more to do a few years later when he starred in *Abbott and Costello Meet Dr. Jekyll and Mr. Hyde*. No stranger to horror spoofs, he had appeared in the wild and wacky *You'll Find Out* (1940) with Kay Kyser and His Orchestra, from the *Kollege of Musical Knowledge* radio show, and *The Boogie Man Will Get You* (1942) with Peter Lorre. He would go on, in the sixties, to appear in Roger Corman's spoof of his own Edgar Allan Poe series, *The Raven* (1963), with Lorre and Vincent Price. The trio added Basil Rathbone to the team when they made *The Comedy of Terrors* (1963) for director Jacques Tourneur. Sara Karloff commented on her father's work in horror spoofs: "I always enjoyed any of the films my father did. And it was fun seeing him in a spoofing situation. I know that he did a lot of radio appearances and a lot of television appearances where he spoofed his own boogie man image. It was just a different venue to see him in, and it was always fun to see him ... do that."[358] Karloff's last great film was Peter Bogdanovich's *Targets* (1968), a fantastic look at modern violence and the fading horror stars of the past. Karloff died on February 2, 1969, of a respiratory illness at the age of 81.[359]

Although Karloff never praised the work of Abbott and Costello, the boys apparently loved working with him, according to Charles T. Barton.[360] Another actor they loved working with was Lenore Aubert. After her great performance in *Abbott and Costello Meet Frankenstein*, Lou wanted her to appear in *Meet the Killer*. One studio executive asked Lou, "What are you trying to do here? Turn this into a trio?"[361]

Other familiar faces make up the supporting cast. Universal regular Alan Mowbray plays the real killer; he had previously been a nemesis to Sherlock Holmes in the 1946 thriller *Terror By Night*. Mowbray had also appeared in *My Man Godfrey* (1936), *Topper* (1937), and *My Darling Clementine* (1946). Roland Winters would go on to play Charlie Chan, taking over the role from Sidney Toler in the Monogram series. Percy Helton was a familiar bit player, notably for his appearance in *Kiss Me Deadly* (1956) as the greasy morgue attendant whose fingers get painfully slammed in a drawer by Ralph Meeker's Mike Hammer.

Furmanek and Palumbo reported a strange story concerning Mikel Conrad, who played Sergeant Stone in the film: During the production of *Meet the Killer*, Conrad was the object of a police manhunt on an assault warrant.[362]

Charles T. Barton again directed; he had helmed the previous seven Abbott and Costello films. This one would, however, be his last Abbott and Costello comedy.

The budget of the film was scaled back because too much had been spent on the previous Universal release, *Mexican Hayride*. The initial budget was only $685,800, with Bud and Lou being paid $113,750 and Boris Karloff receiving $20,000.[363] Karloff's salary was twice what Lugosi had received for his more substantial part in *Abbott and Costello Meet Frankenstein*[364] The picture went $52,000 over budget and 14 days over schedule.

Apparently, the mood on the set was rather somber. Abbott and Costello were concerned about paying off the $80,000 mortgage on the Lou Costello, Jr., Youth Foundation, with Lou in particular spending most of his downtime on the phone trying to raise the necessary funds. Reports of fighting between the two comedians did not help, and, by the time the film wrapped, Costello's health had worsened and he suffered a relapse of rheumatic fever. He told reporters he had had a nervous breakdown and reportedly told director Barton that he was "directing a dead man."[365]

To their credit, the boys still come off well in the film, which opens with a cartoon title sequence (just as its predecessor, *Meet Frankenstein*, did). The boys are painting their names on a wall with blood when a drive-by shooting scatters them (A&C in the Hood?). The bullets spell out "Meet the Killer." The cartoon Lou pops back into frame and says, "You didn't dot the 'i'!" A knife is thrown which does dot the "i," and the cartoon Lou says, "Ooooh!" Blood then drips down to spell Boris Karloff's name. The music accompanying the title credits is lifted from *Meet Frankenstein*, as is most of the film's score.

The story opens on a stormy night. Headlights illuminate a sign for CRANDALL'S LOST CAVERN HOTEL — 3 MILES. The resort, according to the sign, offers golf, swimming, mineral baths, and European cuisine.

In the lobby, reporters wait around for the arrival of famous defense attorney Amos Strickland. Hotel detective Casey Edwards (Abbott) has to ask one of them for that information, to which the reporter replies, "A fine hotel dick — don't you read anything outside the racing form?" Already, the familiar Abbott character is established as a gambler and a con man — after all, why else would someone hire him as a detective and let him talk them into hiring his clumsy cousin as a bellboy?

The reporter tells Casey that Strickland, the number one lawyer in the country, postponed all his important cases to come to the hotel. Something big is obviously in the works. Strickland finally arrives. He is a mean, grouchy old man who yells at the reporters and smashes one of the photographer's cameras. Casey, sensing an opportunity for advancement, helps break up the reporters and leads Strickland to the front desk. Behind a curtain, one of the guests, the beautiful Angela Gordon, watches the proceedings.

Jeff Wilson, the clerk, greets Strickland. (Gar Moore is stiff and wooden in the role, but there is not much material for him to work with.) Strickland asks that the hotel's owner, Lawrence Crandall, be notified of his arrival. Jeff says Crandall is not in but that Crandall's niece Betty would like to talk with him. Strickland is not interested and asks for a room.

Bellboy Freddy Phillips (Costello) brings in Strickland's luggage and hits the lawyer in the leg with his golf bag. "Be more careful!" yells Strickland just before Freddy drops another bag on his foot. Freddy then breaks the lawyer's glasses with his own umbrella. "I'll have your job for this!" fumes Strickland, to which Freddy replies, "Aren't you a little too old for this type of work?" Costello is hilarious here. In less than a minute, he completely destroys this pompous grouch, and his meek little "I'm sorry" makes him so cute that we immediately sympathize with him.

Casey can only shake his head as Freddy accidentally dumps the clubs out of Strickland's golf bag, infuriating the man even more. The hotel manager, Mr. Melton, arrives on the scene. Strickland insists Freddy be fired and Melton easily goes along with this. Freddy threatens Strickland, something unusual for a Costello character but integral to the film's plot. He says he will get even and make Strickland pay. "Are you threatening me?" asks Strickland, to which Freddy replies, "In words of one syllable — YES!"

Unfortunately, Freddy's amusing comeback is ruined when he spins around and trips over Strickland's bags. Casey laughs but Freddy turns on him. "Every dog has its day," he tells the lawyer and barks at him.

Melton tells Casey to take Strickland's bags to his room. In a nice touch, a shocked Casey asks, "Me?" He is obviously not used to manual labor. Strickland is led to his room.

Betty arrives on the scene and is disappointed Jeff did not have Strickland come see her. Betty and Jeff are obviously in love, but Betty is preoccupied with Strickland's arrival at the hotel. Jeff tells her Freddy's been fired, but she is not listening. This is another nice touch — Jeff says Freddy was fired *again*. In other words, this has happened before. Betty says she will speak to her uncle, but will not tell Jeff what she is worried about.

Another guest, Mrs. Grimsby, asks for her key. While Jeff gets it, she peeks at the register to see which room Strickland is in.

A potentially funny scene would have appeared next but was deleted. In it, Freddy wants to apologize to Mr. Strickland and asks Casey to pretend to be the lawyer so Freddy can practice on him. But Casey takes the part too seriously and, when Freddy apologizes, yells at him and beats him up. Then he switches gears and urges Freddy to try again — and again. But each time, Casey violently attacks Freddy. Finally, Freddy says he is sorry for sprinkling ink on his shirt, breaking his glasses, and punching him in the nose. Casey says, "You didn't punch me in the nose," to which Freddy says, "No, but I will if I don't get my job back!"[366]

Later that night, Freddy goes to Strickland's room to apologize. A quick cut to inside the room shows the body of Strickland sitting in a chair, eyes wide open, dead from a gunshot wound. The editing, combined with music from *Abbott and Costello Meet Frankenstein*, delivers a good shock. In fact, the music helps give the entire scene that follows a genuinely creepy feel. Freddy enters the room and, not knowing the lawyer is dead, apologizes to Strickland for causing him so much trouble. When he mentions dropping the golf bag on his foot, he snickers, reinforcing his role as a man-child. He asks Strickland if he will talk to Mr. Melton and help him get back his job. He slaps Strickland on the back and the body falls to the floor. Freddy thinks the lawyer is sleeping and bends down to check his pulse. Lightning from the storm outside illuminates the room and we see a figure behind the curtain (another good shock effect). Freddy does not realize he is checking his own pulse and says out loud that the "guy is pretty sick." The figure behind the curtain reaches for a handkerchief left lying by the body but Freddy picks up the incriminating evidence and fans Strickland with it. When this does not revive the lawyer, Freddy sticks the handkerchief in his pocket. He opens the curtains to get more air and we, of course, expect someone to pop out. But no one is there. After Freddy turns away, the figure is seen moving from one end of the curtain to the other.

Freddy lifts the body up and finally notices the blood from the wound. At last, he realizes Strickland is dead. "That's funny," says Freddy, "I always thought if I was in a room alone with a dead person, I would be scared. Ha ha! But ... CASEY!" He runs out to the lobby.

In the lobby, Freddy runs into Melton and Casey and tries to tell them what he has seen. There is a continuity gaff here that is only recognizable after multiple viewings of the film. Melton is later revealed to be the murderer. And it must be the murderer behind the curtain because he tries to retrieve the incriminating handkerchief. So, if Melton was in the room with Freddy and behind the curtain, then he somehow beat Freddy (who was running) back down to the lobby.

Freddy finally spits out what he has been trying to tell Casey and Melton — that Strickland has been murdered. Alan Mowbray is given a good line here when he replies, "That's impossible! We don't permit murders in this hotel!" With Jeff leading the way, they all head up to Melton's room.

Jeff arrives a few steps before the rest and sees Betty leaving Strickland's room. When the others see the body, Casey orders everyone not to touch anything. Melton wants to keep it quiet in order not to alarm the guests. Naturally, a maid arrives just then and Freddy tells her to leave an extra sheet to cover the dead body. The maid hears this, screams, and runs off. This attracts the attention of Crandall, his niece, and several other guests, who arrive as Casey phones the police.

Betty acts surprised to see the body (though rather unconvincingly acted here by Donna Martell), and Crandall has Jeff take her to her room. Beautiful Angela Gordon remarks how sad it is to see such a nice man murdered and asks Freddy for a handkerchief. Freddy almost gives her the incriminating one but at the last second substitutes another. Angela starts to depart and Freddy whisks his handkerchief back (a good bit). On the way out, Angela and Mr. Brooks share a meaningful glance. Across the hall, Swami Talpur pokes his head out and Angela tells him what has happened. She also tells Mrs. Grimsby, who is accompanied by a timid woman, Mrs. Hargreave.

Casey continues trying to reach Inspector Wellman. Brooks tries to make off with Strickland's briefcase but Freddy catches him. Melton breaks them up and Brooks accuses Freddy of trying to steal the briefcase. Freddy accuses Brooks but Melton naturally disbelieves him. He orders Freddy to apologize. "Mr. Brooks," says Freddy. "I'm sorry you're a crook." But Brooks gets back at him. "Pighead!" he says, making sure to spit in Freddy's eye. Costello makes an odd noise here ("P-p-p-p-ing!") and wipes his eye, but he is clearly the victor.

Crandall tells Melton to keep the goings-on quiet and takes the briefcase, planning to lock it up until the police arrive. Casey finally reaches Inspector Wellman and tells him to come over.

A man named Relia arrives and tells Casey that his gun has disappeared; he wants to inform the police in case it turns out to be the murder weapon. Casey reasons that anyone could have taken it, even a maid or a bellboy because they would have passkeys. Freddy agrees and begins to incriminate himself. Melton tells Casey to search Freddy for the gun. In a great bit, Casey only finds on Freddy a small viewer, which he peeps into. A sound effect makes a loud "BOING" as Casey sees a dirty picture inside. Without any words, Casey slaps Freddy. But Freddy quickly grabs the peeper back whispering, "It's mine." While it may not sound that funny on paper, this gag rarely fails to elicit a laugh from the viewer.

Melton insists that Freddy is the killer and tells Casey not to let him out of his sight until the police arrive. They go to their room.

Freddy is worried. Casey thinks he is innocent but admits things look bad for him. He explains that Freddy does have two things going for him: they found no bloodstains on Freddy, and the gun is still missing. As Casey mentions the blood stains, Freddy wipes his brow with the handkerchief and sees blood on it. He hides it. When Casey mentions the gun, Freddy pulls down his bed covers and finds the gun there. He hastily wraps up the bed coverings, making Casey suspicious. The gun falls out and Casey demands to know where he got it. Freddy doesn't know. Casey realizes it was planted and tells Freddy they must return it to Relia's room.

Freddy cannot understand why someone would want to frame him. "When we find that out, we'll find the culprit," says Casey. "Who's the culprit?" asks Freddy. "The culprit and the murderer are the same!" says Casey. This is the start of one of the film's running gags, although not a very funny one. It tries too hard to use the same type of wordplay as "Who's on First?" or "Watts Are Volts," but it does not work as easily. Whereas the other routines were verbally smooth, this one comes off as forced.

"Come on, shake a leg," says Casey. Freddy literally does so, and the two set off for Relia's room. Again, Lou takes Bud literally at every turn.

On the way, Casey and Freddy see Angela leaving her room, so they hide until she has passed. Casey does not trust her but Freddy is obviously attracted to her. He tries to follow in order to "question" her. Casey, of course, leads him in the opposite direction.

At Relia's room, the two decide to go inside. If Relia is there, they will pretend they have the wrong room. No one answers their knock so Casey tries a key, but it does not work.

"Here, try this," says Freddy, giving Casey another key.

"Where'd you get that?" asks Casey.

"Red."

"Red who?"

"Skelton. It's a skeleton key — opens any door."

Bud does a double take and the two proceed inside.

In the room, our heroes find the place ransacked. Casey finds a telegram from Mr. Strickland to Relia saying Strickland wants to use Relia's case in his memoirs. The telegram orders Relia to come to the hotel. This makes Casey suspicious and he plans to check up on Relia. He tells Freddy to make sure the coast is clear while he plants the gun.

Freddy opens the door and finds the Swami there. Like Dracula in *Abbott and Costello Meet Frankenstein*, the Swami hypnotizes Freddy. Also like in the previous film, Costello's character is immediately susceptible to the hypnotism. The Swami repeats over and over again, "You didn't see me. You didn't see me. I wasn't here." He leaves Freddy in a daze.

When Casey is ready to go, he finds Freddy in a deep sleep.

"What's the matter with you?" Casey asks.

"I didn't see him," says Freddy.

"Who?"

"The man who wasn't there."

Casey is frustrated and tells Freddy to close the door. Freddy steps back into Relia's room, then closes the door. Casey returns and drags Freddy out. Costello next performs a hilarious bit of physical comedy as he moves off down the hall: still in a daze, his hand turns his head, which forces the rest of his body to follow, and that is how he turns the corner.

Inspector Wellman and Sergeant Stone have arrived at the hotel and they meet with Melton and Milford (Strickland's secretary) in Strickland's room while the doctor takes the body out. Milford explains he was Strickland's secretary for over twenty years and, although the lawyer had enemies, he knows of no one who would resort to murder. What is Milford talking about? Strickland was a criminal lawyer who defended murderers! And there is an entire hotel of suspicious crooks in the vicinity!

Melton still insists Freddy is guilty, but the Inspector wants to handle the investigation his own way. He orders Freddy to be brought in. Stone fetches Freddy, and Casey tells his friend to be firm. But immediately upon entering, Freddy breaks down and drops to his hands and knees, begging the Inspector not to whip him with a rubber hose. Casey slaps him, telling him that Wellman did not even touch him. Freddy lets out a typical Costello remark: "What kind of third degree is this?"

Dialogue was omitted here that had Casey try to tell Wellman that Freddy is too dumb to commit a murder. He goes on and on, calling Freddy a pathetic imbecile and a spineless, yellow, chicken-livered, cowardly moron. Freddy finally says, "Thanks, Casey. I knew you'd go to bat for me." What remains is Casey simply stating Freddy is too dumb to commit a crime.

Freddy lets slip about the telegram they found in Relia's room. This arouses Wellman's suspicions and he puts Freddy in Casey's custody. He says Freddy is to remain at the hotel as a guest of the State. When Freddy realizes that this means everything is paid for, he is extremely happy. The duo leave but Freddy is caught eavesdropping at the door, a great capper to the scene.

A very important scene contained in the original script (but not found in the finished film) would have appeared at this point. It is too bad it was cut because it would have explained a lot of back-story and made clear some of the action to come. In the missing scene, Strickland's former clients relax around the pool while Freddy enjoys a shave and manicure as a guest of the State. The guests realize they all have motives to keep their pasts hidden and any one of them might have killed Strickland. Angela was accused of poisoning her husband, Brooks' wife fell out of a window a week after he took out an insurance policy on her, and three wealthy women left their fortunes to the Swami before committing suicide. They realize they are safe as long as the police suspect Freddy, so they decide to pin the crime on him. Angela feels she can entice Freddy to sign a confession.[367]

In the actual film, Freddy enjoys all the comforts of the hotel while exasperating Casey. Angela calls Freddy and makes plans to get together in his room. Casey warns Freddy that the special treatment will not last, especially after he shows Wellman the report he has on Mike Relia. Freddy says he will never be an ordinary bellhop again — he has a date with Angela! Following the formula of the monster spoof, Bud's character is confused and shocked over the attention Lou receives from beautiful women. He never realizes the women are just using Lou.

Someone knocks at the door and Freddy, thinking Angela has arrived, opens the door and says, "Hello darling." It is none other than Bobby Barber, making a cameo as another bellhop. "Darling?" he snarls. "Here's your suit!" When the real Angela arrives, Freddy makes Casey leave, though the ever sly Casey seems to be taking a good look at Angela's derriere on the way out.

Freddy and Angela sit on the couch where Freddy acts coy. Angela brings up the murder. Freddy comments, "If they ever give me the gas chamber, they'll be hanging the wrong man." This is very similar to a joke used in *Who Done It?*

Angela then asks Freddy if he knows who did it, bringing up the murderer/culprit running gag. Freddy says the murderer is the culprit. Angela quickly turns the gag around to her favor, stinging Freddy with his own punchline (and confusing him at the same time). She tells Freddy he should find out who the killer is and become a hero because she just adores heroes. She has him write out a confession he can give to the murderer to sign. It reads: "I hereby confess to the murder of Amos Strickland." She then has Freddy sign the confession as a witness. He does it and she takes the note, telling him not to tell Casey about it. At this point, the champagne cocktails she ordered are brought to the room.

Meanwhile, Wellman meets with the suspects, telling them he has a report on each one of them. Casey arrives and, in the hall, tells Wellman that Relia (who is missing) is the killer. Casey sent in Relia's fingerprints and discovered that Strickland defended Relia on a murder charge in 1940. But Wellman already knows this — all the suspects received telegrams similar to Relia's and all were once defended by Strickland. Even Crandall received a telegram. "Sorry, Casey. Keep trying," says Wellman. This is an interesting moment — Wellman is like a father figure happy to see Casey trying to help, while Casey simply shrugs off his attempt to solve the crime as a shot in the dark.

Rejoining the others, Wellman wants Stone to find Relia and Angela. Casey realizes that Angela is with Freddy, and soon learns that Angela was accused of feeding her husband poisoned champagne cocktails. Casey says the two are having champagne right now, and Crandall blurts out that there is a poison antidote kit in the doctor's office. They all race out. The music in this scene helps tremendously by building in tempo as the suspense in the scene mounts.

Meanwhile, Freddy refuses to drink the cocktail because he never touches alcohol. Angela's attempts to coerce him continually fail. When she says to do it for little Angela, Freddy replies, "I wouldn't do it for *big* Angela!" Hmmm...

When Casey, Wellman, and the others burst in, Freddy has a glass in his hand and he has spilled some of the champagne on himself. Thinking the worst, Casey drags him into the bathroom. A very funny sequence follows, one of the best in the film. Wellman and Milford grill Angela while Stone hands Casey special concoctions designed to make Freddy throw up (mustard and milk, oil and water, sweet oil and vinegar, etc.). Off-camera, Casey shoves the liquids down Freddy's throat, and the unfortunate continually staggers back into view of the camera, whining that he has a date. He's like a little kid, embarrassed to be caught with a female. "What are you doing?" he cries out, "I have a girl here!"

In between, Milford tells Angela that he has filled Wellman in on all of her playmates, including the fake swami from Brooklyn. Milford, who before had defended Strickland's clients, does an about face and seems very venomous towards Ms. Gordon. Angela tells Wellman she will cooperate as long as her name is kept out of the papers — she is engaged to be married. She says she does not know who killed Strickland, nor did she put anything in Freddy's cocktail.

A dejected Casey finally emerges, telling them that nothing worked. Freddy staggers out crying. He finally tells them he did not even drink from the cocktail. Casey asks why he did not tell them sooner. "Everytime I opened my mouth," explains Freddy, "you kept pouring something down into it."

Later, Angela meets with the other suspects while they play bridge. Mrs. Grimsby says the confession is no good if Freddy is still hanging around. Angela explains how she only intended to get Freddy drunk and put him on the slow boat to Shanghai. (Ironically, Bud Abbott had been shanghaied at the age of 16 on a boat going to Norway. He was gone a whole year.[368]) Swami Talpur opts for something more permanent and decides Freddy will have to commit suicide.

That night, a noose hangs from the ceiling of Freddy's room while the Swami sits by the bedside hypnotizing Freddy. He says Freddy's future is black and there is only one escape — death. He has Freddy stand on the foot of the bed and put his head in the noose. On the count of three, he is to jump. Freddy loses his balance, though, and hangs on to the rope, pulling it down from the ceiling.

The Swami tries a new tactic. He asks Freddy if he has a gun. Freddy says yes and the Swami orders him to get it from the next room. Freddy walks into the door on his way out of the room, a wonderful comic touch that is, unfortunately, barely noticed. The gun turns out to be a spray gun and is harmless to Freddy. The Swami asks Freddy how he would like to die. Costello has one of the film's best lines here when he replies, "Old age."

The Swami opens the window and has Freddy climb onto the sill. When he orders him to jump, Freddy jumps back into the room. When he orders him to climb up again, Freddy refuses. The Swami takes a knife and says, "You'll commit suicide if it's the last thing you do." Boris sounds very much like the Grinch here, a character he would provide the voice for in the TV special *How the Grinch Stole Christmas* (based on the book by Dr. Seuss).

The Swami gives Freddy the knife and tells him to use it. Freddy picks his fingernails with it. The Swami forces Freddy into the next room where he corners him and tells him to plunge the knife into his heart. Freddy again refuses. "Amazing," says the Swami, "even under hypnosis, the will of an idiot to cling to life." Noticing Freddy's reflection, the

Swami asks Freddy if he would plunge the knife into the heart of the man he sees in the mirror. But Freddy sees the reflection of the Swami in the mirror and quickly shakes his head yes. When the Swami orders him to do so, Freddy chases him with the knife (note Costello's evil grin). The Swami leaves and Casey arrives. Freddy sees Casey in the mirror and chases *him* with the knife. Casey snaps Freddy out of his trance and demands to know what is going on. Freddy blames it all on sleepwalking.

Casey explains that Relia has run out and they have to find him and make him talk. Freddy starts getting dressed, but when he goes in the closet to get his suit, he finds the dead body of Relia hanging on a clothes hook. Freddy shows the body to Casey, who notices Relia was stabbed. Casey wonders whether Freddy killed Relia while running around with the knife. He decides to plant the body back in Relia's own room and leaves to get a laundry cart. Abbott seems to be showing more loyalty to Costello than he normally does. Usually he is ready to turn Costello in or to quickly accuse him of something he did not do. Here, even though Costello's character looks very suspicious, Abbott stands up for him and tries to help him. Contrast this to his behavior in *Africa Screams* when he abandons Costello in the middle of Africa after realizing he has lost his precious diamonds. Perhaps Abbott helps Costello here because he will receive no kind of reward by turning him in.

A cute moment occurs at the conclusion of the previously mentioned scene that might have been ad-libbed by Costello. After Casey leaves, Freddy looks at Relia's body and imitates for the camera the state of the corpse. Then he softly cries, "Mama." It is a funny scene.

Casey returns with a laundry cart while Freddy dresses up like a maid. (He puts his all into the role, even adopting an annoying falsetto.) He and Casey then head for Relia's room with the body concealed in the cart. In the hall, they run into Wellman, who asks for an extra towel. Casey and Wellman discuss the case and Wellman says he is waiting for a call that will pin the murder on the bellboy. Freddy gets the towel, not realizing he has gotten it wrapped around the exposed arm of Relia. Verbal cues from Casey alert Freddy to his predicament ("Everything's in hand!") and he finally gives Wellman a towel. A phone call distracts the Inspector, and Casey and Freddy take the opportunity to make a hasty exit. Wellman seems uncharacteristically dense here. Casey explains that Freddy is the stupidest maid in the whole hotel and should really be fired. Wellman replies by saying, "Maybe she knows where the bodies are buried."

The boys finally plant the body in Relia's room, leaving it in the closet. Unbeknownst to them, the slamming of a door causes the body to fall back into the laundry cart. They leave, but Casey realizes that if Wellman finds the cart in the room he may connect it with Casey and the "maid." Freddy retrieves the cart (with Relia inside) and leaves it in a hall closet.

The two return to their room to rest. Casey tells Freddy to hang his clothes up in the closet. Inside, Freddy finds the body of Milford. In a daze, he silently retrieves the laundry cart and brings it back into the room. A great gag follows. Freddy yells, "CASEY!" Casey comes running, takes one look at the body, yells "No!" and runs out to get the cart. He comes back in and sees that Freddy has already done so.

"Scared you, didn't it?" asks Freddy.

"Mm-hmm," replies Casey. "I'll confess."

"YOU did it?" asks Freddy.

This is a throwback to their running gag about the culprit and the murderer. It also foreshadows Lou's belief at the film's conclusion that Casey is the real murderer.

Freddy readies the cart for Milford's body and finds Relia inside. The two are now totally confused. They decide to take both bodies to the card room since no one is down there so late at night.

In the card room, a clever shot shows a knife appear over a table, followed by the appearance of night manager Abernathy harmlessly eating an apple. When Freddy enters dressed as the maid, Abernathy starts flirting with him. Freddy is, in fact, sexually harassed by Abernathy! He holds back his urge to punch him when Abernathy pinches his cheek. Abernathy asks Freddy to keep him company, saying, "Things have been dead around here all night." Unfortunately, this funny line is ruined by Freddy's reply of "Much deader than you think." This is too obvious a response that painfully hammers home the joke. A surprised and wordless reaction from Costello would have been a lot funnier.

Casey enters, catching Abernathy hugging Freddy. The desk phone distracts Abernathy and he leaves. Casey and Freddy try to get rid of the bodies. On the phone, Inspector Wellman asks Abernathy if he has seen Freddy. Abernathy tells him the only person he has seen is Casey, so Wellman decides to come down.

With Abernathy on his way back into the room, Casey and Freddy set up the dead bodies as if all four are playing a game of bridge. Amazingly, Abernathy falls for it. This scene inspires a few chuckles, but it goes on too long and some of the jokes fall flat. All in all, it is unconvincing and unbelievable. Abernathy comments that one man's hand is dead, to which Freddy replies, "They're both dead." Abernathy continues to flirt with Freddy, forcing Freddy to drag the man out of the room before their ruse is revealed.

Outside, Abernathy asks for a little "smack." Freddy has him close his eyes and POW! (In a well-staged moment, we, like Casey, only hear the punch from inside the other room.) Freddy rejoins Casey to clean up the room. Casey checks to see if the coast is clear and sees Wellman and Stone heading for the card room. He tries to stall them while Freddy hides the bodies.

Casey intercepts Wellman, who asks about Freddy's whereabouts. Casey feigns ignorance. Meanwhile, Freddy ditches his maid costume and hides the bodies in a freight elevator. Wellman berates Casey for letting Freddy get away and decides to put out a dragnet for the bellboy. Freddy, meanwhile, heads for the passenger elevator, where he finds the bodies! He quickly shuts the door.

Wellman, Stone, and Casey meet up with Freddy at the elevator. They interrogate Freddy while he desperately tries to keep the elevator door from opening. Wellman reveals to Freddy and Casey that they found the ashes of a burnt handkerchief with bloodstains on it. Freddy admits he burnt the handkerchief. Casey yells at him — with the handkerchief they could have found a clue to the murderer's identity. Stone thinks they have and glares at Freddy. The two policemen finally push their way into the elevator (which had gone upstairs), and Freddy is shocked to see that the bodies have disappeared once again. A scream is heard and everyone runs off to find out what is happening.

A maid in Milford's room screams and points at a blood stain on the floor. Everyone gathers around, including suspects Angela, the Swami, Mrs. Grimbsy and the others. The Inspector sends the maid away and asks if anyone has seen Milford. He also wonders why everyone is fully dressed so late at night. They say they were all playing cards in Mr. Brooks' room. Crandall claims he went for a walk and Betty says she was with him. Betty and Jeff are sent out and, in the hall, Jeff asks her why she lied and did not admit to being with him. She asks him to trust her and go along with her for the time being. These scenes with Betty and Jeff are all fine and dandy but they go nowhere. Betty's motives are never quite made clear. We know she is worried about her uncle (who we later learn was being blackmailed) but there's so little back-story (regarding both her and Crandall) that it's difficult to even care about what they are doing. Of course, Abbott and Costello are the centers of attention, but there should be an attempt to flesh out the other characters. Even in *Who Done It?* we knew about the pasts of the romantic leads and even knew why they were bickering all the time.

Wellman says everyone in the room has a motive, but Melton again insists Freddy is the killer. Wellman says Freddy has an airtight alibi and sends everyone but Casey out of the room. Freddy sticks around to laugh at Casey, thinking his cousin is now one of the suspects. Wellman tells Freddy not to laugh—he's in this thing up to his neck. But there was something strange about everyone being dressed so late at night, so he is willing to give Freddy one more chance to clear himself. The real killer will want the handkerchief, not knowing Freddy has burned it. He is to put the fictional handkerchief up for sale for $5,000. The killer will either buy it or try to off Freddy.

Wellman asks Freddy if he is smart enough to pull off the scam and Freddy assures him he is. "Oh, yeah?" asks Wellman. "Where's your hotel key?" Freddy cannot find it and Wellman whips it out. He laughs at Freddy and shows him his badge, but the badge is gone. Freddy has lifted the badge. This is an old but funny bit that Abbott and Costello used many times, including in *The Naughty Nineties*.

Outside, Freddy tells Casey he hid the bodies in the elevator, not knowing Mrs. Grimsby is eavesdropping. But they find the elevator to be empty. Casey reminds Freddy that he must find someone to buy the handkerchief. Freddy realizes the killer may try to kill him in order to get it, which worries him. But Casey, keeping in typical Abbott character, is not worried, saying that at least Freddy will be cleared. "Ain't I a lucky stiff," replies Freddy. "Lucky stiff?!? I shoulda never left Patterson." Paterson, New Jersey, is Costello's hometown and he took every opportunity on radio, television, and, to a lesser extent, the movies to make mention of it or throw it in as an in-joke.

The next day, Freddy tries to sell the handkerchief to the Swami, who is not interested. He tells Casey no one wants to buy it. A vase falls from a balcony and almost hits Freddy. He thinks the killer is making an attempt on his life but Casey points out it was just a cat who knocked it off. Then an arrow narrowly misses the nervous Freddy. "Now they've got the Indians after me!" he says. One immediately thinks of *Ride 'Em Cowboy*, though it's doubtful the connection was intentional. A little boy dressed as an Indian runs over and demands his arrow back. Freddy is too weak to pull the arrow out but the kid has no problem whatsoever. This is a weak gag and does not fit.

The characterizations of our comedy duo seen in the monster spoofs is in full force here. Costello is nervous, knowing someone is out there waiting to get him. Bud, on the other hand, merely shows annoyance and impatience. He actually wishes aloud that the killer would hurry up and make his move because he is tired of waiting!

Freddy realizes he forgot to try to sell the handkerchief to Mr. Brooks, who is in the health club. Freddy goes inside and takes a steambath next to Brooks. Brooks naturally turns down Freddy's handkerchief offer and exits with the attendant, leaving Freddy alone and locked in his steambath. A creepy moment occurs when a gloved hand reaches around the corner and turns up the steam — the killer is making his move! Freddy is too scared to scream for help and steam quickly fills the room. Instead of using real steam in this scene, the special effects men immersed dry ice in water, releasing clouds of white carbon dioxide vapor. Though not poisonous, the gas did cut off the oxygen supply in the cabinet. After being in it for fifteen minutes, Costello complained of a headache and then passed out! He was revived with no ill effects.[369]

Some effective editing and direction occurs as the scene cuts to Wellman and Stone talking to Casey. Stone says he can force a confession out of Freddy if he *sweats* him enough. Wellman agrees to this but only if their handkerchief plan does not pan out. They have until that night, then all the suspects will be leaving on the nine o'clock train. Wellman will be unable to hold them any longer.

A scream breaks the moment — a woman has seen all the steam coming out of the health club. Wellman, Stone, and Casey rush in and rescue Freddy from the cabinet. In a funny moment, Freddy rushes over to the water cooler and drinks the whole thing while the other three characters watch in amazement.

Freddy explains what happened but the police officers think his story is phony. Freddy gets mad and tells off Wellman. He tells him that his taxes pay Wellman's salary so Wellman is actually working for him.

"So?" snarls Wellman.

"Get me another bottle of water," replies Freddy.

"OK — WHAT?!?" yells Wellman. It is a funny gag, but one the boys used many times before (as in the film *In Society*).

On their way back to their room, Casey warns Freddy that he will be charged with the murder if nothing happens by nine. Freddy stops

Casey from entering the room, explaining he has set a trap by the door. "It's a booby trap," says Freddy, "for boobs." He has also set traps by the windows — should someone open the window a hammer will swing down and conk the intruder on the head. Freddy also explains why he has not set a trap by the other windows — they are three flights up and no one can get him there. Suddenly, gunshots crash through the window. Casey is ecstatic and he congratulates Freddy. He laughs as he calls Wellman. In a strangely touching moment, Freddy wonders aloud why everyone is so happy that someone is trying to kill him. Casey tells him to lie down and relax.

In the bedroom, Freddy prepares to hang his clothes in the closet. He breaks the fourth wall (a favorite Costello trick) and says that every time he opens a door he finds a dead body. So he knocks and asks if anyone is inside. Satisfied there is not, he hangs his clothes up and goes to bed. Climbing into bed, he finds himself next to Milford's body. Freddy thinks it is Casey, but when he turns down the covers and sees Milford he panics. Freddy rushes out to get Casey. As the door closes behind him, we see in the mirror's reflection that someone was hiding behind the curtains. This is a clever touch and actually makes this bit both spooky and funny at the same time.

When Freddy returns with Casey, the body is gone. Freddy is speechless, so Casey orders him to drink a glass of water. In the bathroom, Freddy sees Milford again. He leaves to get Casey but when they come back the body is gone. As they leave the bathroom, the adjoining bathroom door opens ever so slightly...

To satisfy the frantic Freddy, Casey agrees to look around the room. While he does this, he wants Freddy to call Wellman and make sure he is on his way up. Freddy goes to the next room to use the phone and sees Milford at the desk. When he brings Casey into the room, the body has again disappeared. This is just another variation of the "Changing Room" routine. It has the same premise as the moving candle and the casino room scenes in previous horror spoofs — some strange phenomenon keeps occurring, but only Costello can see it. Every time he brings Abbott into the room, things are back to normal. The humor comes more from Costello's frustration with Abbott than it does from his fear of the supernatural. Incidentally, this scene was not in the shooting script.[370]

Casey berates Freddy and decides to prove once and for all that there are no bodies in the room. He takes him around, asking again and again, "Is he there?" while pointing to all the places Freddy claimed to have seen Milford. Finally, Casey points to the bed and asks, "Is he there?" "YES!" says Freddy. Sure enough, the body is on the bed. This is an unexpected twist ending to the bit. In previous film incarnations of the routine, Costello never proves that he was seeing something out of the ordinary until the very end.

Casey realizes someone is trying to scare Freddy out of the room. Wellman knocks at the door and Casey tells Freddy that they have to get rid of him. If he finds the bodies, he will arrest Freddy for sure. Wellman and Stone enter and Casey says he made a mistake in calling them. But Freddy ruins Casey's cover-up by pointing out the bullet holes in the wall. Wellman investigates and finds Relia's body behind the couch. He sends Stone into the bedroom to get a sheet and his partner finds Milford's body. Freddy says he was framed and explains how he booby-trapped the room. The only door he did not booby-trap was the door to Crandall's room (their rooms adjoin), but Freddy trusts Crandall. Crandall makes a sudden entrance and admits to having planted the bodies. He says he did not kill the two men but found the bodies in his room. He became frightened and put the bodies in Freddy's room. Freddy then blows it when he asks Crandall, "How could you have found the bodies in your room? I put them in the elevator!"

That does it. Wellman sends Crandall out and places Freddy under arrest. Freddy gives up. Since all the evidence points to him, he is ready to go to jail and face trial. On the way out, a mysterious voice calls out, "Freddy Phillips," over and over again. It is coming from a vent. "Did I scare you with the bodies?" asks the voice. "Then listen carefully. If you don't want to die, come to the caverns at 7:30 tonight. Bring the handkerchief. I'll be on the west bank of the bottomless pit. Tell nobody and come alone." Wellman figures the voice is a phonograph record in the basement. Casey urges Freddy to go. Even Wellman agrees this is his last chance to clear himself.

"Would you rather die like a hero or live like a rat?" asks Casey. "Well?"

"Get the cheese ready," answers Freddy in a painfully predictable joke.

That night, Wellman, Stone, and Casey accompany Freddy to the entrance of the caverns. By this time, most viewers have forgotten the opening shot of the film which shows the name of the hotel: CRANDALL'S LOST CAVERNS. This was probably just an excuse to give the picture a strong horror finish and use the caverns as a creepy setting in which Costello can fool about. The set is admittedly incredible. Numerous stalactites and stalagmites line the ceiling and floor, and there is a healthy amount of fog. More music lifted from *Abbott and Costello Meet Frankenstein* also adds to the general atmosphere of the cave.

Wellman and Stone send Freddy in alone, promising to stay close behind so they can nab the killer. Freddy reluctantly proceeds ahead. Seeing two glowing eyes, he asks if the mystery figure is the man who wants to buy the handkerchief. "Who?" says the glowing eyes. Naturally, it is just an owl. (There had been similar trouble with an owl in *Hold That Ghost*.) Scared by the bird, Freddy runs off ahead, losing the police officers.

In an unusual twist, Casey is also scared by the owl as they try to catch up to Freddy. The killer outsmarts the detectives by closing a gate, keeping them from getting to Freddy. Casey says there is another entrance a half mile down, but before they can get there he twists his ankle on a rock. Barely able to walk, Casey sends the detectives on without him while he heads back to the hotel. This hints that perhaps Casey is scared of meeting up with the killer himself and had faked the accident in order to get out of a possible confrontation.

The killer spies on Freddy and drops a stalactite, which narrowly misses him. Freddy calls for Casey and runs off. He hears his voice echo and decides to test it out. He hums three times at different pitches but there is no echo. Instead, the hums come all at once, echoing together in harmony. Freddy screams for help and the echoes ring out, hurting his ears. "I'm all alone," he whines. In another eerie moment, a voice replies, "Oh no you're not."

Running away, Freddy almost falls down into the bottomless pit— a giant cavern with what looks like bubbling lava lining the bottom (another extremely impressive set). He regains his balance and stumbles around in the dark. After lighting a match, he is able to read a sign: IF LOST CALL FOR A GUIDE. Freddy futilely calls for "Mr. Guide," then sits down to wait for one. He puts the candle on a rock and watches in amazement as the candle literally crawls away. He has actually put the candle on the back of a turtle. This ancient gag can also be seen in the Our Gang short "The First Round-Up" and in the delightfully daffy *Sh! The Octopus* (1938), in which Hugh Herbert does the same thing.

The killer (wearing a slicker, a hat, and a rubber mask) peers out and spies on Freddy. Freddy watches as the turtle slides down into the bottomless pit. Now needing another candle, Freddy does not realize the killer has put a stick of dynamite in with the candles. He lights it but when it sparks out of control and he cannot blow it out, Freddy tosses it behind him. The dynamite explodes, bringing out a sleeping bear who scares Freddy. Bears seem to pop up a lot in Universal comedies. Abbott and Costello shared scenes with a bear in both *Ride 'Em Cowboy* and *The Naughty Nineties*, while Olson and Johnson acted opposite Lon Chaney, Jr., as a bear in *Ghost Catchers*.

Freddy slides down toward the pit but catches a stalagmite at the last minute. The killer appears, urging Freddy to be careful. He offers to save his life in exchange for the handkerchief. (The killer's voice sounds a bit like Karloff's here; perhaps he dubbed it in.) Freddy slips and slides down the ramp. But instead of falling into the pit, he shoots across it (an unconvincing but funny moment) and lands on a ledge on the opposite side of the pit. He narrowly misses impaling his posterior on a stalagmite—a risqué gag since he comments, "This coulda been serious."

The killer reappears above the pit, peeking through a small hole from which a waterfall trickles. He throws a rope down and tells Freddy to catch it and tie it around his waist. After a few tries, the frustrated Freddy finally gets the rope but swings across the pit on it. His exclamatory "Whoa!" is dubbed in from *Abbott and Costello Meet Frankenstein*.

Freddy gets back to the ledge and ties the rope around his waist. The killer pulls him up and out of the cavern. But Freddy gets stuck halfway through the ceiling hole. The killer demands the handkerchief, so Freddy tells him it is in his room. He offers to take him there but the killer says he will find it himself. He then takes an axe to the limestone around the waterfall, causing the water to gush out and fill in around Freddy. "In two minutes the water will be over your head," says the killer before leaving. Freddy screams for his life, and Wellman and Stone hear him. The water covers Freddy and his last (poorly dubbed) words are: "A fine way to end up—a drainplug."

Wellman and Stone rescue Freddy at the last minute and he tells them what happened. Wellman and Freddy rush back to Freddy's room to catch the killer. When they get there, Freddy sees that one of his booby traps worked and actually caught someone. It is Casey! Freddy thinks Casey is the killer and the two argue. Even Wellman is temporarily suspicious, though Casey explains that his ankle hurt and he came in to lie down. Freddy continues making accusations, which makes Casey nervous. For Freddy, the tables have at last turned. It seems likely that he knows Casey did not do it but cannot resist the opportunity for a little revenge. He wants Casey to know what it is like to be suspected of murder.

All the suspects suddenly arrive in the room and Wellman has them sit down. As in traditional mystery films, the suspects gather so the detective can explain the solution and point out the killer. Still, the timely arrival of the suspects is a little too convenient. The script could have at least thrown in a joke for Freddy by having him comment on the sudden presence of the rest of the cast.

Wellman reveals the story: Strickland was murdered to keep him from finding out that Milford was blackmailing Crandall in his name (though we never find out what Milford had on Crandall). When Crandall phoned Strickland and told him he was not going to pay another dime, Strickland was understandably confused. Strickland came to the hotel to find out what was going on. But Milford was 400 miles away when Strickland was murdered, so he must have had a partner who was at the hotel and in on the blackmail.

Freddy interrupts (his first of many interruptions) and accuses Casey of blackmail. That is why he is able to smoke twenty-cent cigars, says Freddy. Casey admonishes, "Freddy, you shouldn't talk that way. We're cousins. We have the same blood in our veins." "Yes," replies Freddy. "And I want to keep mine." This joke seems more appropriate for *Abbott and Costello Meet Frankenstein*.

The killer rounded up many of Strickland's former clients in order to throw suspicion in different directions. There was never going to be any memoirs. Any criminal lawyer who would publish a book like that would never have another client. (Today, such a statement would not hold true.)

Freddy again interrupts and accuses Casey. A small gag occurs here that is easily missed. After showing a reaction shot of Karloff as the Swami, the film cuts back to the Inspector and Freddy. Freddy looks at the Swami suspiciously. The Swami reacts by raising his hand as if he is going to hypnotize Freddy who flinches at the thought of it. It is a nice bit of business from these two fine actors.

Wellman continues. He thought Relia was the killer until Relia turned up dead. He had to look in a different direction. Freddy again accuses Casey but Casey insists he is innocent. Freddy is outraged.

"You're innocent?!? You're innocent?!? ... I forgot what I was going to say. You lucky boy." It is funny how Freddy continually annoys Wellman during this scene, subtly spoofing this detective film convention. He bumps into him, interrupts, and acts as a general nuisance.

Wellman continues with his story, but Melton interrupts with a theory of his own. He believes Relia was killed because he discovered who took his gun. Freddy again accuses Casey.

Wellman explains the killer became nervous when Freddy was no longer under suspicion. So he planted the bodies in Crandall's room. The only remaining problem was the handkerchief. Freddy says Casey came back to the room to get it. Wellman finally proves Casey's innocence to Freddy—Casey could not be the killer because he was one of only four people to know there was no handkerchief. Freddy had burned it.

Stone enters with a bundle. The Inspector admits he has a confession to make. Freddy quickly asks, "*You* did it?" This is a great capper to the "culprit/murderer-confession" running gag.

Wellman says that he stalled and kept everyone here together so Stone could search the rooms. There is a distinctive mineral mud in the caverns and whoever went after Freddy would have the mud on their shoes.

Melton pops up with a gun and grabs Freddy. He makes everyone go to one side of the room while he heads for the glass doors. When he opens the door, Freddy's booby trap springs and a hammer swings down, conking Melton on the head. Freddy then hits him with a tiny hammer he has in his pocket. "That's in case the big one didn't work," he explains.

Freddy is congratulated and Crandall gives him his job back. Freddy tells everyone to go down and have a lemonade on him (in *Wistful Widow of Wagon Gap* he made everyone drink milk). He also tells Casey that he never once suspected him, and the two make up. Wellman congratulates Freddy and tells him that without his booby traps they would never have caught the killer. Freddy thanks him and says he would like to get out of his wet clothes. When he opens his closet door, a boxing glove on a spring pops out and knocks out Wellman. "This one I completely forgot about," says Freddy, and it is THE END.

Remembering that this film was the first "Abbott and Costello Meet" film after *Meet Frankenstein* explains why it lifts music and plot devices from its predecessor. It was clearly designed to cash in on that picture's incredible success. *Meet the Killer*'s trailer even mentions the Frankenstein entry. "Remember the ghoulish time you had when Abbott and Costello met Frankenstein?" it asks. It also emphasizes the horror in the film, even though the horror elements are very scarce: "Yipes ... have you ever felt a shudder ... shiver with glee? You will when Bud Abbott and Lou Costello meet the Killer, Boris Karloff."[371]

This also explains why the film follows the monster spoof formula. Again, we have a beautiful girl pretending to like Costello in order to use him for devious means. We also have Abbott failing to understand why such a girl would fall for his partner. Several times, Costello is the only one who "sees the monster"; in this case, he has trouble with bodies (in a variation of the "Changing Room" gag). He also sees the killer's hand in the health club, but no one believes him. There is a complicated plot on the part of the villain dealing with blackmail, false memoirs, partners in crime, etc. Even the idea of either Abbott or Costello "becoming" the monster is present in the film. Costello is accused of being the killer through most of the picture, while at the end Abbott is also temporarily thought to be the killer (the killer replaces a monster in this film).

Truthfully, the movie is not a horror spoof. It does have a few eerie sequences intermixed with some very funny scenes, but it is more a spoof of the detective film. Like the "horror whodunits" Universal had a habit of producing, the film takes a standard mystery and inserts scenes of horror in order to sell it as a terror picture. But, if anything, the film could be considered a black comedy — or the closest the comedy team ever came to making one. After all, doesn't the switching of bodies seem to precede Hitchcock's blackly funny *The Trouble with Harry* (1955)? And aren't some of the gags, especially when the duo play bridge with the corpses, bordering on the darker side?

The Breen Office certainly thought so. Even before filming began, they were concerned with the black humor in the script regarding corpses. When the film was released, local boards in Australia and New Zealand removed virtually every scene containing a corpse, including the card game (audiences there must have really been confused by the plot!). They also trimmed the climax in the cavern to decrease tension. Because of the previously mentioned card game scene, Denmark banned the film entirely![372]

Abbott and Costello Meet the Killer is one of the team's better vehicles. It possesses a plethora of quotable gags, funny scenes, and creepy moments that work even today. It stands above the later horror spoofs in that it does not become a children's film but uses the black humor to appeal to a more adult crowd.

Not that it is a problem-free picture. One of its major failings (at least in the eyes of horror fans) is the utter wasting of Boris Karloff. The role of the Swami is too small—a cameo. In no way does it warrant billing Karloff in the title. Of course, the title alone is the ultimate red herring, since Karloff is not the killer at all. Fans always grumble about the inaccuracy of *Abbott and Costello Go to Mars* (complaining that they never actually go to Mars but instead land on Venus) yet ignore the incorrect titling of this picture.

Another problem with *Meet the Killer* is the waste of footage involving Crandall's niece and her boyfriend Jeff. The niece is supposedly up to something, but her actions are never explained. Her constant pleadings with Jeff to trust her and not ask questions become tiresome. Who cares? We are never given any reason to care for her character—or, for that matter, the character of her uncle. In fact, it took several viewings before I even realized that Crandall owned the hotel.

Finally, the solution of the mystery causes a minor problem. Inspector Wellman is portrayed as an intelligent character and a good policeman. Unlike the Lieutenant Moran character in *Who Done It?* Wellman is not quick to point the accusing finger. He has his doubts about Freddy being the killer and takes his time to sort clues and do background checks. There is never any doubt he will find the identity of the real murderer. This makes the wrap-up scene even more frustrating. Wellman has sorted the case out pretty accurately, but when he gathers the suspects for the traditional revelation of the guilty, he still does not know the killer's identity. Stone has to search the rooms in order to find the muddy boots which will pinpoint the murderer. (In addition, this evidence seems rather circumstantial—anyone could have gone into the caverns at any time for a tour and muddied his or her boots.) Only then is Melton revealed as the killer (Wellman is as surprised as the rest when Brooks pulls out a gun). Such a mundane solution is not a proper payoff for such a buildup.

Since the film is primarily concerned with spoofing the murder mystery while incorporating horror elements, it does not spend a lot of time building any kind of thematic unity. If there is any kind of message to the picture, it is a simple or obvious one. Like *The Time of Their Lives*, the film puts truth on a pedestal. When ill is thought of Costello's character, the most important thing is to clear his good name. The restoration of truth and the abolition of falsehood is so important that it is worth risking Costello's life in order to carry it out. In a way, the film becomes similar to a good many of Alfred Hitchcock's thrillers. One of Hitchcock's favorite devices was having an innocent man be accused of a crime and forced to catch the real killer in order to prove his innocence (*The Thirty-Nine Steps* [1935], *The Wrong Man* [1956], *Frenzy* [1972]). Like the protagonists of those films, Costello must prove his innocence and catch the real killer. It is the proper thing to do because truth must be upheld. Even Wellman seems to recognize this, giving Freddy chance after chance to clear himself.

A smaller message also makes itself heard here and there throughout the film. The picture warns that danger can strike anyone at anytime. Even the innocent and the ignorant are not exempt. Freddy is both of these (he is so innocent he will not even drink alcohol, and he is so ignorant that Casey repeatedly tells Wellman he is too dumb to commit murder). Yet bad luck befalls the hapless Freddy at every turn — to the point that he is almost shot, asphyxiated, drowned, and so forth. Yet, the film tells us that with perseverance and courage every hardship can be overcome, no matter how simple or common we are. Never is this better stated than when the Swami says, "Amazing! Even under hypnosis, the will of an idiot to cling to life." Even while under attack on all sides, Costello has his little victories and triumphs — and in the end proves to be a real winner.

Though the film itself is also a real winner, reviews from both the present and the past always seem rather lukewarm and never too much on one side or the other. *Variety* felt the picture "will be relished by the comics' following and is okay for the family trade." *The Hollywood Reporter* thought the boys were in "exceptional form." *The Motion Picture Herald* pointed out that the pair have been much funnier in the past but put in a good showing in their present film. Even so, the reviewer complained that "some of the sequences are so farfetched and fantastic that even the most faithful followers of this comedy team are apt to find the film draggy." *The New York Times* found nothing in the film funny and *The New York Post* said the bright moments and laughs in the picture, if counted, would not go over ten.[373] The *Citizen-News* reported: "If you are a kid at heart, you're likely to find this burlesque of the movies' old horror epics a lot of fun. Otherwise the parody may strike you as only mildly entertaining."[374]

Current reviewers have similar reactions, though everyone praises the set design of the cavern/bottomless pit sequences. Jim Mulholland says the film is "strictly routine... The gags are trite, lacking the spark of the Frankenstein film."[375] Leonard Maltin calls it a "pleasant blend of comedy and whodunit,"[376] while the *VideoHound* labels the picture "unremarkable" and "pleasant enough but not one of [Abbott and Costello's] best."[377] Their volume on cult flicks is a bit kinder to the movie, calling it "an entertaining little Abbott and Costello murder mystery ... While not one of A&C's best films, it's far from their worst, worth watching for both fans of the duo and general viewers. Karloff, given little to do, does it well and his legions will want to take it in also."[378] The *Video Movie Guide* simply calls the picture "an enjoyable outing."[379]

The film was heavily promoted, with mentions being made in both *Life* and *Woman's Home Companion* magazines. Boris Karloff promoted the picture on Milton Berle's *Texaco Star Theatre* and a television production of *Arsenic and Old Lace*. But the returns were still disappointing. Executives blamed the title and considered changing it to *Abbott and Costello Meet Boris Karloff* or *Abbott and Costello Meet the Menace, Boris Karloff* until Universal's president Nate Blumberg pointed out that simultaneous playdates with the team's *Africa Screams* put too much Abbott and Costello on the market. (The film's title was originally going to be *Abbott and Costello Meet the Killers* but the "s" was dropped when the wife of Mark Hellinger, the producer of *The Killers* [1946], threatened a lawsuit.[380]) To add further confusion, the title of the movie in Great Britain was *Abbott and Costello in Search of the Killer*.[381]

Still, the film turned out to be one of the studio's most profitable releases that year and helped Abbott and Costello crack *The Motion Picture Herald*'s Poll of the Top Ten box office attractions for a second year in a row.[382] The fans recognized the fun in an Abbott and Costello horror-comedy, even a marginal one such as *Abbott and Costello Meet the Killer, Boris Karloff*.

Critics and pompous film professors may still put the team down as lowbrow, pop comedians, but anyone who has brought so much joy into the lives of as many people as Abbott and Costello have over the years deserves a place in film history. That goes for the monsters, too. I for one embrace these films even more now then I did when I was a child, for there is real magic in each and every one of these pictures — the magic of laughter, scares, and all-around joy. What more does one need?

One final note: Just so you do not think these films are only remembered and loved by me, there are two recent examples of fond references made to the series. A 1997 commercial for Universal Studios in Hollywood's Halloween Haunt featured a quick glimpse of the Frankenstein Monster using Glenn Strange from — what else — *Abbott and Costello Meet Frankenstein*. And on the September 27, 1977, telecast of *Saturday Night Live*, "newsman" Norm MacDonald delivered a story on the new monster stamps released by the United States Postal Service. Showing pictures of Dracula, the Frankenstein Monster, and the Mummy, MacDonald said the stamps were a part of the new series "People Who Abbott and Costello Have Met." The joke seemed to fall flat but I certainly found it funny.

Appendix: Horror, Science Fiction, and Fantasy Scenes in Other Abbott and Costello Films

Keep 'Em Flying (1941) — Due to the popularity of *Hold That Ghost* Universal decreed the duo's next comedy have a scare sequence in which Costello could perform his frightened routine. So, a scene was added that had Bud and Lou fooling around in a carnival funhouse, resulting in Lou being menaced by a gorilla. Paddy Costello recalled the funhouse set: "That funhouse thing — I was very little when they made that film but I can remember on the set they had — it looked like a devil or something…. It had smoke or something like steam coming out and I can remember just standing in front of that thing — I was very little — just looking at it like this and [thinking] 'That's really the devil!'"[383]

Ride 'Em Cowboy (1942) — Lou has a nightmare in which he is menaced by Indians. This bit is a variation of their "Crazy House" routine.

Pardon My Sarong (1942) — Lou, declared the hero of the island, must brave a haunted temple to which many men have traveled but none have ever returned.

Who Done It (1942) — This murder mystery takes place in a radio station and has many horrific touches. Bud and Lou encounter the masked killer throughout the film as they try to solve a murder while masquerading as detectives.

Lost in a Harem (1944)—Bud and Lou are hypnotized into thinking they are termites. Later, they share a cell with an insane prisoner who sees things that are not there (but can be heard). They also do the "Slowly, I Turned" sketch.

Africa Screams (1949)—While on safari in Africa, Lou encounters a giant ape.

Abbott and Costello in the Foreign Legion (1950)—Lost in the desert, Lou suffers hallucinations—including a talking skeleton.

Comin' Round the Mountain (1951)—Abbott and Costello's worst film actually features a wonderful horror sequence. Lou needs a love potion to make his cousin fall for him, so he and Bud visit a backwoods witch (played by Margaret Hamilton). She makes a clay doll of Lou and sticks pins in it until he meets her payment demands. Lou turns the tables by making his own effigy and the two end up in a voodoo battle. Lou also takes a ride on a flying broom.

Jack and the Beanstalk (1952)—While babysitting, Lou falls asleep and dreams the famous children's story. He and Bud climb the stalk and fight the giant, played by Buddy Baer.

Abbott and Costello Go to Mars (1953)—In this sci-fi spoof, Bud and Lou are launched into space in a rocket. First, they land in New Orleans during Mardi Gras and mistake it for Mars. Then, with two escaped convicts, they land on Venus, a planet populated only by women. Lou is made king but cannot remain faithful, so they return to Earth where they are hailed as heroes.

The Thirty Foot Bride of Candy Rock (1959)—Lou made this film without Bud after they broke up. He plays an inventor who turns his girlfriend into a giant. The film is terrible and hard to watch, partly because Costello was so sick during filming. Paddy Costello said, "The very last movie my dad made he shouldn't have done because he was ill. He died right after that ... I can't even bear to watch it because he looks so sick."[384]

The World of Abbott and Costello (1965)—This compilation features scenes from *Hold That Ghost*, *Abbott and Costello Meet Frankenstein*, *Comin' Round the Mountain*, and *Abbott and Costello Meet the Mummy*, among others.

Notes

1. Bob Furmanek and Ron Palumbo, *Abbott and Costello in Hollywood* (New York: Perigee, 1991): 15.
2. Furmanek and Palumbo 16.
3. Furmanek and Palumbo 16.
4. Furmanek and Palumbo 18.
5. Michael Brunas, John Brunas, and Tom Weaver, *Universal Horrors* (Jefferson, NC: McFarland, 1990): 2.
6. Brunas, Brunas, and Weaver 3.
7. Brunas, Brunas, and Weaver 3.
8. Paddy Costello Humphreys, personal interview, 10 May 1997.
9. Humphreys, personal interview.
10. Humphreys, personal interview.
11. Humphreys, personal interview.
12. Furmanek and Palumbo 98.
13. Furmanek and Palumbo 105.
14. Brunas, Brunas, and Weaver 4.
15. Furmanek and Palumbo 185.
16. Humphreys, personal interview.
17. "Lou Costello, 52, Dies on Coast; Comic Had Teamed with Abbott," *New York Times*, 4 March 1959.
18. "Bud Abbott, Straight Man to Lou Costello, Is Dead," *New York Times*, 25 April 1974.
19. Sara Karloff, telephone interview, 7 July 1997.
20. Furmanek and Palumbo 164–165.
21. Furmanek and Palumbo 165–166.
22. Furmanek and Palumbo 166.
23. Bob Thomas, *Bud and Lou: The Abbott and Costello Story* (Philadelphia: J.B. Lippincott, 1977): 154.
24. Furmanek and Palumbo 166.

25. Stephen Cox and John Lofflin, *The Official Abbott and Costello Scrapbook* (Chicago: Contemporary, 1990): 179.
26. Humphreys, personal interview.
27. Furmanek and Palumbo 165.
28. David Quinlan, *Quinlan's Illustrated Registry of Film Stars* (New York: Henry Holt, 1991): 86.
29. Bryan Senn and John Johnson, *Fantastic Cinema Subject Guide* (Jefferson, NC: McFarland, 1992): 579.
30. Karloff, telephone interview.
31. Humphreys, personal interview.
32. Don G. Smith, *Lon Chaney, Jr.* (Jefferson, NC: McFarland, 1996): 103.
33. "Lon Chaney, Jr., Actor Is Dead at 67," *New York Times*, 14 July 1973.
34. Bela Lugosi, Jr., telephone interview, 23 July 1997.
35. Quinlan 294.
36. Lugosi, telephone interview.
37. Gregory William Mank, *Karloff and Lugosi: The Story of a Haunting Collaboration, with a Complete Filmography of Their Films Together* (Jefferson, NC: McFarland, 1990): 282.
38. Senn and Johnson 525.
39. Humphreys, personal interview.
40. Furmanek and Palumbo 167.
41. Furmanek and Palumbo 168.
42. Lugosi, telephone interview.
43. Donald F. Glut, *The Frankenstein Legend: A Tribute to Mary Shelley and Boris Karloff* (Metuchen, NJ: Scarecrow, 1973): 54.
44. Glut, *Legend* 168.
45. Glut, *Legend* 54.
46. Lugosi, telephone interview.
47. Philip J. Riley, ed., *Abbott and Costello Meet Frankenstein Filmbook* (Atlantic City: Magic Image Filmbooks, 1990): 26.
48. Glut, *Legend* 179.
49. Chris Costello, *Lou's on First* (New York: St. Martin's, 1981): 142–143.
50. Cox and Lofflin 50.
51. Senn and Johnson 210.
52. Furmanek and Palumbo 169.
53. Riley 31.
54. Furmanek and Palumbo 169.
55. Riley 32.
56. Lugosi, telephone interview.
57. Lugosi, telephone interview.
58. Humphreys, personal interview.
59. Furmanek and Palumbo 170.

60. Riley 34.
61. Furmanek and Palumbo 170.
62. Costello 173.
63. Humphreys, personal interview.
64. David J. Hogan, "*Abbott and Costello Meet Frankenstein*," in *Bela Lugosi*, Gary and Susan Svehla, eds. (Baltimore: Midnight Marquee, 1995): 200.
65. Hogan, "*Abbott and Costello Meet Frankenstein*" 204.
66. Frederic Rinaldo, Robert Lees, and John Grant, *The Brain of Frankenstein*, script, in *Abbott and Costello Meet Frankenstein Filmbook*, Philip J. Riley, ed. (Atlantic City: Magic Image Filmbooks, 1990, originally written 1948): 6.
67. As seen in *Abbott and Costello in the Movies*, compiled by Sandy Oliveri, Goodtimes Home Video, 1990.
68. Furmanek and Palumbo 172.
69. Rinaldo, Lees, and Grant 11.
70. Lugosi, telephone interview.
71. Lugosi, telephone interview.
72. *Abbott and Costello in the Movies*.
73. Riley 42.
74. Donald F. Glut, *The Dracula Book* (Metuchen, NJ: Scarecrow, 1975): 151–152.
75. Glut, *Dracula* 152.
76. Senn and Johnson 525.
77. *Abbott and Costello in the Movies*.
78. Rinaldo, Lees, and Grant 32.
79. Rinaldo, Lees, and Grant 38–39.
80. Rinaldo, Lees, and Grant 40.
81. Rinaldo, Lees, and Grant 47–48.
82. *Abbott and Costello in the Movies*.
83. Riley 30.
84. Rinaldo, Lees, and Grant 54.
85. *Abbott and Costello in the Movies*.
86. Mank 283.
87. Rinaldo, Lees, and Grant 64.
88. Rinaldo, Lees, and Grant 64–65, and Furmanek and Palumbo 172.
89. Rinaldo, Lees, and Grant 67.
90. Rinaldo, Lees, and Grant 69.
91. *Abbott and Costello in the Movies*.
92. Rinaldo, Lees, and Grant 71.
93. Furmanek and Palumbo 172.
94. Bruce Dettman and Michael Bedford, *The Horror Factory: The Horror Films of Universal, 1931–1955* (New York: Gordon, 1976): 156.
95. Rinaldo, Lees, and Grant 86.

96. Rinaldo, Lees, and Grant 85.
97. Furmanek and Palumbo 172–173.
98. Riley 34.
99. Furmanek and Palumbo 172.
100. Rinaldo, Lees, and Grant 101.
101. Furmanek and Palumbo 168.
102. Furmanek and Palumbo 175.
103. Scott Allen Nollen, *Boris Karloff: A Critical Account of His Screen, Stage, Radio, Television, and Recording Work* (Jefferson, NC: McFarland, 1991): 280.
104. Donald F. Glut, *The Frankenstein Catalog* (Jefferson, NC: McFarland, 1984): 210.
105. Glut, *Catalog* 56.
106. Glut, *Catalog* 59.
107. Glut, *Catalog* 209.
108. Humphreys, personal interview.
109. Glut, *Legend* 185.
110. James L. Neibaur, "'Abbott and Costello Meet' Movies," *Filmfax*, Aug./Sep. 1990: 40.
111. Danny Peary, *Guide for the Film Fanatic* (New York: Simon and Schuster, 1986): 15.
112. David J. Hogan, *Dark Romance: Sexuality in the Horror Film* (Jefferson, NC: McFarland, 1986): 143.
113. Cox and Lofflin 13–14.
114. Review of *Abbott and Costello Meet Frankenstein*, *The Los Angeles Times*, 26 July 1948.
115. Furmanek and Palumbo 173–175.
116. Furmanek and Palumbo 175.
117. Martin Connors, Julia Furtaw, and Terry Schell, eds., *VideoHound's Complete Guide to Cult Flicks and Trash Pics* (New York: Visible Ink, 1996): 1.
118. Furmanek and Palumbo 175.
119. Glut, *Dracula* 152–153.
120. Jim Mulholland, *The Abbott and Costello Book* (New York: Popular Library, 1977): 168.
121. Phil Hardy, ed., *The Encyclopedia of Horror Movies* (New York: Harper and Row, 1986): 94.
122. Les Daniels, *Living in Fear: A History of Horror in the Mass Media* (New York: Da Capo, 1975): 154.
123. Michael R. Pitts, *Horror Film Stars* (Jefferson, NC: McFarland, 1991): 48.
124. Leonard Maltin, ed., *Leonard Maltin's Movie & Video Guide 1997 Edition* (New York: Signet, 1997): 1.

125. Martin Connors, Julia Furtaw, and James Craddock, eds., *VideoHound's Golden Movie Retriever 1996* (New York: Visible Ink, 1996): 135.
126. Mick Martin and Marsha Porter, *Video Movie Guide 1997* (New York: Ballantine, 1997): 1.
127. Hogan, *Abbott and Costello meet Frankenstein* 201.
128. Hogan, *Abbott and Costello meet Frankenstein* 205.
129. Scott Jenkins, Letter, *The Abbott and Costello Quarterly*, Spring 1995: 3–4.
130. "Random Notes," *Rolling Stone*, 23 March 1995.
131. Lisa Kennedy, "Quentin vs. Film Geeks," *Village Voice*, 25 October 1994: 29. Rpt. in *The Abbott and Costello Quarterly*, Spring 1995: 16.
132. Furmanek and Palumbo 173.
133. Furmanek and Palumbo 205–206.
134. Furmanek and Palumbo 206.
135. Brunas, Brunas, and Weaver 228.
136. Furmanek and Palumbo 208.
137. Furmanek and Palumbo 207–208.
138. Quinlan 172.
139. Furmanek and Palumbo 208.
140. Furmanek and Palumbo 207.
141. Humphreys, personal interview.
142. Furmanek and Palumbo 207.
143. Furmanek and Palumbo 208.
144. Costello 188–189.
145. Humphreys, personal interview.
146. Cox and Lofflin 6.
147. Robert Lees, Frederic I. Rinaldo, and John Grant, *Abbott and Costello Meet the Invisible Man* (Final draft of screenplay, 1950): 16.
148. Lees, Rinaldo, and Grant 24.
149. Lees, Rinaldo, and Grant 32.
150. Lees, Rinaldo, and Grant 38.
151. Lees, Rinaldo, and Grant 38.
152. Furmanek and Palumbo 208.
153. Lees, Rinaldo, and Grant 104.
154. Lees, Rinaldo, and Grant 109.
155. Furmanek and Palumbo 209.
156. Furmanek and Palumbo 207.
157. W. E. Oliver, "Boys Serve Merry Mix," *Los Angeles Express*, 4 April 1951.
158. *Abbott and Costello in the Movies*.
159. Neibaur 40.
160. Neibaur 40.

161. Mulholland 191.
162. Furmanek and Palumbo 209.
163. Ruth Waterbury, "Top Comedians Do a Top Job," *Los Angeles Examiner*, 4 April 1951: Sec. 11, p. 7.
164. Mulholland 188.
165. Brunas, Brunas, and Weaver 228.
166. Neibaur 40.
167. Cox and Lofflin 51.
168. Maltin 1.
169. Connors, Furtaw, and Craddock 135.
170. Connors, Furtaw, and Schell 2.
171. John Stanley, *Creature Features Movie Guide Strikes Again* (Pacifica: Creatures at Large, 1989): 10.
172. Mulholland 206.
173. Furmanek and Palumbo 241.
174. Furmanek and Palumbo 241.
175. Quinlan 253.
176. Pitts 81.
177. Karloff, telephone interview.
178. Humphreys, personal interview.
179. Furmanek and Palumbo 241.
180. Quinlan 428.
181. Craig Stevens, telephone interview, 24 July 1997.
182. Stevens, telephone interview.
183. Stevens, telephone interview.
184. Humphreys, personal interview.
185. Stevens, telephone interview.
186. Stevens, telephone interview.
187. Furmanek and Palumbo 241.
188. Furmanek and Palumbo 241–242.
189. Furmanek and Palumbo 242.
190. Lee Loeb and John Grant, *Abbott and Costello Meet Dr. Jekyll and Mr. Hyde* (Final draft of screenplay, 1952): 100 and 17.
191. Loeb and Grant 10–11.
192. Loeb and Grant 17.
193. Loeb and Grant 17–18.
194. Loeb and Grant 31–32.
195. Furmanek and Palumbo 242.
196. Glut, *Legend* 186.
197. Glut, *Legend* 186.
198. Loeb and Grant 47.
199. Loeb and Grant 53.

200. Loeb and Grant 53.
201. Humphreys, personal interview.
202. Loeb and Grant 70–71.
203. Loeb and Grant 72.
204. Loeb and Grant 77–78.
205. Loeb and Grant 89.
206. Loeb and Grant 104–105.
207. Stanley Wiater, *Dark Visions* (New York: Avon, 1992): 79.
208. Connors, Furtaw, and Schell 1.
209. Furmanek and Palumbo 241.
210. Furmanek and Palumbo 243.
211. Furmanek and Palumbo 242.
212. Costello 215.
213. Furmanek and Palumbo 242–243.
214. Mulholland 208.
215. Neibaur 41.
216. Neibaur 42.
217. Connors, Furtaw, and Craddock 135.
218. Martin and Porter 1.
219. Maltin 1.
220. Stevens, telephone interview.
221. Glut, Catalog 210.
222. Don G. Smith, "Frankenstein 1970," in *Boris Karloff*, Gary J. and Susan Svehla, eds. (Baltimore: Midnight Marquee, 1996): 287.
223. Furmanek and Palumbo 254.
224. Mulholland 212.
225. Costello 218.
226. Neibaur 43.
227. Furmanek and Palumbo 251.
228. Humphreys, personal interview.
229. Furmanek and Palumbo 251.
230. Furmanek and Palumbo 249.
231. Costello 227.
232. Costello 217–218.
233. Furmanek and Palumbo 253.
234. Furmanek and Palumbo 251.
235. Furmanek and Palumbo 250.
236. Furmanek and Palumbo 253.
237. Quinlan 482.
238. Furmanek and Palumbo 250.
239. Furmanek and Palumbo 250.
240. Furmanek and Palumbo 250.

241. Costello 228.
242. Costello 228.
243. Furmanek and Palumbo 250.
244. Connors, Furtaw, and Schell 2.
245. Dettman and Bedford 163.
246. Furmanek and Palumbo 251.
247. Furmanek and Palumbo 251, 252–253.
248. Furmanek and Palumbo 253.
249. Furmanek and Palumbo 254.
250. Mulholland 215.
251. Furmanek and Palumbo 253–254.
252. Stanley 10.
253. Mulholland 215.
254. Mulholland 215.
255. Neibaur 42.
256. Brunas, Brunas, and Weaver 483.
257. Brunas, Brunas, and Weaver 483.
258. Connors, Furtaw, and Craddock 136.
259. Maltin 2.
260. Martin and Porter 2.
261. *Men Behaving Badly*, NBC, 14 May 1997.
262. John D. Denne, "Society and the Monster," in *Focus on the Horror Film*, Roy Hoss and T.J. Ross, eds. (Englewood Cliffs: Prentice Hall, 1972): 125.
263. Denne 130.
264. Denne 126.
265. Hogan, "*Abbott and Costello Meet Frankenstein*" 197.
266. Thomas 84.
267. Brunas, Brunas, and Weaver 261.
268. Furmanek and Palumbo 57–58.
269. Furmanek and Palumbo 57.
270. Humphreys, personal interview.
271. Furmanek and Palumbo 58.
272. Mulholland 78.
273. Furmanek and Palumbo 58–59.
274. Mulholland 78.
275. Brunas, Brunas, and Weaver 261.
276. Brunas, Brunas, and Weaver 264.
277. Furmanek and Palumbo 57.
278. Furmanek and Palumbo 57.
279. Furmanek and Palumbo 57.
280. Furmanek and Palumbo 59.

281. John Joseph, *Hold That Ghost* production data, Universal, 15 February 1941.
282. Brunas, Brunas, and Weaver 260.
283. Furmanek and Palumbo 58–59.
284. Furmanek and Palumbo 59.
285. Furmanek and Palumbo 59.
286. Furmanek and Palumbo 60.
287. Furmanek and Palumbo 59, 61.
288. Brunas, Brunas, and Weaver 264.
289. Furmanek and Palumbo 61.
290. *Abbott and Costello in the Movies.*
291. Furmanek and Palumbo 57.
292. Mulholland 74.
293. Brunas, Brunas, and Weaver 263.
294. Furmanek and Palumbo 60.
295. Furmanek and Palumbo 60–61.
296. Mulholland 78.
297. Mulholland 74.
298. Stanley 181.
299. Ted Okuda, "Screamingly Funny!" *Filmfax*, May/June 1986: 38.
300. Maltin 599.
301. Martin and Porter 487.
302. Connors, Furtaw, and Schell 136.
303. Brunas, Brunas, and Weaver 263.
304. Furmanek and Palumbo 61.
305. Brunas, Brunas, and Weaver 439.
306. "The Resurrection of Carlini," *The Greatest American Hero*, ABC, 18 November 1982.
307. Furmanek and Palumbo 141.
308. Quinlan 390.
309. Quinlan 39.
310. *The Time of Their Lives*, preview handout, issued by Universal, 1946.
311. Furmanek and Palumbo 144.
312. Furmanek and Palumbo 141–142.
313. Cox and Lofflin 48.
314. Brunas, Brunas, and Weaver 570.
315. Furmanek and Palumbo 144.
316. Costello 125.
317. Brunas, Brunas, and Weaver 571.
318. Humphreys, personal interview.
319. Furmanek and Palumbo 142.
320. Furmanek and Palumbo 143.

321. Preview handout.
322. Costello 125.
323. Brunas, Brunas, and Weaver 571.
324. Preview handout.
325. Furmanek and Palumbo 143.
326. Furmanek and Palumbo 143.
327. Humphreys, personal interview.
328. Preview handout.
329. Furmanek and Palumbo 143.
330. Furmanek and Palumbo 143.
331. Furmanek and Palumbo 143.
332. Preview handout.
333. Furmanek and Palumbo 144.
334. Cox and Lofflin 50.
335. *Abbott and Costello Meet Jerry Seinfeld*, MCA/Universal Home Video, 1994.
336. Furmanek and Palumbo 143.
337. Mulholland 149.
338. Cox and Lofflin 50.
339. Mulholland 154.
340. Furmanek and Palumbo 143–144.
341. Maltin 1372.
342. Connors, Furtaw, and Craddock 846.
343. Martin and Porter 1087.
344. Stanley 398.
345. Mulholland 149.
346. Furmanek and Palumbo 143.
347. Brunas, Brunas, and Weaver 570.
348. Brunas, Brunas, and Weaver 572.
349. Brunas, Brunas, and Weaver 573.
350. Furmanek and Palumbo 143.
351. *Abbott and Costello in the Movies*.
352. Brunas, Brunas, and Weaver 570.
353. Furmanek and Palumbo 144.
354. Mulholland 180.
355. Furmanek and Palumbo 192.
356. Furmanek and Palumbo 192.
357. Karloff, telephone interview.
358. Karloff, telephone interview.
359. "Boris Karloff Dead; Horror Movie Star," *New York Times*, 4 February 1969.
360. Mank 283.

Notes

361. Furmanek and Palumbo 192.
362. Furmanek and Palumbo 194.
363. Furmanek and Palumbo 193.
364. Mank 283.
365. Furmanek and Palumbo 194.
366. Furmanek and Palumbo 195–196.
367. Furmanek and Palumbo 196.
368. Cox and Lofflin 21–22.
369. Furmanek and Palumbo 194.
370. Furmanek and Palumbo 195.
371. *Abbott and Costello in the Movies.*
372. Furmanek and Palumbo 192.
373. Furmanek and Palumbo 196–197.
374. "Abbott, Costello Cut Capers with Karloff," *Citizen News*, 5 September 1949.
375. Mulholland 179.
376. Maltin 2.
377. Connors, Furtaw, and Craddock 136.
378. Connors, Furtaw, and Schell 2.
379. Martin and Porter 2.
380. Furmanek and Palumbo 194.
381. "Cinema," *News Review*, 17 November 1949.
382. Furmanek and Palumbo 197.
383. Humphreys, personal interview.
384. Humphreys, personal interview.

Bibliography

Abbott and Costello in the Movies. Compiled by Sandy Oliveri. Produced by Film Shows, Inc. Goodtimes Home Video, 1990.

Abbott and Costello Meet Jerry Seinfeld. Written and Directed by Daniel Helfgott. With Jerry Seinfeld. MCA/Universal Home Video, 1994.

Beck, Calvin Thomas. *Heroes of the Horrors.* New York: Macmillan, 1975.

Brunas, Michael, John Brunas, and Tom Weaver. *Universal Horrors.* Jefferson, NC: McFarland, 1990.

Catsos, Gregory J.M. "Children of the Corn: Paddy Costello Humphreys and Bud Abbott, Jr." *Filmfax* (Mar./Apr. 1995): 64–65, 82.

____. "Lou's on First: An Exclusive Interview with Chris Costello." *Filmfax* (Oct./Nov. 1994): 58–61.

Connors, Martin, Julia Furtaw, and James Craddock, eds. *VideoHound's Golden Movie Retriever 1996.* New York: Visible Ink, 1996.

Connors, Martin, Julia Furtaw, and Terry Schell, eds. *VideoHound's Complete Guide to Cult Flicks and Trash Pics.* New York: Visible Ink, 1996.

Costello, Chris, with Raymond Strait. *Lou's on First.* New York: St. Martin's, 1981.

Cox, Stephen, and John Lofflin. *The Official Abbott and Costello Scrapbook.* Chicago: Contemporary, 1990.

Daniels, Les. *Living in Fear: A History of Horror in the Mass Media.* New York: Da Capo, 1975.

Denne, John D. "Society and the Monster." In *Focus on the Horror Film.* Edited by Roy Huss and T.J. Ross. Englewood Cliffs, NJ: Prentice Hall, 1972.

Dettman, Bruce, and Michael Bedford. *The Horror Factory: The Horror Films of Universal, 1931–1955.* New York: Gordon, 1976.

Furmanek, Bob, and Ron Palumbo. *Abbott and Costello in Hollywood.* New York: Perigee, 1991.

Glut, Donald F. *The Dracula Book.* Metuchen, NJ: Scarecrow, 1975.

____. *The Frankenstein Catalog.* Jefferson, NC: McFarland, 1984.

____. *The Frankenstein Legend: A Tribute to Mary Shelley and Boris Karloff.* Metuchen, NJ: Scarecrow, 1973.

Hardy, Phil, ed. *The Encyclopedia of Horror Movies*. New York: Harper and Row, 1986.
Hogan, David J. "Cinema Sourcebook." Review of *Abbott and Costello Meet Frankenstein* filmbook and script. *Filmfax* (Aug./Sep. 1990): 12, 14.
____. *Dark Romance: Sexuality in the Horror Film*. Jefferson, NC: McFarland, 1986.
Humphreys, Paddy Costello. Personal interview. 10 May 1997.
Jenkins, Scott. Letter to *The Abbott and Costello Quarterly*. 24 (Spring 1995): 3–4.
Jones, Stephen. *The Frankenstein Scrapbook: The Complete Guide to the World's Most Famous Monster*. New York: Carol, 1995.
Joseph, John (director of advertising and publicity). *Hold That Ghost* production data from Universal Studios. Issued 15 February 1941.
Karloff, Sara. Telephone interview. 7 July 1997.
Kennedy, Lisa. "Quentin vs. Film Geeks." *Village Voice* (25 October 1994): 29. Reprinted in *The Abbott and Costello Quarterly* (Spring 1995): 16.
Lees, Robert, Frederic I. Rinaldo, and John Grant. *Abbott and Costello Meet the Invisible Man*. Final draft of screenplay. 1950.
Lennig, Arthur. *The Count: The Life and Films of Bela "Dracula" Lugosi*. New York: Putnam, 1974.
Lindsay, Cynthia. *Dear Boris: The Life of William Henry Pratt a.k.a. Boris Karloff*. New York: Knopf, 1975.
Loeb, Lee, and John Grant. *Abbott and Costello Meet Dr. Jekyll and Mr. Hyde*. Final draft of screenplay. 1952.
Lugosi, Bela, Jr. Telephone interview. 23 July 1997.
Maltin, Leonard, ed. *Leonard Maltin's Movie & Video Guide 1997 Edition*. New York: Signet, 1996.
Mank, Gregory William. *Karloff and Lugosi: The Story of a Haunting Collaboration, with a Complete Filmography of Their Films Together*. Jefferson, NC: McFarland, 1990.
Martin, Mick, and Marsha Porter. *Video Movie Guide 1997*. New York: Ballantine, 1996.
Mulholland, Jim. *The Abbott and Costello Book*. New York: Popular Library, 1977.
Neibaur, James L. "'Abbott and Costello Meet' Movies." *Filmfax* (Aug./Sep. 1990): 38–43.
Nollen, Scott Allen. *Boris Karloff: A Critical Account of His Screen, Stage, Radio, Television, and Recording Work*. Jefferson, NC: McFarland, 1991.
Okuda, Ted. "Screamingly Funny!" *Filmfax* (May/June 1986): 38–41, 45.
Peary, Danny. *Guide for the Film Fanatic*. New York: Simon and Schuster, 1986.
Pitts, Michael R. *Horror Film Stars*. Jefferson, NC: McFarland, 1991.
Quinlan, David. *Quinlan's Illustrated Registry of Film Stars*. New York: Henry Holt, 1991.

Riley, Philip J., ed. *Abbott and Costello Meet Frankenstein Filmbook.* (Includes *"The Brain of Frankenstein,"* the original 1948 script by Frederic Rinaldo, Robert Lees, and John Grant.) Atlantic City: Magic Image Filmbooks, 1990.

Senn, Bryan, and John Johnson. *Fantastic Cinema Subject Guide.* Jefferson, NC: McFarland, 1992.

Skal, David J. *The Monster Show: A Cultural History of Horror.* New York: Penguin, 1993.

Smith, Don G. *Lon Chaney, Jr.* Jefferson, NC: McFarland, 1996.

Stanley, John. *Creature Features Movie Guide Strikes Again.* Pacifica: Creatures at Large, 1989.

Stevens, Craig. Telephone interview. 24 July 1997.

Svehla, Gary, and Susan Svehla, eds. *Bela Lugosi.* Baltimore: Midnight Marquee, 1995.

_____. *Boris Karloff.* Baltimore: Midnight Marquee, 1996.

Thomas, Bob. *Bud and Lou: The Abbott and Costello Story.* Philadelphia: J.B. Lippincott, 1977.

The Time of Their Lives. Preview handout. Issued by Universal, 1946.

Warren, Bill. *Keep Watching the Skies: American Science Fiction Movies of the Fifties.* Volume One. Jefferson, NC: McFarland, 1982.

Wiater, Stanley. *Dark Visions.* New York: Avon, 1992.

Index

A-Haunting We Will Go 167
Abbott, Betty 91
Abbott, Betty Smith 6, 67
Abbott, Bud 2, 9, 217–218; as "Abbott" in Meet the Mummy 117–131; as "Bud" in Meet the Invisible Man 68–83; as "Casey" in Meet the Killer 192–211; as "Chick" in Meet Frankenstein 36–58; as "Chuck" in Hold That Ghost 141–161; as "Cuthbert" and "Ralph" in The Time Of Their Lives 169–183; as "Slim" in Meet Dr. Jekyll 93–110; at Universal 12, 14–15, 16–17, 20–21, 22–24, 25–26; biographical information 5–6, 10–12, 20, 27–28; making Abbott and Costello Meet Dr. Jekyll and Mr. Hyde 89–93; making Abbott and Costello Meet Frankenstein 29–31; making Abbott and Costello Meet the Invisible Man 67–68; making Abbott and Costello Meet the Killer, Boris Karloff 191–192; making Abbott and Costello Meet the Mummy 115–116; making Hold That Ghost 138–140; making The Time of Their Lives 166, 168–169

Abbott, Harry 5
Abbott, Norman 167
Abbott, Rae 5
The Abbott and Costello Book 87, 113, 188
Abbott and Costello Go to Mars 25–26, 213, 218
Abbott and Costello in Hollywood 21
Abbott and Costello in the Foreign Legion 24, 65, 218
Abbott and Costello Meet Captain Kidd 25
Abbott and Costello Meet Dr. Jekyll and Mr. Hyde 26, 62, 71, 83, 88–114, 116, 117, 120, 127, 129, 134, 149, 155, 162, 190; budget 92; criticism 111–113; foreign titles 114; reviews 113–114; story and plot 93–110
Abbott and Costello Meet Frankenstein 2–3, 18, 22, 23–24, 29–64, 65, 68, 69, 71, 72, 75, 76, 78, 82–83, 84, 90, 93, 98, 100, 101, 102, 104, 113, 114, 117, 118, 120, 123, 127, 134, 141, 146, 150–151, 152, 162, 164, 168, 169, 187, 188, 190, 191, 192, 194, 196, 208, 209, 210, 211, 216, 218; budget 58; criticism 59–64; foreign titles 59; reviews 63–64; story and plot 36–58
Abbott and Costello Meet Jerry Seinfeld 182

Abbott and Costello Meet the Invisible Man 24, 65–87, 93, 97, 134, 162; budget 66; criticism 83–87; reviews 87; story and plot 68–83
Abbott and Costello Meet the Keystone Kops 26, 124
Abbott and Costello Meet the Killer, Boris Karloff 24, 34, 65, 72, 99, 120, 138, 147, 151, 188–215; budget 191; criticism 211–214; reviews 214–215; story and plot 192–211
Abbott and Costello Meet the Mummy 19, 26, 114–135, 218; budget 115; criticism 132–134; reviews 131–132; story and plot 117–131
The Abbott and Costello Scrapbook 87
The Abbott and Costello Show 89, 181
Ackerman, Forrest J 43
Acquanetta 19, 22
Adams, Julie 26
The Adventures of Sherlock Holmes 16
Africa Screams 24, 53, 79, 201, 215, 218
All Quiet on the Western Front 7
Alyn, Kirk 167
An American Werewolf in London 135

The Andrews Sisters 14, 138, 139, 140, 142, 143, 144, 159, 160
Ankers, Evelyn 14, 15, 19, 140; as "Norma" in *Hold That Ghost* 146–160
Ansara, Michael 166, 177; as "Charlie" in *Abbott and Costello Meet the Mummy* 121–130
Anthony Adverse 167
Army of Darkness 25
Arnold, Jack 25, 26
Arsenic and Old Lace 1, 215
Arthur, Robert 30, 64, 65–66, 89
Ash, Jerome 34, 44
Atomic Submarine 66
Attack of the 60 Foot Centerfold 64
Atwill, Lionel 13, 15, 16
Aubert, Lenore 34, 36, 59, 191; as "Angela" in *Abbott and Costello Meet the Killer, Boris Karloff* 195–211; as "Sandra" in *Abbott and Costello Meet Frankenstein* 38–57
Auer, Mischa 140, 141

Baer, Buddy 24, 218
Baer, Max 24
Ball, Lucille 21
Barber, Bobby 35, 42, 50, 67, 117, 160
Barnes, Binnie 166–167; as "Mildred" in *The Time of Their Lives* 173–183
Barnum and Bailey Circus 5
Barrymore, John 13, 88, 97
Barton, Charles T. 34–35, 36, 51, 57, 168, 169, 191
The Bat (1930) 69
The Bat Whispers 2
Batman (comic book) 69
Beatty, Clyde 24
Bellamy, Ralph 15
Bergman, Ingrid 88
Berle, Milton 167, 215
Besser, Joe 24, 181
Best of Abbott and Costello 59

The Bionic Woman (TV) 116
The Black Castle 24–25
The Black Cat (1934) 9, 90
The Black Cat (1941) 139, 167
Blithe Spirit 138, 166
Blumberg, Nate 22, 215
Blyth, Ann 36
The Body Snatcher 90
Bogdanovich, Peter 190
The Boogie Man Will Get You 190
"Boogie Woogie Bugle Boy of Company B" 14
The Bowery Boys 68, 161, 165
The Bowery Boys Meet the Monsters 3
Bradbury, Ray 25
Bradstreet, Charles (as "Prof. Stevens" in *Abbott and Costello Meet Frankenstein*) 38–58
Bram Stoker's Dracula 51
The Breen Office 89, 141, 144, 160, 174, 212
Brice, Fanny 5
The Bride of Frankenstein 1–2, 10, 90
Brodney, Oscar 30, 189
Broken Arrow (TV) 117
Brooke, Hillary 24, 25
Brown, Johnny Mack 12
Browning, Tod 7
Bruce, David 19
Bruce, Nigel 16
Bruce, Virginia 13
Brunas, Brunas, and Weaver 131, 187
The Brute Man 22
Buck, Frank 24
Buck Privates 14, 45, 68, 74, 79, 80, 83, 138, 139, 140, 141, 163
Buck Privates Come Home 23, 68
A Bucket of Blood 135
Bud and Lou (TV movie) 89
Burton, Val 166

Calling Dr. Death 18
Campbell, Bruce 25
Candido, Candy 27
The Canterville Ghost 186

Captive Wild Woman 19, 140
Carlson, Richard 14, 25, 26, 140; as "the Professor" in *Hold That Ghost* 146–160
Carradine, John 19, 20, 21
El Castillo de los Monstruos 59
The Cat and the Canary (1927) 2, 151, 154
The Cat and the Canary (1939) 138, 167
The Cat People (1942) 34
Cat Women of the Moon 26, 116
Chandler, Jeff 134
Chaney, Lon 15
Chaney, Lon, Jr. 10, 15–16, 17–18, 19, 20, 21, 24, 31–32, 33, 35, 36, 97, 115, 209; as "Talbot/The Wolf Man" in *Abbott and Costello Meet Frankenstein* 38–58, 59
Chaplin, Charlie 6
Charlie Chan in the Secret Service 102
Christie, Howard "Red" 66, 89
Christine, Virginia 19
Clarke, Mae 8
Clive, Colin 8, 10
A Clockwork Orange 73
Cochrane, Robert M. 10
The Cock-Eyed Miracle 138
Cole, Lester K. 66
The Colgate Comedy Hour (TV) 26, 64, 128
Collins, Ted 11
Colona, Jerry 83
Columbia Wheel Burlesque Circuit 5
The Comedy of Terrors 190
Comin' Round the Mountain 24, 33, 87, 218
Coney Island 5
Conrad, Mikel 191
Corman, Roger 117, 135, 190
Costello, Anne Battler 11
Costello, Butch 20
Costello, Carole 91, 124
Costello, Chris 34, 35, 36, 113, 116, 168
Costello, Lou 9, 217–218;

Index

as "Costello" in *Meet The Mummy* 117–131; as "Ferdy" in *Ghost* 141–161; as "Freddy" in *Meet the Killer* 192–211; as "Horatio" in *Time* 169–183; as "Lou" in *Meet the Invisible Man* 68–83; as "Tubby" in *Meet Dr. Jekyll* 93–110; as "Wilbur" in *Meet Frankenstein* 36–58; at Universal 12, 20–21, 22–24, 25–26; biographical information 6, 10–12, 20, 27, 74; comedy style 2; making *Abbott and Costello Meet Dr. Jekyll and Mr. Hyde* 89–93; making *Abbott and Costello Meet Frankenstein* 29, 31, 34–36; making *Abbott and Costello Meet the Invisible Man* 67–68; making *Abbott and Costello Meet the Killer, Boris Karloff* 191–192; making *Abbott and Costello Meet the Mummy* 115–166; making *Hold That Ghost* 138–140; making *The Time of Their Lives* 166, 168–169; stealing props 36, 168–169
Costello, Paddy 12, 14, 15, 27, 31, 32, 33, 35–36, 59, 67, 90, 91, 104, 115, 139–140, 168, 174, 217, 218
Costello, Pat 159
Cowdin, J. Cheever 10
Cox, Stephen 35, 62–62, 87
Crawford, Broderick 139
The Creature Features Movie Guide 87, 131, 163
Creature from the Black Lagoon 26, 119, 140
The Creature Walks Among Us 26
Cristillo, Helene 6
Cristillo, Sebastian 6
Crosby, Bing 25
Culhane, James "Shamus" 37
Culp, Robert 165
Cult of the Cobra 26

Cummings, Bob 12
Curse of the Cat People 34
Curse of the Werewolf 27
Cushing, Peter 27

Dance with Me, Henry 27, 115
Daniels, Les 63
Dark Romance: Sexuality in the Horror Film 61
Davis, Joan 14, 103, 139–140, 180; as "Camille" in *Hold That Ghost* 146–160
The Day Mars Invaded the Earth 116
Deacon, Richard 117; as "Semu" in *Abbott and Costello Meet the Mummy* 121–130
Dead Alive 135
Dead Man's Eyes 18
The Deadly Mantis 90
Del Rio, Dolores 6
Dempsey, Jack 67
Denne, John 133–134
Denning, Richard 26
Denny, Reginald 91–92; as "the Inspector" in *Abbott and Costello meet Dr. Jekyll and Mr. Hyde* 95–110
Denver, Bob 99
Derek, Bo 173
Dettman and Bedford 118–119
Devine, Andy 19
Dierkes, John 92, 155; as "Batley" in *Abbott and Costello meet Dr. Jekyll and Mr. Hyde* 96–106
The Dick Van Dyke Show (TV) 117
Dr. Jekyll and Mr. Hyde (novel) 88
Dr. Jekyll and Mr. Hyde (1931) 92
Dr. Jekyll and Ms. Hyde 81
Dr. Seuss 200
Dr. Strange (TV movie) 59
Dr. Strangelove, or How I Learned to Stop Worrying and Love the Bomb 1
Dodd, Claire 14
Donovan's Brain (novel) 55

Douglas, Melvyn 8
Douglass, Robert 91
Dracula (1931) 7, 10, 13, 15, 161
Dracula vs. Frankenstein (1971) 43
Dracula's Daughter 10
Dressed to Kill (1946) 16
Dumbrille, Douglas 16

The East Side Kids 41
Eating Raoul 1
Edison, Thomas 7
The Encyclopedia of Horror Movies 63
The Evil Dead 2, 135
Ewell, Tom 25

Famous Monsters of Filmland (magazine) 59
The Fearless Vampire Killers, or Pardon Me, But Your Teeth Are in My Neck 135
Ferguson, Frank (as "MacDougal" in *Abbott and Costello Meet Frankenstein*) 38–58
Fields, Sid 89
Fields, W.C. 5
Fireman, Save My Child 89
The First Round-Up 208
Fitzgerald, Ella 16
Florey, Robert 7
Foran, Dick 13, 16
Ford, Wallace 13, 16
Fox, Matty 138
Francis the Talking Mule 134
Frankenstein (1931) 7, 10, 13, 45, 90, 161, 190
Frankenstein Meets the Wolf Man 17–18, 19, 40
Frankenstein 1970 114
Franz, Arthur 24, 66–67, 87; as "Tommy Nelson" in *Abbott and Costello Meet the Invisible Man* 69–82
Frawley, William 24, 67; as "Roberts" in *Abbott and Costello Meet the Invisible Man* 70–82
Frenzy 214
Freund, Karl 9

Index

Friday the Thirteenth 110
From Beyond 113
The Frozen Ghost 18
Frye, Dwight 8
Fulton, John 9
Furmanek and Palumbo 182, 186–187, 191

Garcia, Jerry 64
GE Theater (TV) 27
The George Gobel Show (TV) 116
The Getaway (1994) 59
Ghost 184
The Ghost Breakers 138, 140, 172
The Ghost Catchers 19, 141, 164, 209
The Ghost Comes Home 167
Ghost of Frankenstein 16, 18, 43, 55, 140
Ghosts Can't Do It 173
Gilbert, Billy 6
Gilligan's Island (TV) 99
Gillis, Anne 167; as "Nora" in The Time of Their Lives 169–171, 183
Glut, Don 44, 59, 63
Goddard, Paulette 138
Goetz, William 22, 33
Golden, Al 6
The Golem 7
Gorcey, Leo 165
Gordon, Stuart 110
The Gramercy Ghost 166
Grant, John 34, 89, 92, 116, 164
The Greatest American Hero (TV) 165
Green, Clarence 66
Guild, Nancy 67; as "Helen" in Abbott and Costello Meet the Invisible Man 69–82
Gwynne, Anne 16

Hackett, Buddy 89
Hale, Alan, Jr. 99
Hall, Huntz 165
Hall, Jon 16, 19
Hamilton, Margaret 24, 218
Hammer Films 27
Hanna-Barbera 28
Hardwicke, Sir Cedric 13
Hatton, Rondo 22

Hayden, Harry 147
Healy, Myron 167
Heaven Only Knows 166
Hellinger, Mark 215
Helton, Percy 191; as "Abernathy" in Abbott and Costello Meet the Killer, Boris Karloff 202–203
Herbert, Hugh 139, 161, 208
Here Come the Co-Eds 20, 31, 56, 125
Hey, Hey, Hey—It's Fat Albert (TV) 59
Hit the Ice 17, 67, 121
Hitchcock, Alfred 1, 2, 212, 214
Hogan, David J. 37, 61, 64
Hold That Ghost 2, 14, 25, 40, 41, 50, 52, 76, 103, 120, 137–165, 180, 208, 217; budget 141; criticism 161–163; reviews 163–164; story and plot 141–161
Holiday Inn 166
Hollywood Premiere 164
Holm, John Cecil 166
Hope, Bob 25, 138, 161, 172, 189
Horne, Lena 83
The Horror Show (TV) 59
Horsley, David 34, 44, 92
The Hound of the Baskervilles (1939) 16
House of Dracula 21–22, 38, 44
House of Fear (1939) 8, 150, 188
House of Fear (1945) 16
House of Frankenstein 19–20, 55, 57
House of Horrors 22
How the Grinch Stole Christmas (TV) 200
Howard, Curly 37, 140
Howard, Moe 140
Howard, Shemp 24, 140, 146–147
The Howdy Doody Show (TV) 119
The Howling 135
Hull, Henry 11
The Hunchback of Notre Dame (1923) 15

I Love Lucy (TV) 67
I Married a Witch 186
I Married Joan 139
In Society 20, 167, 205
In the Navy 14, 139, 140
The Incredible Hulk (TV) 110–111, 112, 116
The Incredible Shrinking Man 26–27
Innocent Blood 3
Interview with the Vampire 51
The Invisible Agent 16, 65, 66
The Invisible Man 9, 65, 70, 83
The Invisible Man Returns 11, 65, 66, 70, 72–73, 77, 78
The Invisible Man's Revenge 19, 65, 167
The Invisible Woman 13–14, 65
Irwin, Stan 28
Isle of the Dead 90
It Ain't Hay 17, 18
It Came from Outer Space 25, 140
It's Alive: The True Story of Frankenstein (TV) 59
It's in the Bag 167

Jack and the Beanstalk 25, 218
Jergens, Adele (as "Boots" in Abbott and Costello Meet the Invisible Man) 76–82
Johann, Zita 9
Jones, Allan 12, 83
Journey's End 7
Julius Caesar (1953) 117
Jungle Captive 21–22
Jungle Woman 19

Karloff, Boris 7–8, 9–10, 11, 13, 16, 19, 24, 28, 32, 34, 58, 89–90, 113, 114, 117, 190–191, 215; as "Dr. Jekyll and Mr. Hyde" in Abbott and Costello Meet Dr. Jekyll and Mr. Hyde 95–109; as "Talpur Swami" in Abbott and Costello Meet the Killer Boris Karloff 195–211

Index

Karloff, Sara 28, 31–32, 90, 190
Katt, William 165
Keep 'Em Flying 14–15, 78, 161, 217
Keith, Ian 33
The Killers (1946) 215
The Killing 116
King, Peggy 116, 123
Kiss Me Deadly 191
Knowles, Patric 17, 18
Kosleck, Martin 19, 22
Kruger, Otto 22
Kubrick, Stanley 73
Kyser, Kay 190

Lady and the Tramp 77
Lady Frankenstein 117
Laemmle, Carl 7, 10
Laemmle, Carl, Jr. 7, 10
Lamont, Charles 66, 67, 92, 115, 116, 117, 118
Lanchester, Elsa 10
Lane, Vicky 22
Lantz, Walter 37
Laughton, Charles 8, 24, 25
Laurel and Hardy 2, 68, 161, 167
Lawrence, Marc 140; as "Charlie" in *Hold That Ghost* 143–149
Leave It to Beaver (TV) 117
Lee, Christopher 27
Lee, Gypsy Rose 71
Lee, Rowland V. 13
The Leech Woman 26
Lees, Robert 31, 66, 164
The Left-Handed Gun 92
Leonard, Jack E. 28
Leonard, Sheldon 17, 67; as "Morgan" in *Abbott and Costello Meet the Invisible Man* 74–82
Lewis, Ted 14, 140, 141, 142, 143, 144, 159, 160
Lewton, Val 34
Life Begins at Minsky's 11
Life of Riley (TV) 166
Life Without Soul 7
Little Giant 22–23, 166, 184
The Little Shop of Horrors (1960) 117, 135
Living in Fear (book) 63
Loeb, Lee 89, 116

Lofflin, John 35, 62–63, 87
Lorre, Peter 16, 190
Lost in a Harem 20, 24, 38, 217–218
Lost in Alaska 25, 87, 116
Lou Costello, Jr., Youth Foundation 191
Lou's on First (book) 116
Love at First Bite 2
Lubin, Arthur 141
Lugosi, Bela 7, 8, 9, 10, 13, 15, 16, 17–18, 32–33, 35, 139, 191; as "Dracula" in *Abbott and Costello Meet Frankenstein* 40–58
Lugosi, Bela, Jr. 32, 33, 34, 35, 42
Lugosi, Lillian 35

Ma and Pa Kettle 134
MacDonald, Norm 216
The Mad Ghoul 18–19
Main, Marjorie 23, 31
Maltin, Leonard 63, 87, 114, 132, 163–164, 186, 215
Man Made Monster 15, 140
The Man Who Reclaimed His Head 8
Mancini, Henry 116
Mank, Gregory William 33, 51
Manners, David 9
March, Fredric
Marlowe, Don 33
Martin, Dean 172
Martin and Lewis 83
Martin and Porter's *Video Movie Guide* 63–64, 132, 164, 186, 215
The Marx Brothers 21, 172
The Mask of Fu Manchu 90, 114
Massey, Raymond 8
The Maze 140
Meeker, Ralph 191
Men Behaving Badly (TV) 132
Mexican Hayride 12, 24, 35, 188, 191
MGM 7, 17, 20, 21, 23
Milhauser, Bertram 30
Milland, Ray 166
Ministry of Fear 166
Mr. Blandings Builds His Dream House 91–92

Mr. Peabody and the Mermaid 36
Mr. Wong in Chinatown 114
The Mole People 26
Monogram 7, 166, 191
The Monolith Monsters 26
Monster on the Campus 26, 66
The Monster Walks 140
Moore, Eva 8
Moore, Gar 192
Moreland, Mantan 102
Morison, Patricia 34
Morris, Chester 83
The Mothers-in-Law (TV) 117
Movie Story (magazine) 59
The Movie That Changed My Life (TV) 64
Mowbray, Alan 191; as "Mr. Melton" in *Abbott and Costello Meet the Killer, Boris Karloff* 193–211
Muhl, Ed 30
Muir, Gavin 66; as "Dr. Gray" in *Abbott and Costello Meet the Invisible Man* 69–82
Mulholland, Jim 63, 87, 113, 131, 163, 186, 188, 214
The Mummy (1932) 8–9, 90
The Mummy (1959) 27
The Mummy's Curse 19, 115, 133
The Mummy's Ghost 19, 133
The Mummy's Hand 9, 13
The Mummy's Tomb 16, 133
Murders in the Rue Morgue (1932) 8
Murphy, Audie 134
Murphy, Eddie 88
My Darling Clementine 191
My Man Godfrey (1936) 191

Naish, J. Carrol 20
Napier, Alan 13
Narrow Margin 116
The Nassour Brothers 24
Nat Young's Orchestra 83

Index

Natwick, Grim 37
The Naughty Nineties 20–21, 53, 72, 76, 124, 204, 209
Neibaur, James L. 83, 87, 113–114, 131
A Night at the Opera 172
A Nightmare on Elm Street 110
The Noose Hangs High 23, 153
The Nutty Professor (1996) 88

O'Brien, Hugh 89
O'Driscoll, Martha 21
Of Mice and Men (1939) 15, 31
Okuda, Ted 163
The Old Dark House (1932) 1, 8, 90, 114
Olson and Johnson 19, 94, 141, 164, 209
One Night in the Tropics 12, 67, 138
Our Gang 2, 178, 208
Ouspenskaya, Maria 15, 18

Paige, Janis 83
Paramount 166
Pardon My Sarong 16, 124, 139, 145, 217
Parker, Eddie 92, 97, 100, 117; as "Klaris" in *Abbott and Costello Meet the Mummy* 119–130, 131
Parks, Vic 92, 100, 116, 125–126
Parsons, Louella 164
Pearl of Death 16, 22
Peter Gunn (TV) 90, 91 116
Phantom of the Opera (1925) 15
Phantom of the Opera (1943) 18
Phantom of the Opera (1962) 27
Pierce, Jack 8, 10, 15, 30, 34
Pillow of Death 18
Pitts, Michael R. 63
Poe, Edgar Allan 9, 190
Polanski, Roman 135
Post, Don 33–34
Powell, Dick 14, 139
PRC 22

Presley, Elvis 64
Price, Vincent 13, 33, 58, 190
The Private Life of Henry VIII 167
Psycho 2
Pursuit to Algiers 16

Queen of Outer Space 26

Ragland, Rags 21
Raiders of the Lost Ark 122, 127
Rains, Claude 9, 15, 18, 65, 70
Randolph, Jane 34; as "Joan" in *Abbott and Costello Meet Frankenstein* 46–58, 59
Rathbone, Basil 13, 16, 22, 89, 139, 190
The Raven (1935) 9, 90
The Raven (1963) 190
Raye, Martha 15
Re-Animator 2, 100, 135
Re-Possessed 2
Rebecca 91, 173
Return of the Living Dead 2, 135
Revenge of the Creature 26
Reynolds, Marjorie 23, 166; as "Melody" in *The Time of Their Lives* 169–183
Ride 'Em Cowboy 16, 140, 204, 209, 217
Rinaldo, Fredric 31, 66, 164
Rio Rita 17
The Ritz Brothers 2, 161
Road to Utopia 25
The Robe 117
Robles, German 59
Rogers, Charles R. 10
Rouse, Russell 66
Runyan, Damon 17

Sands of Iwo Jima 66
Saturday Night Live (TV) 216
Sawyer, Joe 21
Scared Stiff (1953) 172
The Scarlet Claw 16
Scream 2
The Secret Life of Walter Mitty 91

Secret of the Blue Room 150
Selleca, Connie 165
Sennett, Mack 113, 139
Sh! The Octopus 208
Shelton, John 167; as "Sheldon" in *The Time of Their Lives* 173–183
Sherlock Holmes and the Secret Weapon 16
Sherlock Holmes and the Voice of Terror 16
Sherlock Holmes Faces Death 16
Sherlock Holmes in Washington 16, 30
The Silence of the Hams 2
Simms, Ginny 17
Siodmak, Curt 17, 55, 66
Sirk, Douglas 134
The Sixth Man 184
Skinner, Frank 34, 93
"Slowly, I Turned" 218
Smith, Alexis 91
Smith, Don G. 32
Smith, Kate 11, 133
The Sniper 116
Snyder, Howard 66, 189
Son of Dracula 18
Son of Frankenstein 13, 32, 55, 90, 114
Son of Kong 13
Sondergaard, Gale 166; as "Emily" in *The Time of Their Lives* 173–183
The Spider Woman 16, 167
The Spider Woman Strikes Back 22, 167
Spielberg, Steven 127
Spitz, Leo 22
Spook Busters 68
Spooks Run Wild 41
Standard Capital Corporation 10
Stanley, John 87
The Steve Allen Show (TV) 27
Stevens, Craig 90–91, 114; as "Bruce" in *Abbott and Costello Meet Dr. Jekyll and Mr. Hyde* 93–109
Stevens, Onslow 17
Stevenson, Robert Louis 93, 111
Strange, Glenn 20, 21, 33–34, 35, 36, 100, 216; as "the Monster" in *Abbott*

and Costello Meet
  Frankenstein 42–58
The Strange Case of Dr. RX
  188
Strange Confession 18
The Strange Door 24
Streets of Paris 11
Strickfaden, Kenneth 55
Stuart, Gloria 8
Superman 122
Superman (TV) 130
Sweet Charity 59

Tarantino, Quentin 64
Tarantula 26
Targets 190
Terror By Night 16, 191
Texaco Star Theater (TV)
  215
Thesiger, Ernest 8, 10
The Thing (1951) 92
The Thirty Foot Bride of
  Candy Rock 27, 218
The Thirty-Nine Step 214
This Island Earth 26
Thomas, Danny 83
The Three Stooges 2, 21, 37,
  66, 94, 99, 149, 161, 170
The Time of Their Lives
  23, 34, 36, 71, 138, 165–
  187, 213; budget 167;
  criticism 184–186; reviews 186–187; story and
  plot 169–183
Toler, Sidney 191
Topper 138, 166, 191
Tourneur, Jacques 190
Tower of London (1939)
  114
Tracy, Spencer 88, 97
Tremors 135
The Trouble with Angels 167

The Trouble with Harry 1,
  212
Turner, Lana 88
20th Century–Fox 16, 139,
  140
Tyler, Tom 13

Ulmer, Edgar G. 9
Universal 12, 31, 68, 88–
  89, 90, 115, 117, 118, 134,
  138, 161, 162, 169, 188,
  189, 216, 217; history 7–
  10, 12–28
Universal Horrors (book)
  87, 164

Vampire in Brooklyn 3
Van, Frankie 12, 67, 79
Van Enger, Charles 167
Van Sloan, Edward 9, 10
Il Vicino di Casa 59
VideoHound 63, 87, 112,
  114, 132, 164, 186, 215

Waggner, George 15
Wagon Train (TV) 27
The Walking Dead 90
Walky Talky Hawky (cartoon) 52–53
Warner, H.B. 117
Warner Bros. 52, 90
Wayne and Shuster Take an
  Affectionate Look at
  Monsters (TV) 59
Wedlock, Hugh, Jr. 66, 189
Weird Woman 18
Welles, Mel 117
Wells, H.G. 65
Wegener, Paul 7
Werewolf of London 9–10
West, Roland 69
Westcott, Helen 90; as

"Vicky" in Abbott and
  Costello Meet Dr. Jekyll
  and Mr. Hyde 93–109
Westmore, Bud 33, 34, 92
Whale, James 1, 7, 8, 9, 10,
  65
Wheeler and Woolsey 2
Whispering Ghosts 167
Who Done It? 17, 69, 97,
  98, 99, 120, 121, 122, 176,
  189, 198, 204, 213, 217
White, Jesse 67
"Who's on First?" 11, 21
Wilder, Gene 47–48
Williams, Grant 26–27
Windsor, Marie 116; as
  "Rontru" in Abbott and
  Costello Meet the
  Mummy 119–136
Winters, Roland 191; as
  "Mr. Brooks" in Abbott
  and Costello Meet the
  Killer, Boris Karloff 195–
  211
The Wistful Widow of Wagon Gap 23, 33, 76, 211
The Wolf Man 15, 54, 140
The Wolf Men (TV) 59
Woman in Green 16
Wood, Edward D., Jr. 8
The World of Abbott and
  Costello 28, 58–59, 115,
  131, 164, 218
The Wrong Man 214

You'll Find Out 190
Young Frankenstein 2, 47–
  48, 59

Ziegfeld, Flo 17
Zucco, George 13, 18–19,
  20

www.ingramcontent.com/pod-product-compliance
Ingram Content Group UK Ltd.
Pitfield, Milton Keynes, MK11 3LW, UK
UKHW041939140426
5217IPUK00014B/565